CLASSIC FURNITURE PROJECTS

Measured Shop Plans &
Simplified Construction Techniques

Thomas H. Jones

Drawings by Mel Erikson & John Johnston

 Sterling Publishing Co., Inc.   New York

Library of Congress Cataloging-in-Publication Data
Jones, Thomas H., 1926–
  [Heirloom furniture you can build]
  Classic furniture projects : measured shop plans & simplified
construction techniques / Thomas H. Jones ; drawings by Mel Erikson
& John Johnston.
     p. cm.—(Popular science)
  Reprint. Originally published: Heirloom furniture you can build.
New York : Popular Science Books, c1987.
  Bibliography: p.
  ISBN 0-8069-6987-3
  1. Furniture making. I. Erikson, Mel. II. Johnston, John.
III. Title. IV. Series: Popular science (Sterling Publishing
Company)
TT194.J663   1989
684.1'042—dc199   88-33656
                                          CIP

1 3 5 7 9 10 8 6 4 2

Published in 1989 by Sterling Publishing Co., Inc.
Two Park Avenue, New York, N.Y. 10016
Originally published in hardcover by Grolier
Book Clubs, Inc., copyright © 1987 by
Thomas H. Jones, under the title
"Heirloom Furniture You Can Build"
Distributed in Canada by Oak Tree Press Ltd.
% Canadian Manda Group, P.O. Box 920, Station U
Toronto, Ontario, Canada M8Z 5P9
Distributed in Great Britain and Europe by Cassell PLC
Artillery House, Artillery Row, London SW1P 1RT, England
Distributed in Australia by Capricorn Ltd.
P.O. Box 665, Lane Cove, NSW 2066
Manufactured in the United States of America
All rights reserved

Sterling ISBN 0-8069-6987-3 Paper

This Book Is For

Marjorie Ann
Whelan

CONTENTS

PREFACE

What is heirloom furniture? Strictly speaking, an heirloom is something that belonged to an ancestor and has been handed down through generations of the same family. By that definition, one could not build heirloom furniture today in a home shop. However, this book shows you how to build a variety of furniture pieces that could *become* heirlooms—perhaps because they were made for someone special, with dedication, care, and craftsmanship.

The furniture in this book is a mixture of reproductions, adaptations, and new designs. Some projects are based on classical period pieces by Chippendale, Hepplewhite, and Sheraton. Others are derived from a general type of furniture made during a certain period—a Queen Anne table, an Early American credenza, a Shaker shelf, a Federal tambour desk, and modern furniture such as an oak and cane coffee table. And there are original designs—a tall clock and a jewelry box.

Most of these pieces can be built by serious woodworkers with a modestly equipped shop and a knowledge of basic cabinetmaking techniques. A few are for advanced hobbyists who are looking for real challenges. Each project includes complete construction drawings, materials and cutting lists, explanatory text, and captioned photos of important steps in building the piece. Since I designed all of these projects, I know the pitfalls and problems of each. These I have described in the instructions, along with all the other details that went into construction and finishing.

Although I've included my own finishing schedule at the end of each project, the reader may have different ideas. To help you to formulate them, I've included a special chapter on finishing furniture which contains general information on the applicaton of the various types of finishes.

Special thanks are due to my wife, Carolyn, for the help she has given me in constructing and finishing the furniture in the book, for reading and rereading the manuscript, and for allowing me to include two projects, the Shaker shelf and the Canadian wall secretary, which she built herself.

Thomas H. Jones

HEIRLOOM FURNITURE YOU CAN BUILD

1

❦❦❦

QUEEN ANNE TABLE

This small Queen Anne table with its graceful and simple lines can add elegance to a corner of almost any room. As the table is decorated on all sides, it can also be reversed and used as an occasional table against a wall.

It is an easy piece of furniture to build because the legs can be purchased. There are several sources for Queen Anne legs, and you can get them in mahogany or walnut instead of the ash I used. The shape of the legs is not standard, however, and buying them for your table should be the first step. You might have to change the dimensions of the apron pieces to match them.

You will need about 4 board feet of $3/4''$ ash lumber for the top and aprons. Lay out all the pieces before doing any cutting. If possible, for easier clamping, leave the ends of the top pieces squared until after you glue up the top.

Sand the glued-up top flat and dress the edges square and to accurate dimension for routing the edge thumbnail molding. I used a ball-bearing piloted, $1/2''$-radius, corner-rounding bit for the top, and a piloted $1/4''$-radius, corner-rounding bit for the bottom of the edge. Sand the edges to remove tool marks, and round off the corner for safety.

Blank the aprons and dress them to $11/16''$ thickness (don,t scroll the edges yet) and square and bevel the ends to the angles shown. The $11/16''$ thickness is necessary if the legs are to be at tached to the aprons with $3''$ hanger bolts—longer bolts will allow thicker aprons. Slot the aprons for the table-top fasteners. Draw full-size patterns for the lower edges and saw the edges. A band saw, scroll saw, or sabre saw can be used. Sand the edges with a drum sander.

The corner blocks can be made from any hardwood. Blank them and bevel the ends as shown. Drilling mating holes for the screws must be done carefully if the table is to go together accurately (Fig. 1). The angle of the holes is also important because the wrong angle will make driving the screws difficult. Initially, for #10 screws, drill pilot holes in the blocks using a #28 drill.

The tops of two legs have to be trimmed to match the 45-degree apron angle. Note that all this leg trimming is on the outside exposed surfaces—the sides of the legs that mate with the aprons are not touched. Remove material with chisel and Surform rasp, then sand smooth. Drill holes in the legs for the hanger bolts. Either

EXPLODED VIEW

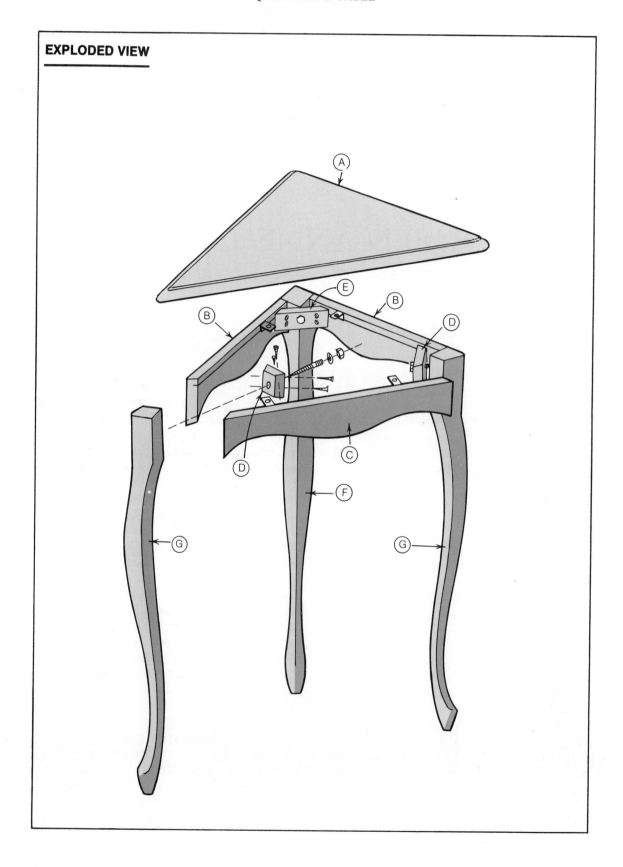

Fig. 1. Pilot holes in corner blocks are enlarged and countersunk after drilling mating holes in aprons. Body drill should produce a loose fit for screw. C-clamp provides safe handle for holding small part.

size bolt can be used. For a neater job when threading in the hanger bolts, counterbore clearance holes in the legs $\frac{1}{4}''$ deep before drilling the pilot holes.

The aprons and blocks must be positioned in a jig for assembly (Fig. 2). To make a jig, I clamped a triangle of 2-by-2s to my bench, to surround the legs and aprons. The aprons were then clamped to the 2-by-2s with $\frac{1}{8}''$ thick shims, as I wanted the aprons set back from the legs. The legs are used to line up the aprons, but they are not part of the assembly at this time and are not clamped. Check the ends of the aprons—the curve of the scrolled edges should flow into the curve of the legs nicely.

Position the blocks and drill oversized clearance holes for the hanger bolts; then bolt the blocks in position, finger-tightening the nuts. With the blocks held in position against the aprons, pass the #28 drill through the holes in the blocks and drill mating holes in the aprons (Fig.3).

Remove the blocks, drill body clearance holes and countersink; then glue and screw the blocks to the aprons (Fig. 4). When the glue is dry, you

MATERIAL LIST

QUANTITY	ITEM
4 board feet	$\frac{3}{4}''$ ash
3	27$\frac{1}{4}''$ ash Queen Anne legs
4	$\frac{1}{4}$ x 3$''$ or $\frac{5}{16}$ x 3$''$ hanger bolts
4	Steel tabletop fasteners
	Legs were purchased from the Door Store of Washington, DC.

CUTTING LIST

KEY	QTY.	PART NAME	SIZE AND DESCRIPTION
A	1	Top	$\frac{3}{4}''$ ash, 12$\frac{3}{4}$ x 25$\frac{1}{2}''$
B	2	Side Apron	$\frac{3}{4}''$ ash, 3 x 11$''$
C	1	Front Apron	$\frac{3}{4}''$ ash, 3 x 16$\frac{3}{4}''$
D	2	Corner Block	$\frac{3}{4}''$ hardwood, 1$\frac{7}{8}$ x 2$''$
E	1	Corner Block	$\frac{3}{4}''$ hardwood, 1$\frac{7}{8}$ x 4$\frac{1}{2}''$
F	1	Back Leg	27$\frac{1}{4}''$ ash Queen Anne leg
G	2	Front Leg	27$\frac{1}{4}''$ ash Queen Anne leg (modified)

TABLETOP

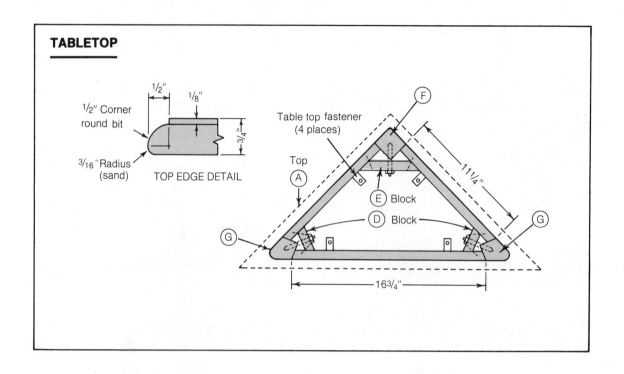

¹/₂″ Corner round bit

³/₁₆″ Radius (sand)

TOP EDGE DETAIL

Table top fastener (4 places)

Top Ⓐ

Ⓕ

Ⓔ Block

Ⓓ Block

Ⓖ

Ⓖ

11¹/₄″

16³/₄″

PATTERN FOR APRON

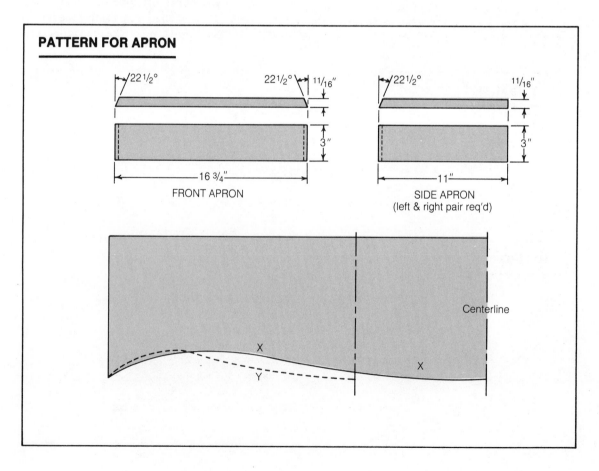

22¹/₂°   22¹/₂° 11/₁₆″

3″

16 ³/₄″

FRONT APRON

22¹/₂°   11/₁₆″

3″

11″

SIDE APRON
(left & right pair req'd)

Centerline

X

X

Y

CORNER CONSTRUCTION

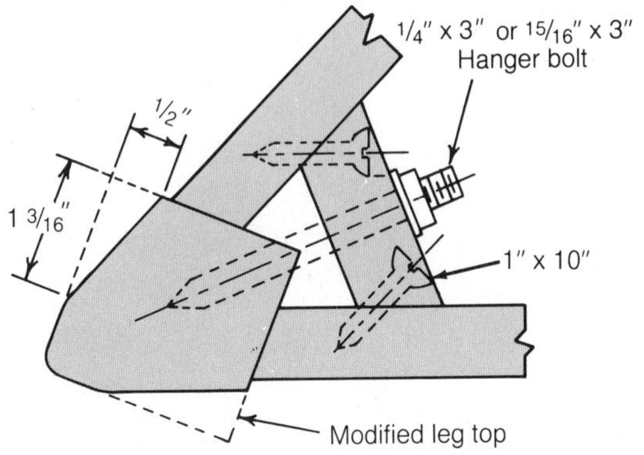

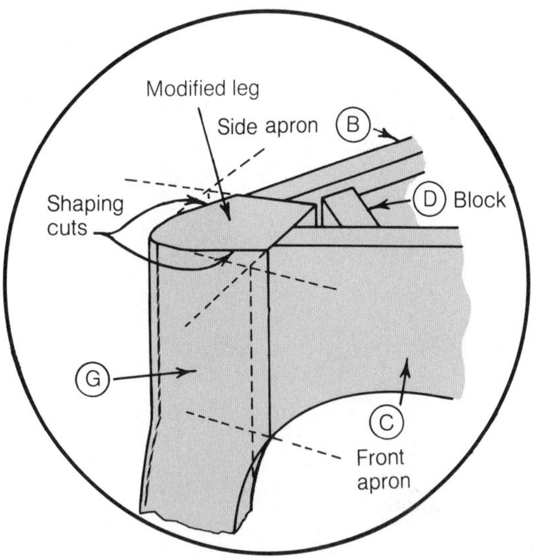

$1/4'' \times 3''$ or $15/16'' \times 3''$ Hanger bolt

$1/2''$

$1\ 3/16''$

$1'' \times 10''$

Modified leg top

Modified leg

Side apron

(B)

Shaping cuts

(D) Block

(G)

(C) Front apron

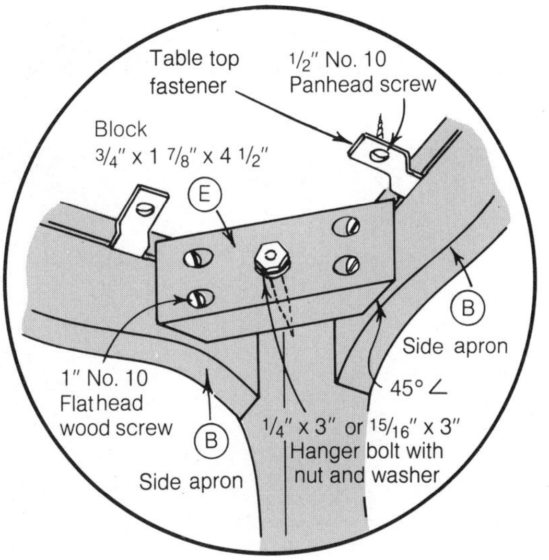

Table top fastener

$1/2''$ No. 10 Panhead screw

Block $3/4'' \times 1\ 7/8'' \times 4\ 1/2''$

(E)

Side apron

$45°\angle$

(B)

1'' No. 10 Flathead wood screw

(B)

Side apron

$1/4'' \times 3''$ or $15/16'' \times 3''$ Hanger bolt with nut and washer

90° ANGLE CORNER

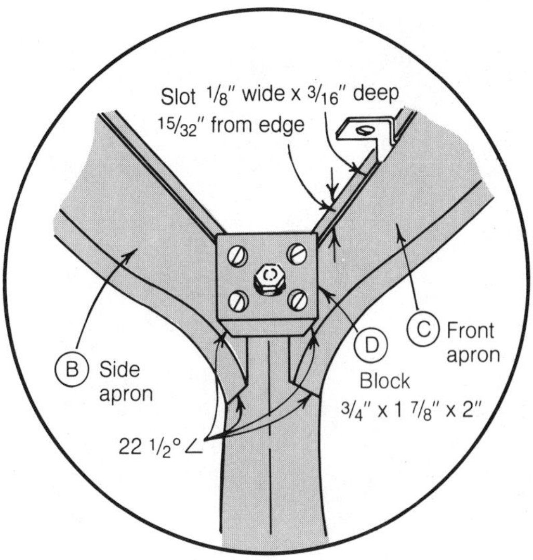

Slot $1/8''$ wide x $3/16''$ deep $15/32''$ from edge

(B) Side apron

(D)

(C) Front apron

Block $3/4'' \times 1\ 7/8'' \times 2''$

$22\ 1/2°\angle$

45° ANGLE CORNERS

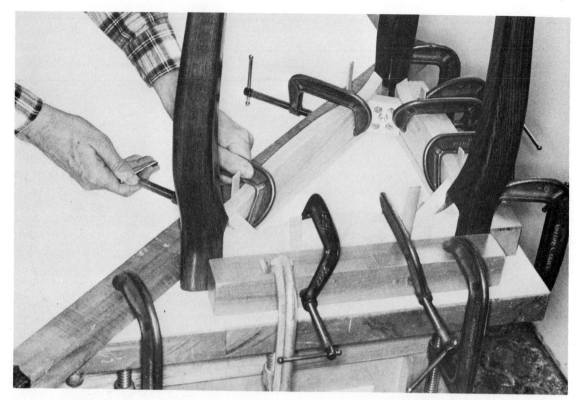

Fig. 2. Clamp a jig of three 2-by-2s to the workbench to surround and position the legs and aprons. Clamp the aprons to the jig with ⅛″-thick shims, as shown, to set back the aprons. The legs are held against the apron ends with corner blocks and hanger bolts. Check apron scroll-work for fit against the legs and trim if necessary.

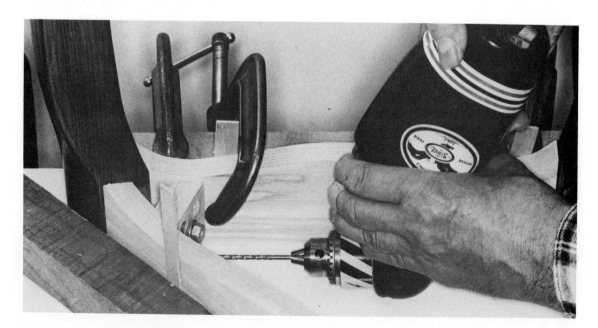

Fig. 3. A #28 (for #10 woodscrews) drill is run through drilled pilot holes in corner block and into the apron.

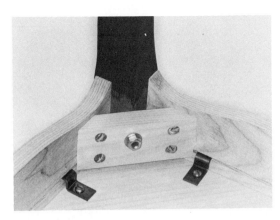

Fig. 4. Apron and corner blocks are assembled with screws and glue. Pull each leg tightly against the ends of the aprons by means of a hanger bolt threaded into the leg and secured to the corner block with a nut and washer. The leg is not glued to the aprons. Steel fasteners hooked in slots in the aprons attach the top.

can glue the legs to the aprons if desired: I did not as I wanted to be able to disassemble the table.

We finished the ash table with brown mahogany stain, walnut paste wood filler, two coats of ZAR Quick Dry Varnish and two coats of ZAR Gloss Polyurethane Varnish. Both varnishes were sanded between coats, and the final coat was steel-wooled (#000) before waxing. The underside of the top received all varnish coats.

After finishing, the top is attached to the frame with steel top fasteners that seat into the slots in the inside surface of the aprons. These fasteners allow the top to move with changes in humidity and thus prevent cracking.

A three-legged table has a unique advantage—no matter how uneven the floor, it won't wobble!

Fig. 5. Thumbnail molding on edge of tabletop can be routed using a ball-bearing piloted ½″ rounding-over bit from the top, and a piloted ¼″ bit from the bottom.

2

EARLY AMERICAN CREDENZA

A credenza is an attractive and useful addition to any living room, hallway, or family room. If it's put in a dining room, a credenza becomes a buffet. This Early American cherry credenza was designed to go into our dining room and to fit in with, but not exactly match, our existing cherry china cabinet.

The construction is divided into major assemblies: base, floor, partitions and ends, top frame, top, doors, and drawers. This makes the credenza easy to build in a small home shop. Each of the assemblies can be handled in the shop by one person, and each can be completely finished before final assembly of the credenza.

The Early American cherry credenza has the customary raised-panel doors and thumbnail molding around the edge of the top.

You will need about 50 board feet of $13/16''$ or $3/4''$ cherry. The exact need will depend on the random width and length lumber you get, and how much waste there is. Half-inch oak is used for drawer sides and backs, and $1/4''$ plywood for the back and drawer bottoms.

BASE

The base is made of six major pieces: center rail, wing rails, end rails, end frames, back rail, and bearer rails. The back is rabbet-and-dadoed into the ends, but only after the joints on the front of the base have been assembled.

The end-to-wing rail joints should be splined, then reinforced with glue blocks and screws near the bottom edge. The base end frames are doweled to the base wing rails, then screwed to the base end rails.

Center-to-wing butt joints also have to be doweled or splined; either way these joints should be reinforced with blocks glued and screwed on the inside. Birch aircraft plywood in $1/8''$ or $3/32''$ thickness makes excellent splines. It can be obtained in small pieces at hobby shops.

Begin base construction by blanking the six pieces to width and slightly over length. Set your table saw for 7 degrees and trim both ends of the base center rail, and one end of each of the base wing rails.

EXPLODED VIEW

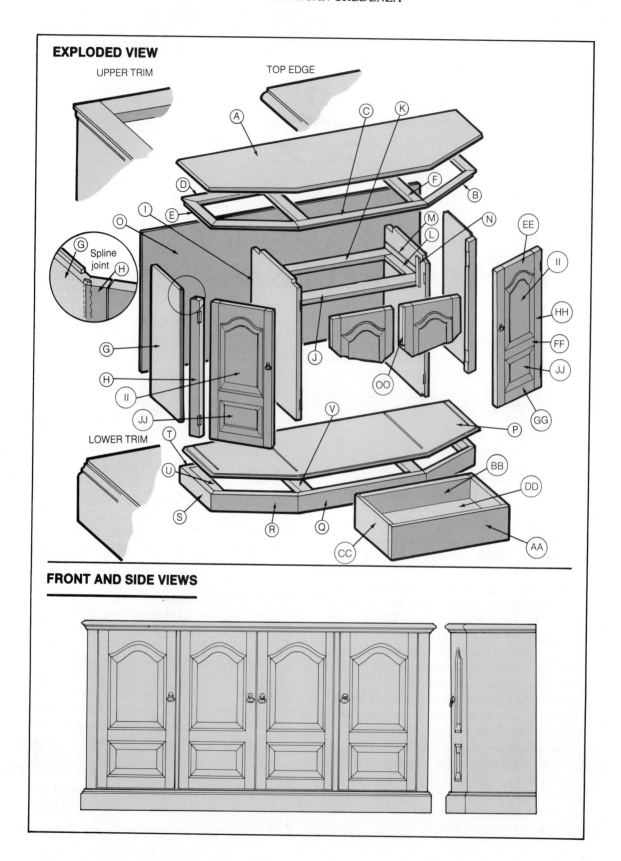

UPPER TRIM

TOP EDGE

Spline joint

LOWER TRIM

FRONT AND SIDE VIEWS

MATERIALS LIST

QUANTITY	ITEM
50 board feet	13/16" cherry
4 board feet	¾" hardwood (any economical)
3 board feet	½" oak
1 panel, 48 x 96"	¼" birch or lauan plywood
6	Drawer and door pulls: Amerock #886
4 pair	Hinges: Amerock #2355

CUTTING LIST

KEY	PART NAME	QTY.	MATERIAL	BLANK DIMENSIONS
A	Top	1	¾" cherry	15⅜ x 61¾"
B	Frame Wing Rail	2	¾" cherry	2½ x 16½"
C	Frame Center Rail	1	¾" cherry	2½ x ⅝"
D	Frame Back Rail	1	¾" hardwood	2 x 58¼"
E	Frame End Rail	2	¾" cherry	2½ x 11¼"
F	Frame Bearer Rail	2	¾" hardwood	2 x 12¼"
G	End Panel	2	¾" cherry	10⅞ x 27¼"
H	End Post	2	¾" cherry	2 x 26¾"
I	Partition	2	¾" cherry	14½ x 27¾"
J	Front Drawer Rail	1	¾" cherry	1½ x 28½"
K	Rear Drawer Rail	1	¾" hardwood	1½ x 28½"
L	Drawer Support	2	¾" hardwood	1½ x 10"
M	Drawer Guide	2	hardwood	¼ x ¾" x 12"
N	Drawer Trim	2	cherry	¼ x ¾" x 5¾"
O	Back	1	¼" plywood	27 x 61"(approx.)
P	Floor	1	¾" cherry	15⅜ x 61¾"
Q	Base Center Rail	1	¾" cherry	3 x 29⅝"
R	Base Wing Rail	2	¾" cherry	3 x 16¾"
S	Base End Rail	2	¾" cherry	3 x 11½"
T	Base Back Rail	1	¾" hardwood	3 x 61½"
U	Base End Frame	2	¾" hardwood	2 x 10¾"
V	Base Bearer Rail	2	¾" hardwood	2 x 14¼"
W	Center Shelf	1	¾" cherry	13 x 27⅞"
X	Side Shelf	2	¾" cherry	13 x 14⅝"
AA	Drawer Front	1	¾" cherry	5 x 27⅜"
BB	Drawer Back	1	½" oak	4 x 26¾"
CC	Drawer Side	2	½" oak	4¾ x 12¼"
DD	Drawer Bottom	1	¼" plywood	12 x 26¾"
EE	Door Top Rail	4	¾" cherry	5¼ x 11¾"
FF	Door Center Rail	4	¾" cherry	2½ x 11¾"
GG	Door Bottom Rail	4	¾" cherry	2⅛ x 11¾"
HH	Door Stile	8	¾" cherry	2⅛ x 26⅝"
II	Door Upper Panel	4	¾" cherry	10 ⅜ x 5 ⅜"
JJ	Door Lower Panel	4	¾" cherry	10⅜ x 15⅜"
KK	Door Edge Trim	1	cherry	⅜ x ¾" x 26⅝"

Without changing the angle, lower the blade and saw the kerfs for the splines using a tenoning jig to hold the pieces (Fig. 1).

Reset the saw to 38 degrees and trim the other ends of the wing rails, and one end of each end rail; then lower the blade and saw the kerfs for the splines.

Cut splines and clamp the five base pieces together (dry) with the splines and check the accuracy of your joints. If angles are slightly off, adjust the length of the base back to compensate, rather than try to correct the bevels. When the frame parts are positioned for tight miter joints, trim and dado the ends of the back.

With the assembled base clamped to your bench (dry), cut and fit glue blocks, and drill the holes for the screws. Fit the base end frames and the braces, and drill blind dowel holes to attach these parts to the base center and wing rails, and through dowel holes to attach them to the back. You are now ready to assemble the base.

Using ³/₄″ plywood, make an accurate 14-76-90- degree triangle about 12″ long to help get the joints of the base and frame lined up accurately. Don't attempt to glue the whole base in one shot.

Start by gluing the center and sides together with the reinforcing glue blocks. Use the rest of the still-assembled base as a jig. Next glue up one end-to-wing joint, with the glue block doweled and screwed. Glue and dowel both bearer rails, or braces, to the front of the base, with the rest of

Fig. 1.　Sawing the spline kerf for the angled front corner joint of the base. A Rockwell tenoning accessory provided the necessary accuracy for this operation. First set the blade angle to miter the ends of the frame members, then without resetting angle, lower blade and saw kerf.

the base assembled dry for accurate positioning.

Now, in one shot, glue up the other end-to-wing joint, and glue the back between the ends and to the bearer rails. When clamping, use the plywood triangle to check the front joints, and a square for the back corners. Always double-check alignment to be sure your clamps aren't pulling the frame parts out of position or bend-

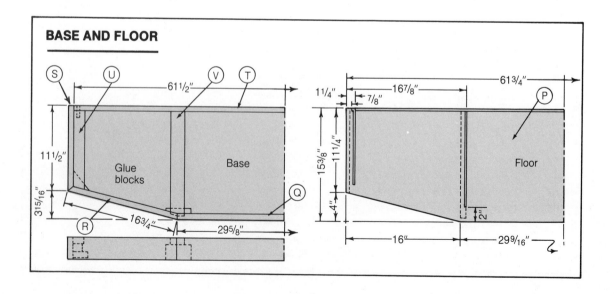

ing the back piece. Keep the base clamped flat on your bench overnight.

FRAME

The frame, like the base, is made of six back rails, pieces—center, wing, end and back rails, plus two cross-bracing bearer rails. The back is tenoned into the ends; the rest of the rails are assembled with stopped splined miter joints. You could also dowel or mortise-and-tenon these joints, but be careful you don't end up with something impossible to assemble. I used splines, with my router set up as a shaper to make the stopped mortises.

Blank the six exposed frame rails to width and slightly overlength. Miter the ends of the center, wing, and end rails and rout the stopped mortise to receive the splines. The back rail is tenoned to the ends, so mortise the ends for these tenons also. Next, mortise the back and center rails for the bearer rail tenons. These bearer rails must be

positioned accurately as their outer edges position and provide attachment for the tops of the partitions. Note that the back rail is inset $3/8''$. This is to provide a nailing surface for the plywood back.

Frame assembly is not easy because it is awkward to apply clamping pressure properly to the odd-angled joints. Exactly how you do it will depend on your clamp supply. Proceed cautiously. I began by gluing the center, bearer, and back rails together, with the rest of the frame clamped up dry to serve as a jig to assure correct alignment of the glue joints. When these joints were dry, I glued ends and wings together, using the rest of the frame as a jig. When these were dry, I glued them to the center and back rails.

Now glue up blanks for the top, floor, partitions, ends, shelves, drawer fronts, and door panels. Assemble the drawer frame. Use either dowels or mortise-and-tenon joints. If sanding the surfaces flat and smooth is not your favorite activity, do as I did—take the blanks, frame, and

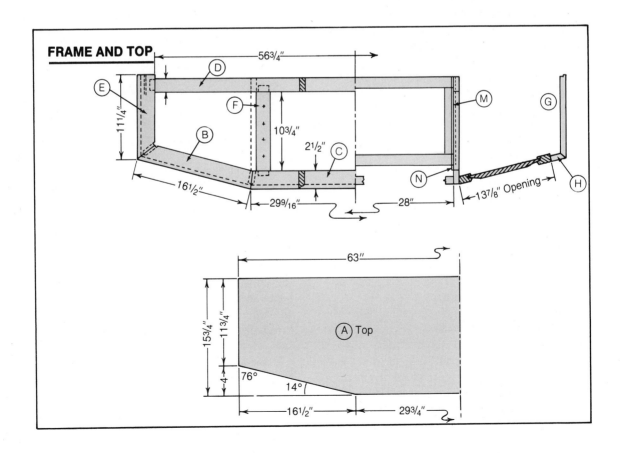

Fig. 2. Assembling the carcase. If great care is taken getting the first partition glued absolutely square, the rest of the assembly will be easy. The angle clamping fixtures assist in getting the partition vertical, but final checking is done with 24″ carpenter's square. Excessive clamping pressure can bow the parts and deform the fixtures.

drawer frame (but not the base) to a cabinet shop which has a wide-belt sander. The time saved and the accuracy of the sanding is well worth the cost.

When sanding is completed, lay the frame on the base and check the alignment of the wing angles. The frame should be ¼″ smaller than the base at the front and ends, with the back surfaces of the ends even. If necessary, bring the wings into alignment by trimming the edges of the frame.

Lay the frame on the glued-up floor blank and trace the outline of the frame; these parts have identical outline dimensions.

Trim the floor to dimension, then clamp the floor and frame on your bench back-to-back and lay out the stopped mortises for the end panel and partition tenons. Rout these mortises, and rout the stopped rabbet in the back of the floor to receive the cabinet back panel. (Remember that the back of the frame is already set ⅜″ in for the same purpose.)

ENDS AND PARTITIONS

Rabbet the top and bottom of the end panels, and the bottom of the partitions to form tenons. Cut blanks for the end posts. Bevel the mating edges of the end panels and end posts to form a mitered joint. This joint should be reinforced with a spline. Rabbet the back edge of the end panels to receive the back panel. Before going further with assembly, rout mortises for the hinges in the end posts and partitions.

The molded edges of the frame and floor are the same, but inverted. I clamped both to my bench so they could be routed at the same time—walking round and round. Doing them together saved trying to reset the router for successive cuts.

Place the frame on top of the credenza floor again (be sure top sides are both up) and trace the location of the outboard edge of the frame bearer rails on the floor to locate the dadoes for the partition tenons. Next, flip the frame over

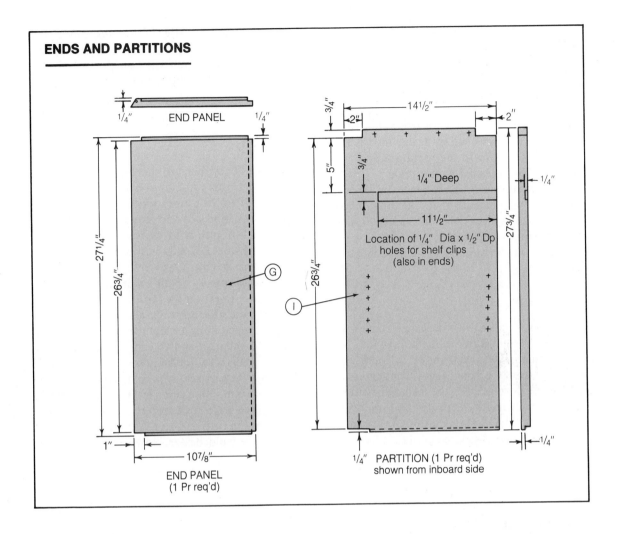

ENDS AND PARTITIONS

END PANEL

END PANEL
(1 Pr req'd)

1/4" Deep

Location of 1/4" Dia x 1/2" Dp holes for shelf clips (also in ends)

PARTITION (1 Pr req'd) shown from inboard side

(bottom up), lay it back to back with the floor, and clamp in alignment. Now mark both to locate the dadoes for the end assembly tenons. Rout all six dadoes.

Clamp the two partitions to your bench, aligned back to back with center sides up. Rout the stopped dadoes to receive the drawer frame. Notch the front ends of the drawer frame to fit the dadoes in the partitions. Drill and countersink screw holes in the partitions for the screws that will go into the drawer frame and into the top frame bearer rails.

CARCASE ASSEMBLY

Clamp the partitions to the top frame bearer rails and fasten with screws. Now fasten the drawer frame between the partitions with screws. Fit the partition bottom tenons into the dadoes in the floor. Clamp sufficiently so the assembly won't fall apart, then fit the end assemblies to the frame and floor. Check this trial assembly to be sure the partition and the front and back edges of the end frame are located correctly in relation to the edges of the floor and frame at both front and back.

Note: You should have eight pipe or bar clamps for the final carcase assembly step. You can get by with six if you have heavy clamping cauls available so you can use only one clamp on each end.

Disassemble the carcase. Begin assembly by gluing and screwing one partition to the frame. (The carcase is assembled upside down.) Block the partition and frame carefully so that this first joint goes together absolutely square. When the glue is dry, glue and screw the end of the drawer frame to the same partition (support the other end with the other partition), then add the second partition to the assembly, using the unglued floor as a jig for alignment. Next glue the end panel and end post assemblies to the frame, one at a time, still using the floor as a jig. Last, glue the floor to the partitions and ends. Fill the screw holes in the partitions.

Place the top blank on the bench upside down and position the carcase on it. The top should be $5/8''$ larger than the frame on front and sides. Draw the finish outline of the top and cut to size. Rout the thumbnail molding on the edge of the top.

DRAWER

The front of the single drawer extends downward, covering the drawer frame; the sides of the opening for the drawer are trimmed in to keep the drawer clear of the door hinges. The sides of the drawer are dovetailed to the front. These dovetails can be handcut, or routed with a dovetail attachment. The back is dado-rabbeted to the sides. The bottom fits into slots in the front and sides and under the edge of the back. I used side drawer guides, with guides and drawer supports faced with nylon self-stick strips for smooth operation. You could substitute a center guide and rail.

DOORS

Make the frame-and-raised-panel doors with two panels separated by a rail because a single panel will not be proportioned attractively. The frames are mortised and tenoned together, and the panels fit into grooves in the stiles and rails. Make the stiles and rails before tackling the panels. Be sure you leave enough room in the grooves for panel expansion in humid weather. It is better to err on the loose side.

Blank the stiles and rails in back-to-back pairs for ease in handling, except the center rails which should be blanked end-to-end. Saw and sand the top rail curve to finished dimension, then saw and rout the grooves for the panels and shape the decorative molding (Fig. 3). (For the groove in the curved edge at the top rail, you will need a $3/16''$ slotting cutter.) Use a $3/8''$ rounding-over bit to rout the molded edge. Now separate the parts.

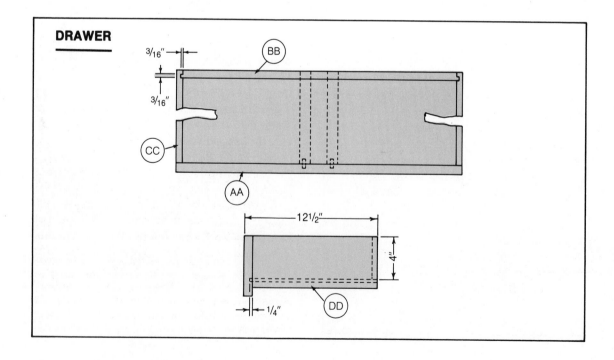

MOLDING DETAIL

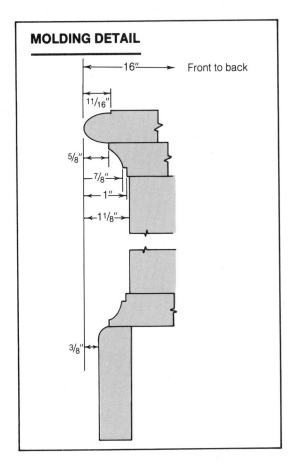

16"   Front to back

11/16"

5/8"

7/8"

1"

1 1/8"

3/8"

Fig. 3. After shaping the molding and routing the groove for the panels, recesses in the molding for the ends of the rails were routed out on the table saw, then routed clean with a cobbled-up fixture. Fences were next clamped to the bench on either side of the fixture for routing mortises for the rail tenons.

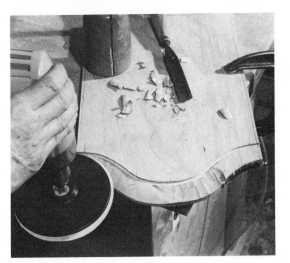

Fig. 4. The straight sides of the panels were easily raised on the table saw, but the curved tops had to be done by hand. The edge of the panel was first formed by routing against a templet, then most of the waste was chiseled away. The surface was finished first with a disc sander (coarse and fine), then with an orbital pad sander.

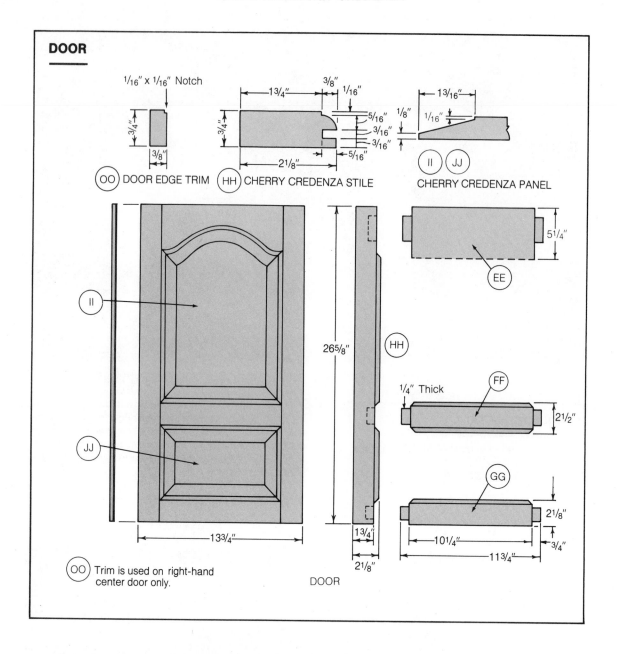

DOOR

OO DOOR EDGE TRIM   **HH** CHERRY CREDENZA STILE   CHERRY CREDENZA PANEL

OO Trim is used on right-hand center door only.

DOOR

Form the tenons on the rails, and miter the molded edges on both the rails and stiles with a saw. To remove the waste from the stiles, chisel most of it away, then set up a fixture and clean out the rest of the wood with a router. Last, drill and chisel out the mortises in the stiles.

Assemble all doors dry to be sure of fits, then trace the outline of the opening in the door frames on paper, add $3/16''$ all around and you have patterns for the panels.

The straight sides of the panels can be easily raised on a table saw. The procedure for forming the curved part of the raised panel requires several steps, but it is not difficult, and it should be done first.

Start by making a plywood or hardboard template to guide a router equipped with guide bushing to make a cut to form the top edge of the raised panel. Next, saw the edge of the panel to rough but oversize dimension.

Fig. 5. Mortise-and-tenon joints were used to assemble the door, although dowels would have done as well. Be sure panel fits loosely, and that the groove is deep enough to allow some expansion.

Using a gouge, rough out the bevel. (If you don't have a gouge, rough out with a coarse-grit sanding disc on an electric drill.) After roughing by either method, smooth the bevel to dimension with a fine-grit sanding disc on the drill (Fig. 4).

Trial fit the top door rail to the panel. Sand the bevel until the panel fits loosely into the groove with 1″ of the bevel exposed. Now complete the panel raising by sawing bevels on the bottom and sides of the panel in the usual manner.

Before gluing up the door frames and panels, make sure the panels will fit loosely, particularly if you are doing your building in cold. low-humidity weather (Fig. 5). Before gluing the frames together (the panels are not glued in), stain the panels. This will avoid the sudden appearance of unstained wood if the panels shrink with changing weather.

The right center door has a trim strip glued to the free edge to give the appearance of a narrow center stile when the door is closed.

After sanding, fit the doors in the openings and mortise for hinges. The open edges of the two side doors must be beveled 14 degrees in order to lie flat against the partitions. Last, install magnetic catches.

FINISHING

Sand thoroughly. Sand everything you can before assembly—partitions, ends, door panels, interior drawer surfaces. Make the back from ¼″ luan plywood; leave it oversize until the credenza is assembled so it can be fitted tightly in order to give the credenza maximum racking resistance.

I used UGL's Zar Natural Teak #120 satin stain on the cherry credenza. The top coat was Constantine's Wood-Glo, three coats, lightly sanded between coats.

3

⧓

TRADITIONAL AND REGENCY CREDENZAS

At the time I built the Early American style cherry credenza described in the previous chapter, I also made two other versions—one in traditional oak design, the other in English Regency style, which is similar to American Federal. All three credenzas were built to the same basic plan. The changed styles were accomplished by relatively minor structural and detail modifications.

The Early American cherry credenza was built first. The traditional oak credenza incorporated only a few design changes. To reduce cost, the floor was replaced with a frame identical to the top frame. Floors were used only in the wings. Three flush drawers replaced the doors and hidden drawer in the center section of the cherry version.

English Regency is a style that came along in the early 19th century after Queen Anne, Chippendale, Hepplewhite, and Sheraton. It was adapted by American furniture makers, including Duncan Phyfe, after the American Federal style, and before the arrival of the many Victorian styles.

This Regency mahogany credenza is actually closer to the basic cherry credenza in construction than is the oak one. The door design was changed and the doors were shortened. The only other changes were the addition of a 1½″-wide apron around the top under the frame molding, a different molding on the frame and floor, and none on the edge of the top.

You will need about 50 board feet of $^{13}/_{16}″$ or $^3/_4″$ lumber for either credenza. Half-inch oak is used for drawer sides and backs, and $^1/_4″$ plywood for the backs and drawer bottoms.

The construction of the credenza was described in detail in the last chapter; the changes for the other two versions follow.

TRADITIONAL OAK CREDENZA

In this version, the center doors and single inside drawer have been replaced with three flush drawers. Instead of a full floor, a second frame identical to the top frame is used. Because

EXPLODED VIEW

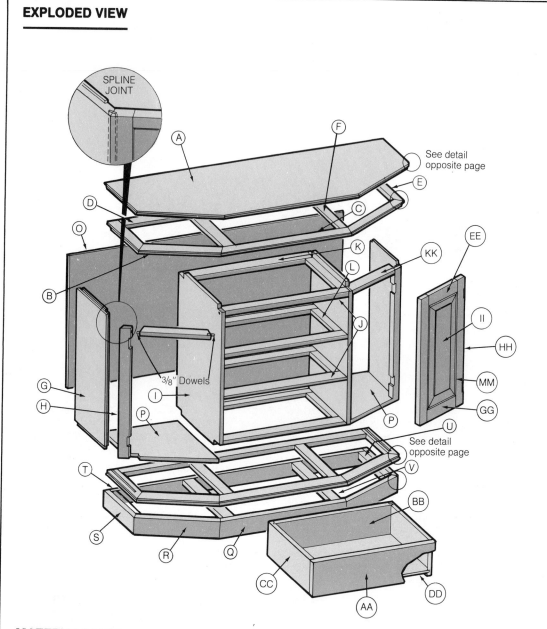

SPLINE JOINT

See detail opposite page

³⁄₈″ Dowels

See detail opposite page

MATERIALS LIST

QUANTITY	ITEM	QUANTITY	ITEM
50 board feet	³⁄₁₆″ oak	6	Drawer pulls: #71B-AE (Smith supply)
8 board feet	¾″ hardwood (any economical)	2	Door pulls: #33B-AE (Smith supply)
10 board feet	½″ oak		
1 panel, 48 x 96″	¼″ birch or lauan plywood	2 pair	Hinges: Amerock #2355

CUTTING LIST

KEY	PART NAME	QTY.	MATERIAL	BLANK DIMENSIONS
A	Top	1	¾" oak	15⅜ x 61¾"
B	Frame Wing Rail	2	¾" oak	2½ x 16½"
C	Frame Center Rail	1	¾" oak	2½ x 29⅝"
D	Frame Back Rail	1	¾" hardwood	2 x 58¼"
E	Frame End Rail	2	¾" oak	2½ x 11¼"
F	Frame Bearer Rail	2	¾" hardwood	2 x 12¼"
G	End Panel	2	¾" oak	10⅞ x 27¼"
H	End Post	2	¾" oak	2 x 26¾"
I	Partition	2	¾" oak	14½ x 28¼"
J	Front Drawer Rail	4	¾" oak	1½ x 28½"
K	Rear Drawer Rail	4	¾" hardwood	1½ x 28½"
L	Drawer Support	8	¾" hardwood	1½ x 10"
M	Drawer Guide			Not Used
N	Drawer Trim			Not Used
O	Back	1	¼" plywood	27 x 61" (approx.)
P	Floor	2	¾" oak	14½ x 14½"
Q	Base Center Rail	1	¾" oak	3 x 29⅝"
R	Base Wing Rail	2	¾" oak	3 x 16¾"
S	Base End Rail	2	¾" oak	3 x 11½"
T	Base Back Rail	1	¾" hardwood	3 x 61½"
U	Base End Frame	2	¾" hardwood	2 x 10¾"
V	Base Bearer Rail	2	¾" hardwood	2 x 14¼"
W	Center Shelf			Not Used
X	Side Shelf	2	¾" oak	13 x 14⅝"
Y	Kicker			Not Used
AA	Drawer Front	3	¾" oak	7¾ x 27¾"
BB	Drawer Back	3	½" oak	6¾ x 27⅛"
CC	Drawer Side	6	½" oak	6¾" x 12¼"
DD	Drawer Bottom	3	¼" plywood	12 x 26¾"
EE	Door Top Rail	2	¾" oak	2⅛ x 11¾"
FF	Door Center Rail			Not Used
GG	Door Bottom Rail	2	¾" oak	2⅛ x 11¾"
HH	Door Stile	4	¾" oak	2⅛ x 26⅝"
II	Door Panel	2	¾" oak	10⅜ x 21¾"
JJ	Door Panel			Not Used
KK	Wing Apron	2	¾" oak	1 x 15"
LL	Center Apron			Not Used
MM	Bead (Door)		12' oak	½ x ½"
NN	Bead (Case Trim)			Not Used
OO	Center Door Edge Trim			Not Used

TOP EDGE

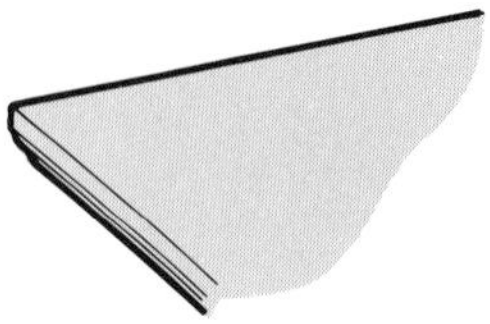

UPPER TRIM

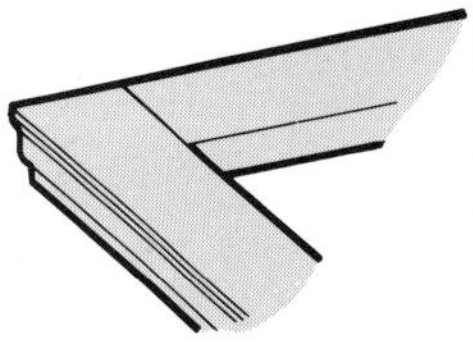

LOWER TRIM

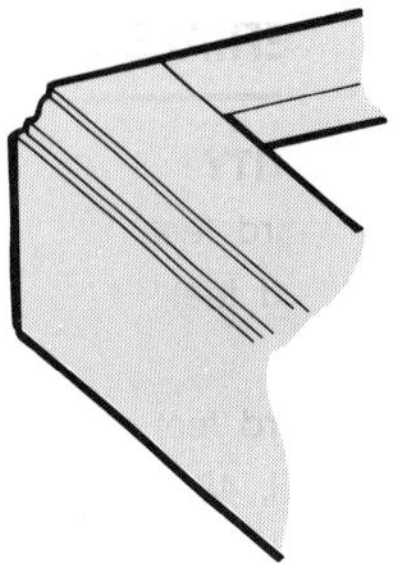

FRONT AND SIDE VIEWS

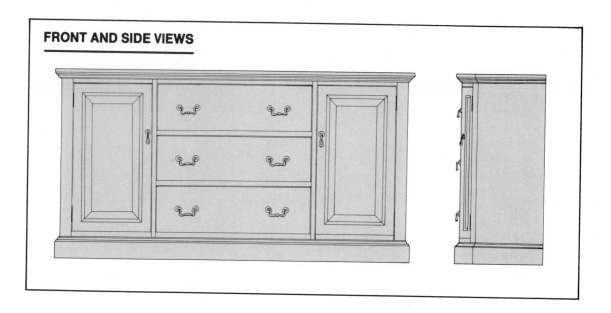

of this, the partitions do not have rabbeted tenons on the bottom and must be blanked with an extra ½″ in height so they can be fastened to the sides of both the top and bottom frame-bearer rails.

The floors in the wing sections floors fastened to the top of the bottom frame. The center section has a drawer frame below the bottom drawer, and above the top drawer. Trim is used under the top frame in the wings for balanced appearance. This added trim gives a more massive appearance to the moldings, in keeping with the use of oak.

A different method is used to secure the panels in the door frames. The raised panels are held in stepped rabbets with separate moldings, and can be installed after the door frame is assembled and all parts are finished (Fig. 5). Having the panels mounted this way allows panel movement without resultant loosening of the molding. The molding can be shaped with a combination of router cuts, sanded smooth, ripped from supporting boards, then nailed in place.

The drawer construction is the same as for the cherry credenza except there is no overlapping lip on the bottom edge. The width has also been changed and the trim at the sides of the opening is not used as there are no hinges to clear. If desired, dust panels of ¼″ plywood can be set in grooves in three of the drawer frames.

MOLDING DETAIL

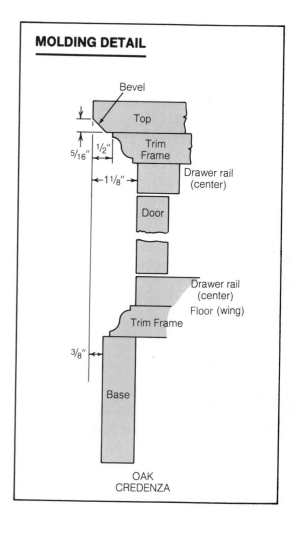

Fig. 1. Routing the edge molding on the base and top trim frames of the oak credenza. Clamp the frames on the bench back-to-back so that the successive routing operations in forming the molding can be done simultaneously, reducing the chance for setting differences.

Fig. 2. Parts of the carcase for the traditional oak credenza, sanded and ready for assembly.

Fig. 3. Assembling the carcase of the oak credenza. First, glue the right end partition to the base trim. One at a time, glue and screw the drawer frames to this partition, using the second partition and the top trim (not shown) as a jig to assure alignment. In the step shown, the second partition is being affixed to the frames and the base trim.

Fig. 4. Assemble the top trim frame dry to the glued carcase. This assures proper alignment of the partitions. Note, however, that the ends of the carcase must be glued to the lower trim frames before the top frame can be added and attached permanently.

Fig. 5. The panels of the oak credenza doors are retained with separate nailed-on moldings. Panels should be finished before nailing them into the frames.

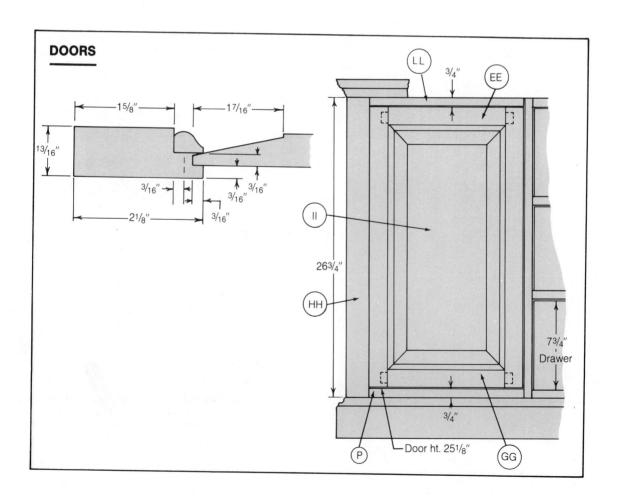

DOORS

MAHOGANY REGENCY CREDENZA

The only change in carcase construction from the Early American cherry credenza is the addition of an apron 1 x ½" deep across the front below the top frame. The end posts are 1½" shorter to accommodate the apron. Half-round ¼" molding is nailed and glued around the carcase. (Make the molding by forming the edge of ¼" wood, then rip the molding from the board.)

The frames of the side and center doors are essentially the same. The dadoes in the center doors are wider to accommodate the grille, and the bottoms of these doors are permanently removable, held to the stiles by screws through the tenons. The right center door also has a trim strip glued on.

The panels of the side doors are ¼" luan plywood veneered on the front with matched mahogany crotch veneer, and on the back with plain mahogany veneer. The center door panels are ⅛" plywood, veneered on the front with avodire, and on the back with mahogany. Thinner panels were used to allow space for the metal grille.

This bright brass grille (it also can be obtained

EXPLODED VIEW

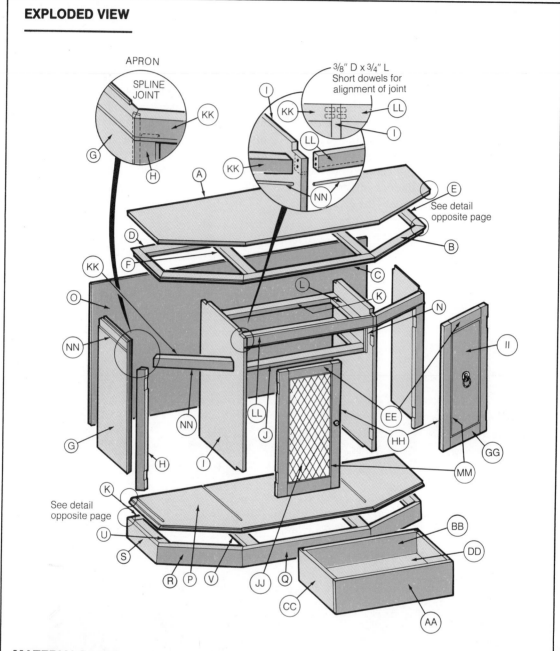

APRON

SPLINE JOINT

³⁄₈″ D x ³⁄₄″ L
Short dowels for
alignment of joint

See detail
opposite page

See detail
opposite page

MATERIALS LIST

QUANTITY	ITEM	QUANTITY	ITEM
50 board feet	³⁄₁₆″ mahogany	2	Door pulls: #1588 knob (Smith supply)
5 board feet	³⁄₄″ hardwood (any economical)		
3 board feet	½″ oak	4 pair	Hinges: amerock #2355
1 panel, 48 x 96″	¼″ birch or lauan plywood	2 pieces	Brass grille, 11⅜ x 22¾″#D4904
	Door pulls: #4619X3 ring pulls (Smith supply)		(not exactly the same grill used) The Woodworker's Store

CUTTING LIST

KEY	PART NAME	QTY.	MATERIAL	BLANK DIMENSIONS
A	Top	1	¾" mahogany	15⅜ x 61¾"
B	Frame Wing Rail	2	¾" mahogany	2½ x 16½"
C	Frame Center Rail	1	¾" mahogany	2½ x 29⅝"
D	Frame Back Rail	1	¾" hardwood	2 x 58¼"
E	Frame End Rail	2	¾" mahogany	2½ x 11¼"
F	Frame Bearer Rail	2	¾" hardwood	2 x 12¼"
G	End Panel	2	¾" mahogany	10⅞ x 27¼"
H	End Post	2	¾" mahogany	2 x 25¼"
I	Partition	2	¾" mahogany	14½ x 27¾"
J	Front Drawer Rail	1	¾" mahogany	1½ x 28½"
K	Rear Drawer Rail	1	¾" hardwood	1½ x 28½"
L	Drawer Support	2	¾" hardwood	1½ x 10"
M	Drawer Guide	2	hardwood	¼ x ¾" x 12"
N	Drawer Trim	2	mahogany	¼ x ¾" x 5¾"
O	Back	1	¼" plywood	27 x 61"(approx.)
P	Floor	1	¾" mahogany	15⅜ x 61¾"
Q	Base Center Rail	1	¾" mahogany	3 x 29⅝"
R	Base Wing Rail	2	¾" mahogany	3 x 16¾"
S	Base End Rail	2	¾" mahogany	3 x 11½"
T	Base Back Rail	1	¾" hardwood	3 x 61½"
U	Base End Frame	2	¾" hardwood	2 x 10¾"
V	Base Bearer Rail	2	¾" hardwood	2 x 14¼"
W	Center Shelf	1	¾" mahogany	13 x 27⅞"
X	Side Shelf	2	¾" mahogany	13 x 14⅝"
Y	Kicker	2	¾" hardwood	1 x 12"
AA	Drawer Front	1	¾" mahogany	5½ x 27⅜"
BB	Drawer Back	1	½" oak	4 x 26¾"
CC	Drawer Side	2	½" oak	4¾ x 12¼"
DD	Drawer Bottom	1	¼" plywood	12 x 26¾"
EE	Door Top Rail	4	¾" mahogany	1½ x 12¼"
FF	Door Center Rail			not used
GG	Door Bottom Rail	4	¾" mahogany	1½ x 12¼"
HH	Door Stile	8	¾" mahogany	1½ x 25⅛"
II	Door Panel	2	¼" plywood	11¼ x 22⅝"
JJ	Door Panel	2	⅛" plywood	11¼ x 22⅝"
KK	Wing Apron	2	¾" mahogany	1½ x 15"
LL	Center Apron	1	¾" mahogany	1½ x 28"
MM	Bead (Door)	24'	mahogany	¼ x ⅜"
NN	Bead (Case Trim)	8'	mahogany	¼ x ¼"
OO	Center Door Edge Trim	1	¾" mahogany	⅜ x 25⅛"

TOP EDGE

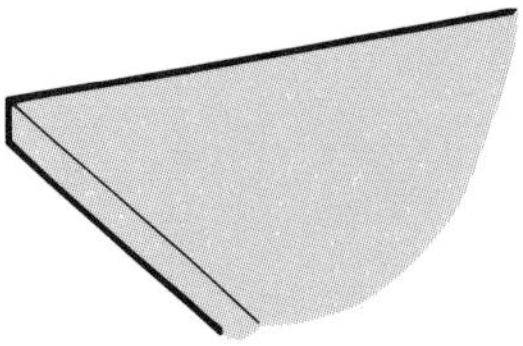

UPPER TRIM

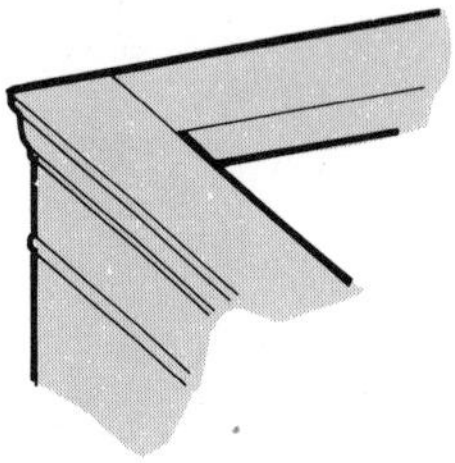

LOWER TRIM

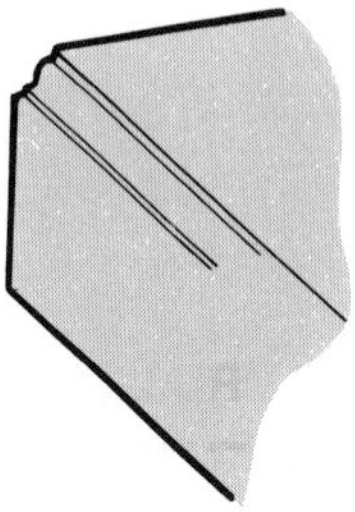

FRONT AND SIDE VIEWS

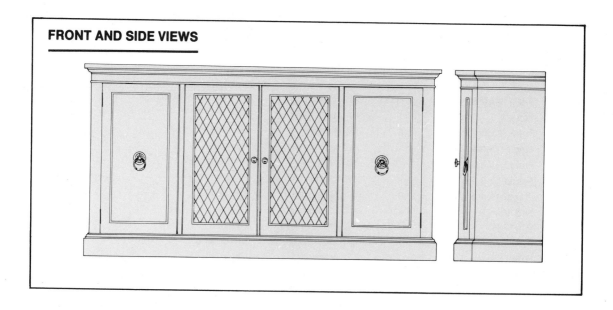

DOORS

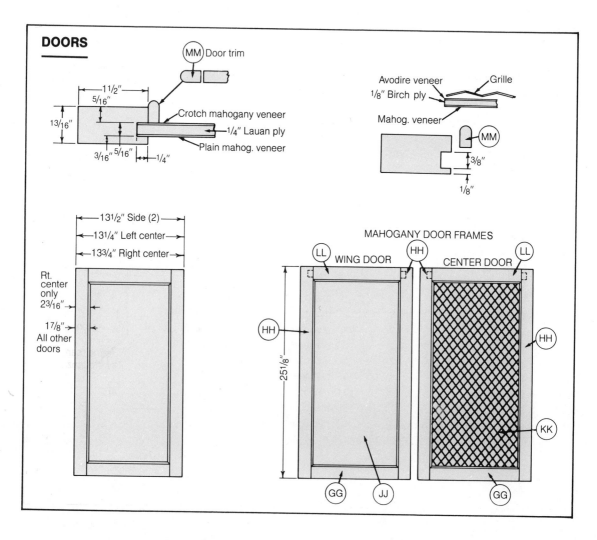

MM) Door trim

Crotch mahogany veneer

1/4" Lauan ply

Plain mahog. veneer

11/2"
5/16"
13/16"
3/16" 5/16"
1/4"

Avodire veneer   Grille
1/8" Birch ply
Mahog. veneer

MM
3/8"
1/8"

131/2" Side (2)
131/4" Left center
133/4" Right center

Rt. center only 23/16"

17/8" All other doors

MAHOGANY DOOR FRAMES

LL WING DOOR   HH   CENTER DOOR LL

HH

251/8"

HH

KK

GG   JJ   GG

antiqued) is actually square steel wire brass-plated and lacquered, and it is hard work to cut. I used a "jab" hacksaw to cut pieces from stock, then heavy diagonal cutters to trim ends. In the sawing, I notched the wire, then broke it by carefully bending the whole grille. It is important when cutting the grille to have it fit symetrically in the door, and to have both grilles identical.

FINISHING

Sand thoroughly. Sand everything you can before assembly—partitions, ends, door panels, interior drawer surfaces. Make the back from $1/4''$ luan plywood; leave it oversize until the credenza is assembled so it can be fitted tightly in order to give the credenza maximum racking resistance.

I used Constantine's Brown Mahogany NGR stain on the English Regency mahogany credenza, and Sherwin-William's Fruitwood on the traditional oak version. The mahogany and oak surfaces were filled with paste filler. The top coat on both was Constantine's Wood-Glo, three coats lightly sanded between coats.

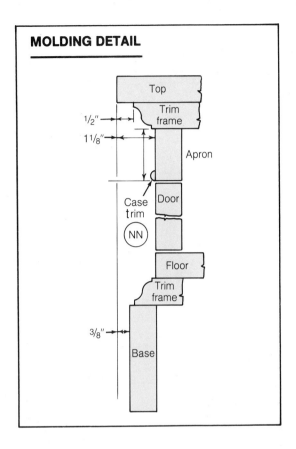

MOLDING DETAIL

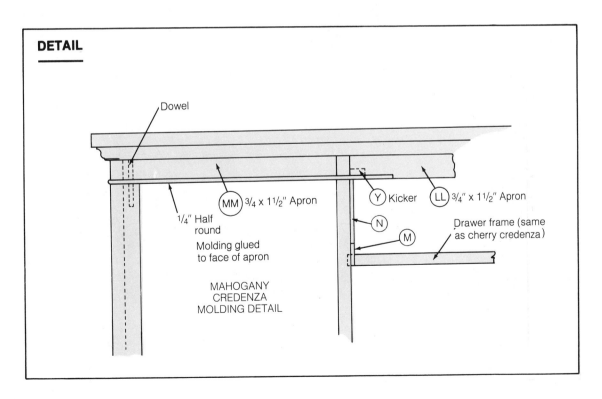

DETAIL

4

CONTEMPORARY TALL CLOCK

Oiled walnut, bronze-tinted Plexiglas, and gleaming polished brass are combined in this handsome contemporary-styled clock. Although the smooth, clean lines of the case contrast sharply with the traditional grandfather and grandmother clocks, the high-quality German movement marks the quarter hours with full Westminster chimes and strikes the hours with a deep melodious tone.

The case is constructed of $3/4''$ and $1''$ walnut (cherry or mahogany would be two other good choices), assembled with dowel and spline joints, and finished with Watco Oil. The seatboard for the movement and the face is $1/4''$ clear, polished Plexiglas, the doors clear $1/10''$ Plexiglas. The sides, back, and top panels of the case are $1/8''$ bronze-tinted solar-control Plexiglas.

A clock can be only as good as its movement. When I designed and built the clock I chose one of the better ones available at the time—Mason & Sullivan's model H60K. This weight-driven 8-day movement has a Graham escapement with pallets that can be adjusted to compensate for wear, hard brass wheels and plates, and pinions and pivots of hardened steel. The pendulum can be zero-beat with a simple knurled screw adjustment rather than the usual bending or shimming. Weights are encased in polished brass shells. (This is a "grandmother" movement; the case is not tall enough for a grandfather movement—the weights would have to be pulled up twice a week).

The movement I used is no longer available, but Mason & Sullivan has a "drop in" replacement, the model 3260X. It is not of the same quality. If I were designing the clock today, I would do it around a movement with a nest of bells rather than chime rods, such as the Mason & Sullivan model 3318X or 3319X. These movements weren't available when I built the clock.

This brings up a really important point. Always design and build your clock case around a movement, never the other way around. And always have the movement in your hand before you start cutting wood. Mason & Sullivan's "drop in" replacement listed is not 100% inter-

EXPLODED VIEW

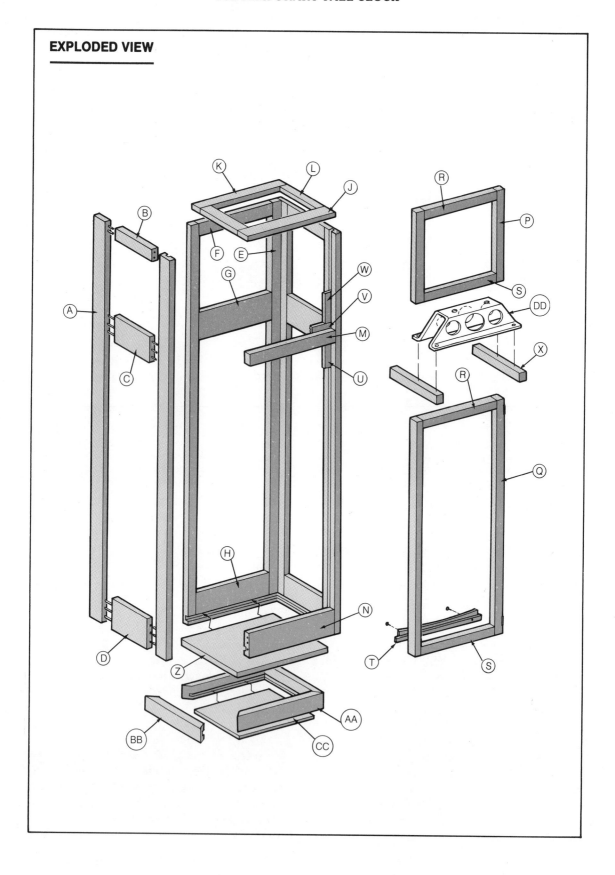

CUTTING LIST

KEY	QTY.	PART NAME	MATERIAL	BLANK DIMENSIONS
A	4	Side Post	walnut	¾ x 2 x 67"
B	2	Side Top Rail	walnut	¾ x 2 x 7"
C	2	Side Waist Rail	walnut	¾ x 4½ x 7"
D	2	Side Bottom Rail	walnut	¾ x 5¼ x 7"
E	2	Back Post	walnut	¾ x 1¼ x 67"
F	1	Back Top Rail	walnut	¾ x 2 x 14"
G	1	Back Waist Rail	walnut	¾ x 4½ x 13"
H	1	Back Bottom Rail	walnut	¾ x 5¼ x 13"
J	1	Top Front Rail	walnut	¾ x 2 x 13"
K	1	Top Back Rail	walnut	¾ x 1¼ x 15½"
L	2	Top Side Rail	walnut	¾ x 1¼ x 15½"
M	1	Front Waist Rail	walnut	1 x 2 x 15½"
N	1	Front Bottom Rail	walnut	¾ x 4 x 15½"
P	2	Upper Door Stile	walnut	1 x 1¼ x 15½"
Q	2	Lower Door Stile	walnut	1 x 1¼ x 45"
R	2	Door Top Rail	walnut	1 x 1¼ x 13"
S	2	Door Bottom Rail	walnut	¾ x 1¼ x 13"
T	2	Glazing Retainer	walnut	¼ x 1¼ x 13"
U	2	Door Stop	walnut	5⁄16 x ¾ x 45"
V	4	Door Stop	walnut	5⁄16 x ¾ x 17"
W	2	Door Stop	walnut	5⁄16 x ¾ x 15"
X	2	Seat Board Support	walnut	1 x 1½ x 9¼"
Y	1	Chime Block	walnut	1½ x 4 x 5"
Z	1	Case Floor	plywood	¾ x 9⅞x 15⅞"
AA	2	Base Front Back	pine	¾ x 2½ x 15½"
BB	2	Base Side	pine	¾ x 2½ x 9½"
CC	2	Base Floor	plywood	¾ x 8½ x 14½"
DD	18'	Quarter Round Molding	pine (or walnut)	½ x ½"
EE	1	Clock Face	CT acrylic	¼ x 13 x 13"
EE	1	Seat Board	CT acrylic	¼ x 15 x 16"
GG	1	Upper Door Panel	CT acrylic	1⁄10 x 14½ x 14½"
GG	1	Lower Door Panel	CT acrylic	1⁄10 x 14½ x 42½"
JJ	2	Upper Side Panel	Bronze acrylic	⅛ x 8½ x 15¾"
KK	2	Lower Side Panel	Bronze acrylic	⅛ x 8½ x 46½"
LL	1	Back Panel	Bronze acrylic	⅛ x 15 x 64¾"
MM	1	Top Panel	Bronze acrylic	⅛ x 8½ x 15¼"
NN	13'	Spline	Hardware	⅛ x ⅜"

MATERIALS LIST

QUANTITY	ITEM	SOURCE
12 board feet	¾" walnut	
1 piece	1" walnut, 7 x 48"	
1 piece	¼ x 16 x 30" clear transparent Plexiglas G	
1 piece	¹⁄₁₆ x 15 x 60" clear transparent Plexiglas G	
1 piece	⅛ x 15 x 72" #2304 bronze solar control Tinted Plexiglas G	
5	Brass butt hinges 1½ x 1¼"	
1	Brass knob, ¾" dia.	
6"	Brass rod, 1" dia.	Small Parts, Inc.
3	Brass tube, ³⁄₃₂ OD x 12"	Small Parts, Inc.
1	Brass rod, ¹⁄₁₆ x 12"	Small Parts, Inc.
1	Brass rod, ⅛ x 12"	Small Parts, Inc.
1	Bag (25 pounds) #9 lead shot	Local Gun Shop
	Clock movement. The following are suggested (all have three weights, strike the hours, play Westminster chimes on the quarter hour):	
	Model 3260x	Mason & Sullivan
	Model 3261x	Mason & Sullivan
	Model 13001	Klockit
	Model 136-8610 (this movement seems to be the closest to the one I used.)	
	Model 089342S.	S. LaRose, Inc.
	(cable driven, triple chime, lyre pendulum)	S. LaRose, Inc.
	Model 089584 (triple chime)	S. LaRose, Inc.

hangeable—some of the holes in the top of the seatboard will have to be repositioned, and the distance from the bottom surface of the movement to the hand shaft axis is slightly different.

Several alternate movements are suggested at the end of the chapter.

CLOCK CASE

The clock case consists of two side frames, back and top frames, a waist rail, a bottom rail, and a bottom panel, or floor. Each of the frames is assembled with doweled joints. Spline joints are then used to align and join the side, top, and back frames (Fig. 1).

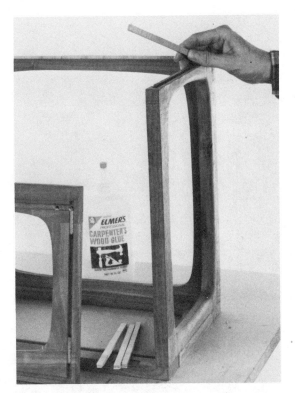

Fig. 1. Case frames are assembled with splined joints for positive alignment, strength, and economy in the use of expensive walnut. Joints should be assembled and clamped dry first to be sure they can close tightly.

Begin construction with the side frames. Mark dowel locations on the four 3/4″ x 2″ x 67″ corner posts. As the posts and rails do not have a square cross section, the dowels are not located on the centerlines of the frames, but are located 5/16″ from the inside surface. Bore dowel holes to the depths indicated; then with dowel centers, transfer the dowel hole locations to the top, waist, and bottom rails, and bore mating holes.

Before proceeding, assemble the frames dry to be sure all parts line up properly. At this point, you should also mark the inside surface of both frames permanently, as once the frames are glued up, you will have no way of knowing which is the inside.

Make cardboard patterns for marking the frames and doors for the openings. This is done by first locating the 7/8″ corner circles and the midpoints between, then connecting the circumference of the circles and the points with smooth curves. Dowel and glue case frames and doors before sawing the openings.

The back frame and the top frame are made up in the same manner as the sides. Make the back frame first, then cut the front and back rails of the top to length. After the back is assembled, cut the waist and bottom rails to the measured width of the back.

Rout grooves for the splines joining the top, back, and side frames. These grooves are all 1/4″ wide and 3/16″ deep. Except for the groove on the back of the top frame, all are stopped. Also, rout the grooves in the side frames for the doorstops. Bore holes in the side frames for the waist and bottom rail dowels, and mortise for door hinges. Bullet or magnetic catches can be used to latch the doors. Drill appropriate mounting holes.

Assemble the clock frames with splines without glue, and transfer dowel locations to the waist and bottom rails, and bore mating holes. (The waist rail is made of 1″ stock; the bottom rails can be 1″ or 3/4″ with a 1/4″ filler strip as shown in the drawing.) Disassemble, rout grooves for doorstops and the bottom panel, and mortise the right side (as you face the clock) for hinges.

DOOR FRAMES

The sides and tops of both doors are constructed in the same manner from 1″ stock. The bottom rails are 3/4″-thick. Saw 1/8″-wide slots for the Plexiglas glazing in the side and top frames. If you have substituted 1/8″ Plexiglas for the 1/10″ in the materials list, put a micrometer to the edge all the way around. The thickness tolerance on acrylic sheet is very loose and in spots it may be more than 1/8″, which means you will have to make the slot wider, which will be easier to do now than later.

Because of the small joint cross section, the door corner joints are each assembled with two 1/4″ dowels instead of 3/8″ dowels. After assembling the door frames, fit the rabbeted retainers made from 1/4″ stock. These retainers hold the Plexiglas in place and are attached with wood screws.

The openings in the case door frames should now be shaped. Begin by drum-sanding to finish dimension the portion of the inner edges that

CASE AND BASE DETAILS

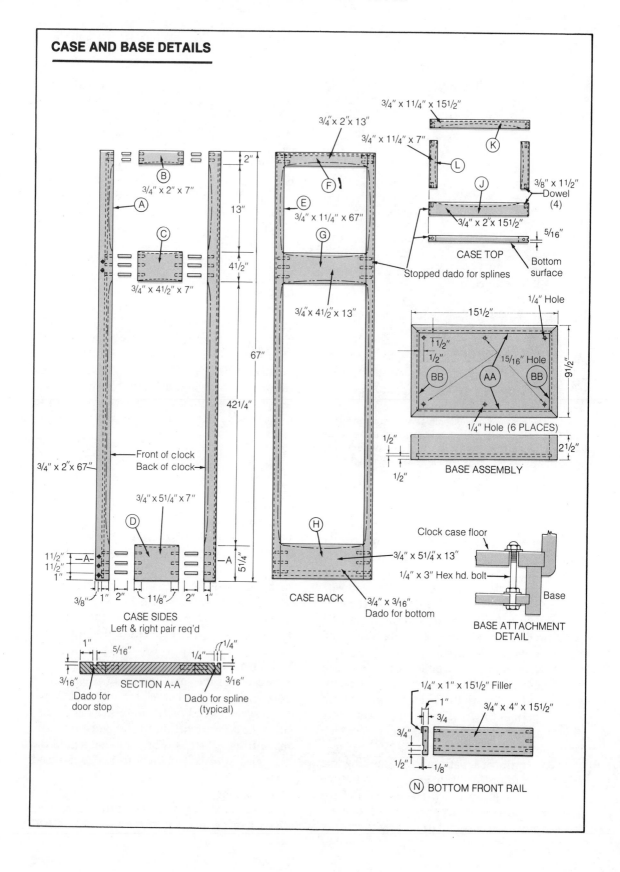

3/4" x 2" x 13"

3/4" x 1 1/4" x 15 1/2"

3/4" x 1 1/4" x 7"

B

3/4" x 2" x 7"

A

F

K

L

J

E

3/8" x 1 1/2" Dowel (4)

3/4" x 1 1/4" x 67"

C

3/4" x 2" x 15 1/2"

3/4" x 4 1/2" x 7"

G

5/16"

CASE TOP

Bottom surface

Stopped dado for splines

2"

13"

4 1/2"

3/4" x 4 1/2" x 13"

67"

42 1/4"

1/4" Hole

15 1/2"

1/2"

1/2"

15/16" Hole

9 1/2"

BB

AA

BB

1/4" Hole (6 PLACES)

Front of clock

Back of clock

3/4" x 2" x 67"

3/4" x 5 1/4" x 7"

D

H

1/2"

1/2"

2 1/2"

BASE ASSEMBLY

Clock case floor

3/4" x 5 1/4" x 13"

1/4" x 3" Hex hd. bolt

Base

5 1/4"

1 1/2"
1 1/2"
1"

-A-

-A

3/8" 1" 2"   1 1/8"   2" 1"

CASE SIDES
Left & right pair req'd

CASE BACK

3/4" x 3/16"
Dado for bottom

BASE ATTACHMENT
DETAIL

1"

5/16"

1/4"
1/4"

3/16"

1/4"

3/16"

SECTION A-A

Dado for
door stop

Dado for spline
(typical)

1/4" x 1" x 15 1/2" Filler

1"

3/4

3/4" x 4" x 15 1/2"

3/4"

1/2"

1/8"

N BOTTOM FRONT RAIL

DOOR DETAILS

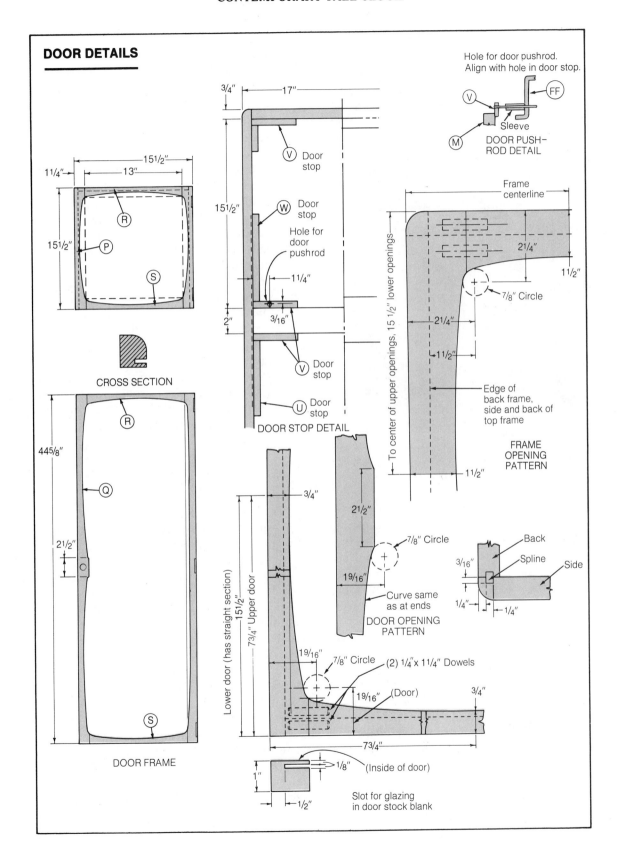

Hole for door pushrod.
Align with hole in door stop.

Ⓥ — FF
Ⓜ — Sleeve
DOOR PUSH-ROD DETAIL

151/2"
13"
11/4"
Ⓡ
Ⓟ
151/2"
Ⓢ

CROSS SECTION

DOOR FRAME
Ⓡ
Ⓠ
445/8"
21/2"
Ⓢ

3/4"
17"
Ⓥ Door stop
Ⓦ Door stop
Hole for door pushrod
151/2"
11/4"
2"
3/16"
Ⓥ Door stop
Ⓤ Door stop
DOOR STOP DETAIL

Frame centerline
21/4"
11/2"
7/8" Circle
21/4"
11/2"
To center of upper openings, 15 1/2" lower openings
Edge of back frame, side and back of top frame
FRAME OPENING PATTERN
11/2"

3/4"
21/2"
7/8" Circle
19/16"
Curve same as at ends
DOOR OPENING PATTERN

Back
Spline
Side
3/16"
1/4"
1/4"

Lower door (has straight section)
151/2"
73/4" Upper door
19/16"
7/8" Circle
(2) 1/4" x 11/4" Dowels
(Door)
19/16"
3/4"
73/4"

1"
1/8"
(Inside of door)
1/2"
Slot for glazing in door stock blank

Fig. 2. Routing outside edges of assembled case. Do this after final assembly, so as to leave a square surface for clamping the spline joints. Use a 1/2" radius ball-bearing piloted rounding-over bit.

side frames, and should be installed first.

Now rout the outside edges of the case (Fig. 2) and finish-sand all external surfaces. Fit the doors, mortise them for hinges, and finish-sand.

THE BASE

The base of the clock is a simple box held to the case bottom panel with three through-bolts, one at the center of the front, and at each of the back corners. The base will contain a sack of lead shot to give the clock stability when the weights are pulled up. Any free-standing tall clock tends to be decidedly topheavy. The base and the case bottom panel are painted black

The clock stands on three feet—actually, hex-head bolts passed through the bottom of the box and threaded into T-nuts on the underside of the case bottom panel and locked after adjustment with a nut on top. This arrangement facilitates accurate leveling. Having only three feet prevents any rocking which would interfere with time-keeping. The clock should stand on a bare floor for best time-keeping.

MOUNTING THE MOVEMENT

The clock movement is mounted on a formed Plexiglas seatboard which is bolted to wood supports. These wood supports are glued and doweled to the sides of the clock.

Plexiglas is Rohm and Haas's trade name for acrylic, a thermoplastic that can be bent if first heated, and will stay bent if held in the bent position until cooled. Heating can be done with a strip heater. A strip heater element, and plans and directions for making a strip heater, can be obtained from the Brisk Heat Corporation. You will also need special drills for drilling the plastic, and a buffing kit. These can be obtained from plastics distributors listed in the Yellow Pages.

Heat-bending 1/4" acrylic is an art you might not get perfect the first time out. The seatboard supports should be located and doweled to the clock case after the seatboard is bent, making adjustment in the location to compensate for dimensional errors in the seatboard. The top of the seatboard must be flat and perfectly level.

remain square. This surface can then be used to guide the ball-bearing pilot of a 1/2"-radius, rounding-over router bit to form the curved part of the surface. Sand and scrape smooth. Do not profile the outside edges at this time—they should be left square to provide a clamping surface for case assembly. Now finish-sand all inside surfaces.

Begin assembly by gluing the back to one side using the top frame and the bottom panel to hold the two parts square. Clamp the frames together first without glue to make sure the spline joint will go together tightly.

Next add the top frame to the assembly, then the bottom panel floor and rail, then the waist rail, each time using the second side of the clock case as a fixture to assure alignment. Last, add the second side to the case assembly.

Fit the doorstop. Note that the ends of the horizontal doorstops fit into the dadoes in the

CLOCK MOVEMENT AND CHIME ASSEMBLY

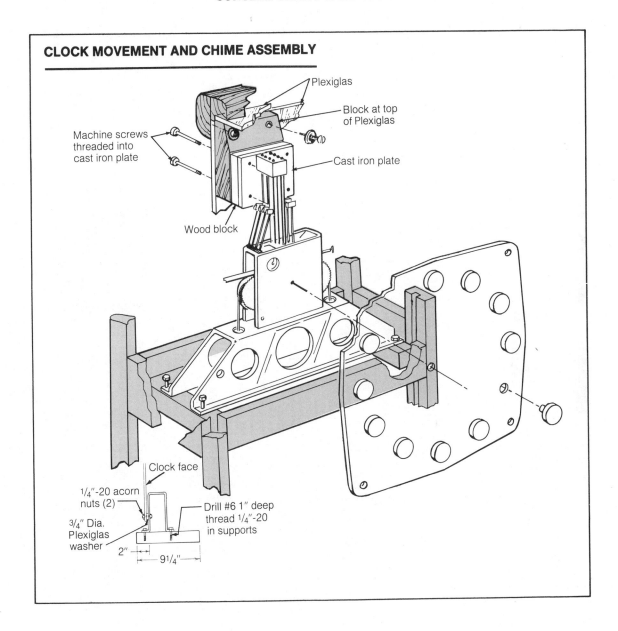

Plexiglas

Block at top of Plexiglas

Machine screws threaded into cast iron plate

Cast iron plate

Wood block

Clock face

1/4"-20 acorn nuts (2)

Drill #6 1" deep thread 1/4"-20 in supports

3/4" Dia. Plexiglas washer

2"

9 1/4"

Directions for bending come with the element, but two comments should be added. It is better to overheat than underheat because bubbles caused by overheating won't show while cold-bending craze marks will. Also, you have to hold the acrylic at the required 90° angle while cooling, and it is going to take some muscle to restrain it, as the plastic, if left alone, will revert to its original unbent position as it cools. I clamped a wood box to the bench to form a 90° corner jig into which I could force and clamp the plastic.

Warning: *Do not attempt to heat thr plastic in your kitchen oven. It does not work because you cannot concentrate the heat along the bend line and the fumes genertated and possibility of fire are real hazards.*

Trace the outline of the seatboard on the acrylic protective paper and mark locations of all holes except the guide holes for the trip and mute rods, and the two holes for attaching the face. These will be located later. Be particularly careful locating the holes for the chains. Polish

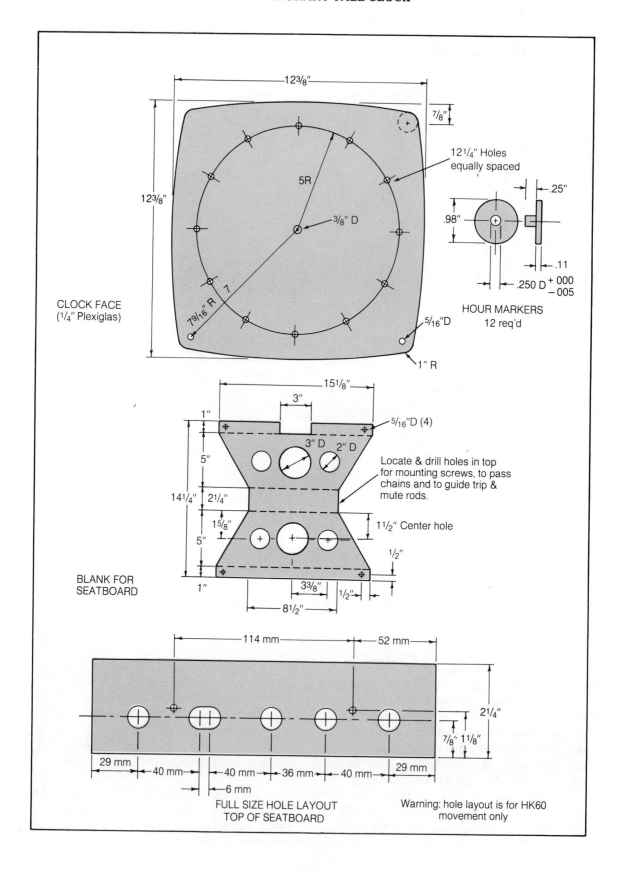

CLOCK FACE
(1/4" Plexiglas)

12 3/8"

12 3/8"

5R

3/8" D

7 9/16" R   7

5/16"D

1" R

7/8"

12 1/4" Holes
equally spaced

HOUR MARKERS
12 req'd

.25"

.98"

.11

.250 D +000 / −005

BLANK FOR
SEATBOARD

15 1/8"

3"

5/16"D (4)

1"

5"

14 1/4"

2 1/4"

1 5/8"

5"

1"

3" D   2" D

Locate & drill holes in top
for mounting screws, to pass
chains and to guide trip &
mute rods.

1 1/2" Center hole

1/2"

3 3/8"   1/2"

8 1/2"

114 mm

52 mm

2 1/4"

7/8" 1 1/8"

29 mm   40 mm   40 mm   36 mm   40 mm   29 mm

6 mm

FULL SIZE HOLE LAYOUT
TOP OF SEATBOARD

Warning: hole layout is for HK60
movement only

Fig. 3. Sand the top surface of the seatboard flat after the acrylic is formed so there will be no unevenness to twist the movement when it is clamped down. Wet-sand all exposed acrylic edges and the sanded top surface and polish to a transparent finish.

all edges before removing the protective paper and bending. After bending, sand and polish the top of the seatboard flat so the movement can be mounted without being distorted out of square by the mounting bolts (Fig. 3).

Now clamp the seatboard supports to the sides of the case and position them and the seatboard so the handshaft of the clock is lined up exactly in the center of the door opening, and the movement plates are level both side-to-side and front-to-back. The front surface of the seatboard (not the bottom flange) should be exactly 2″ behind the back surface of the waist rail (not the door-stop). Drill and tap the seatboard supports for 1″ ¼-20 bolts.

The upper door does not have a knob, but is opened by an inside pushrod reached by opening the lower door. (Once the clock is set up and adjusted, there is little reason to open the top door, as the weights are drawn up from below.) Drill aligned loose holes in the doorstop and the seatboard for the ⅛″ diameter rod. The rod

requires a thick center section to keep it from falling in or out. I crimped on a short piece of brass tubing.

The chime bar assembly is mounted on a wood block that is attached to the top of the back frame with wood screws and to the back acrylic panel with four through bolts. It is important that the chime rod assembly be solidly fastened to the back acrylic panel, as the panel acts as a sounding board. The mounting block is dimensioned to fit; I used two scraps of ¾″ walnut glued together.

CLOCK FACE

Make the clock face from ¼″ acrylic. Drill holes as shown and polish edges. The hour markers are turned from 1″ brass rod (Fig. 4). Six inches of rod is enough, but there is no excess for error. After turning, polish the markers and wash them in lacquer solvent. Dip them in a 1:1 mix of lacquer and solvent to preserve the finish.

Fig. 4. The markers for the clock face can be turned on a metalworking lathe from 1″ diameter brass rod. Bosses on the back of the markers fit into holes in the clock face. Glue them with clear epoxy.

The face is mounted to the seatboard with two pieces of threaded rod capped with acorn nuts on either end. You will probably need spacers between the face and the seatboard to keep the face clear of the movement. Make spacers in the form of washers from 1/4" Plexiglas. If by chance the front of the seatboard is not exactly vertical. taper the washers to compensate.

FINISHING AND GLAZING

Now remove everything from the interior of the case for finishing after which the acrylic glazing can be fitted. Walnut received the Watco Danish Oil finish only, following can directions. If you use pine quarter-round, it must be stained walnut first.

Begin the glazing with the back, which is made in one piece. Its actual maximum width is determined by the diagonal of the top case opening because that is how it has to be inserted., The glazing is held in place with 1/2" quarter-round molding, except behind the doorstop, where 1/8" x 3/8" flat strip is used.

To keep the acrylic panels from interfering with the retaining screws used with the quarter-round molding, glue a series of strips of 1/8" square and 1/8" x 1/4" balsa in the back case corners, and in the corners between the sides and the top. Fit the acrylic panels loosely to allow for expansion and contraction with changes in temperature.

Mute and strike control rods were made from 3/32" OD brass tube with a short length of 1/16" rod soldered in the top that can be bent to engage the movement-control arm. The rings on the bottom are picture-frame hangers epoxied into the tubes. Drill loose-fit holes in the seatboard to allow the rods to hang straight down from the movement connection. The chime trip rod has to be bent sideways below the seatboard hole so it will clear the time weight when the weight is drawn all the way up.

Fig. 5. Bronze-tinted Plexiglas panels are used to glaze the top, back, and sides of the case. Clear Plexiglas is used for the doors. The holes in the top of the back panel are for mounting the chime-rod assembly.

SETTING UP THE CLOCK

Directions for setting up and adjusting a movement are packed with it. If this is your first clock, a couple of precautions are in order. Once the movement is set up, never remove the pendulum rod with the weights in place. Without the restraint of the pendulum, the high-speed rundown can damage or destroy the escapement. And never move the clock—even a short distance—without first removing all three weights and then the pendulum rod, in that order.

For good time-keeping performance, and for the best sounding chimes and strike, any tall clock should stand on a bare floor. The additional weight of the 25 pounds of lead in the base will also reduce any tendency of the clock to sway (Fig. 7). Next best is a cotton shag rug. Standing a tall clock on a thickly piled wool or blend carpet with a cushion under it causes the clock to sway slightly in opposition to the pendulum swing, even causing the mechanism to stop.

Fig. 6. Before installing the movement, it should be bench-tested. It is easier to locate and drill holes in the seatboard for the mute and strike-control rods with the movement out in the open than in the case.

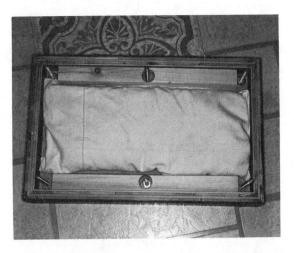

Fig. 7. Base of the clock case, showing the 25 pounds of lead shot that provide stability when the weights are pulled up, and the three adjustable feet at the front corners and at the center of the back. The other three bolts attach the base to the case floor. Note: the lead has been rebagged to lay flat in the base.

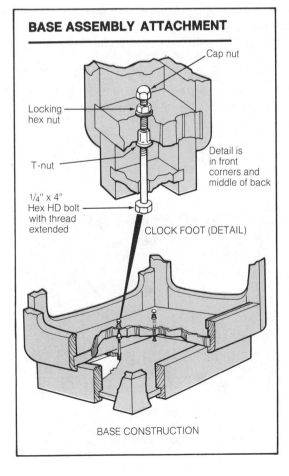

BASE ASSEMBLY ATTACHMENT

Cap nut

Locking hex nut

T-nut

Detail is in front corners and middle of back

1/4" x 4" Hex HD bolt with thread extended

CLOCK FOOT (DETAIL)

BASE CONSTRUCTION

(The hard vibration transmitted to the clock by someone walking on a bare floor does not affect timekeeping.) Also, with the clock so well cushioned from the floor, the chimes and strike are somewhat muted.

If a grandfather or grandmother clock has to stand on heavy-piled carpet, the case should be tipped back so the top rests against the wall. This will reduce the tendency to sway.

WORKING WITH SHEET ACRYLIC

Acrylic is a rigid, resilient thermoplastic material that is available in colorless and tinted transparent sheets, translucent and opaque colored sheets, and all of the above in a variety of textured surfaces. The two most prominent trade names are Plexiglas and Lucite.

Sheet acrylic in glazing grade (Plexiglas G, for example), is clear, durable, and lightweight (compared to glass of the same thickness). It is also resistant to yellowing, weather, and corrosion, and is easy to clean.

Acrylic is not as dimensionally stable as glass with changes in temperature. When fitted in a frame, a $1/16''$ gap per $12''$ of width and length must be allowed for expansion. This may require wider rabbets than you would make for glass.

CUTTING

Do not remove protective masking paper from sheet acrylic before cutting. If you must cut an unmasked sheet, center masking tape on the cut line on both sides. This will keep hot acrylic chips from gumming on the surface behind the blade and marring the surface, and prevent scratching the surface with the saw or saw table.

When sawing curves with a sabre, band, or scroll saw, use a fine-toothed metal-cutting blade with little set (14 tpi for $3/16''$ and $1/4''$ acrylic, 32 tpi for thinner sheets. A band-saw blade should have at least 10 tpi).

Make straight cuts with a circular saw, using a blade made for cutting acrylic, or a fine-toothed plywood or veneer blade (Fig. 8). All the teeth should be the same size, height, and point-to-point distance. Set the blade just slightly more than the thickness of the material to prevent chipping. Hold the work firmly, use clamps whenever possible, and feed slowly.

It is also possible cut acrylic by scoring and breaking. I seldom do it because sawing gives a cleaner cut and is faster. Special scribing tools are available. Clamp a straightedge to guide the scriber, and draw the tool the full edge-to-edge length of the cut, with a firm pressure, from five to ten times, depending on the thickness of the material.

Place the scribed line face up over a $3/4''$ diameter wood dowel running the length of the intended break. To break, hold the sheet with one hand and apply downward pressure on the short side of the break with the other. The hands should be kept adjacent to one another and successively repositioned about $2''$ in back of the break as it progresses along the scribed line. The minimum cut-off width is about $1 1/2''$. Patterned acrylic sheet cannot be scored and broken.

Fig. 8. Straight cuts can be made in acrylic with any circular saw with a fine-toothed plywood or veneer blade, or a special acrylic blade. Use a sabre, scroll, or band saw for sawing curves.

DRILLING

Standard twist drills can be used to drill acrylic sheet, but they don't work too well. Back the plastic with wood, clamp and drill at a slow speed with minimum pressure.

If you drill at too high a speed the acrylic sheet will climb the drill. If you apply too much pressure, you will chip the back side of the hole even before the drill penetrates the material.

Specially ground drills should be used to drill acrylic. Use a high speed, up to 3000 rpm, for holes under $3/8''$. For larger holes, use a slower drill speed, 1000-2000 rpm. Do not force feed. Slow the feed as the drill point penetrates the second surface.

EDGE FINISHING

This is done in three stages: smooth finish, satin finish, and transparent finish.

Smooth finish. Remove file, saw, and other tool marks by scraping, draw-filing, or sanding with 80-grit abrasive paper. If you use a disc or belt sander, stop often to remove the waste acrylic adhering to the work edge.

Satin finish. To improve the appearance of the edge and prepare it for cementing, sand it with 250-, then 320-grit wet-or-dry paper. If the joint will be cemented, be careful not to round the edge, as this will result in bubbles in the cemented joint.

Transparent finish. For a transparent, high-gloss edge, sand the stain edge with *wet* 400-, then 500-grit wet-or-dry paper. Buff the edge with a muslin wheel charged with buffing compound.

CEMENTING

Capillary cementing (Plexiglas G and equivalent acrylics only). Capillary cementing is done with a solvent (IPS Weld-ON #3 Solvent for Cementing Plexiglas, Methylene Chloride MDC, Ethylene Dichloride EDC or 1-1-2 Trichlorethane). It is an easy method of joining two pieces of Plexiglas G. Note: Plexiglas K (glazing grade) and equivalent acrylic sheets cannot be cemented this way.

The edges to be solvent-cemented must have very accurate and square satin edges. Do not polish the edges. Remove protective paper. Hold pieces together with strips of masking tape. Apply solvent to joint with the Hypo RH-200 Solvent Applicator (Fig. 9). Always keep the solvent-cemented joint horizontal. Let the joint dry thoroughly before moving it, or removing the tape.

Thickened cement. IPS Weld-On #16 Thickened cement produces high-strength joints with good outdoor weather resistance on both types of acrylic.

Satin finish edges. Do not polish. Remove protective masking paper. Check for good fit of parts. Apply a small bead of cement to joint.

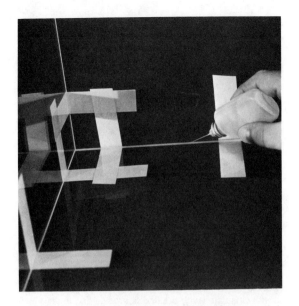

Fig. 9. To cement sheets of acrylic, tape finished edges and apply solvent to horizontal joint. Capillary action draws the solvent into the joint where it dissolves plastic at edges, which then fuse together.

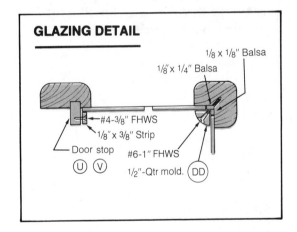

GLAZING DETAIL

1/8 x 1/8″ Balsa
1/8″ x 1/4″ Balsa
#4-3/8″ FHWS
1/8″ x 3/8″ Strip
Door stop
#6-1″ FHWS
U V
1/2″-Qtr mold. DD

Gently join pieces being cemented. Clamp or hold firmly until set. Let joint cure thoroughly, at least 2 hours.

Caution: *Solvents may be toxic if inhaled for extended periods of time or if swallowed; many are also flammable. Use in a well-ventilated area; keep away from children.*

SURFACE REPAIR

Use thickened cement. Several applications may be required to fill a scratch. Allow 24 hours

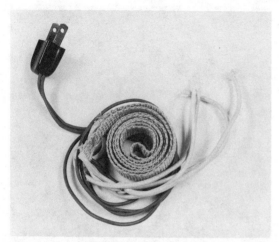

Fig. 10. BriskHeat RH-36 element is designed for bending plastic sheets in strip heater. The tape element consists of finely stranded resistance wires doubly insulated with braided fiberglass and knitted into flat tapes with fiberglass yarn. The heating element is 1/2" wide and 36" long. It is wired to a standard two-prong 110-volt plug.

drying time between applications. Sand with a very fine wet-or-dry paper and buff to transparency as in edge finishing.

STRIP-HEAT FORMING

Acrylic sheet may be formed along a straight line by strip-heating using a strip heater element in a shopmade fixture (Figs. 10, 11).

To strip-heat and bend acrylic, first remove the protective paper. Mark a line on the acrylic where you want to bend with a china marker and place the acrylic on the heater with the line to be bent centered over the heating element. Allow the material to heat thoroughly until it softens or wilts in the area to be formed, about 5–6 minutes for $1/8$" thick material and 12–15 minutes for $1/4$"). Bend to the desired angle, keeping the heated side of the material on the outside of the bend, and hold firmly until cool (Fig. 12).

The acrylic will tend to return to its prior flat

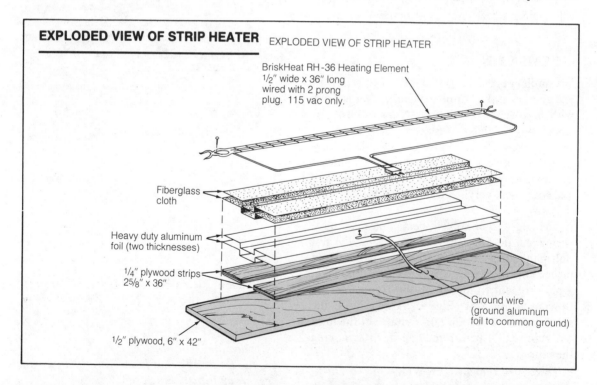

EXPLODED VIEW OF STRIP HEATER

BriskHeat RH-36 Heating Element
$1/2$" wide x 36" long
wired with 2 prong
plug. 115 vac only.

Fiberglass cloth

Heavy duty aluminum foil (two thicknesses)

$1/4$" plywood strips
$25/8$" x 36"

Ground wire
(ground aluminum
foil to common ground)

$1/2$" plywood, 6" x 42"

Fig. 11. A strip heater to accommodate the BriskHeat element can be made in your shop. Center and nail two plywood strips on a plywood base, leaving a 3/4"-wide channel along center of base. Cut two 6" by 36" pieces of heavy-duty aluminum foil; place over strips and form into the channel. Attach a ground wire to the aluminum foil with a washer and screw (in use, ground the strip heater to the outlet coverplate screw). Insulate with fiberglass cloth pressed into channel. Staple fiberglass cloth and foil to plywood strips with staples. Lay BriskHeat element in channel. Drive a nail 1½" from each end of the base and tie the end strings of the element to nails.

condition until it cools. For accurate work make an angle jig to hold or clamp the plastic while it cools.

Bending material before it is thoroughly heated will result in crazing (small internal fractures) along the bend. Overheating may cause scorching and bubbling; if this occurs, check to be sure that the distance between the heating element and and the acrylic sheet is approximately $\frac{1}{8}''$. Practice on scrap material first. Acrylic thicker than $\frac{1}{4}''$ requires a commercial strip heater for bending.

Safety. *Work in a well-ventilated area. Have a general-purpose ABC rated (dry powder) fire extinguisher nearby. Do not heat acrylic with an open flame or in a kitchen oven. Kitchen ovens are not equipped with adequate temperature controls and safety devices for this type of work.*

Heating acrylic in an oven produces monomer bleed-off. These gases are combustible, and if ignited, can cause severe explosions. Kitchen ovens and other heating devices, which do not circulate air to prevent accumulation of these gases, and which are not equipped with proper temperature controls and safety devices for this type of work, should not be used.

CLEANING ACRYLIC

Dusting. Always damp-dust acrylic. For best results, mix a solution of one teaspoon dishwashing liquid and water; apply this solution to Plexiglas with a spray bottle and wipe until dry and glossy smooth with a clean cotton-flannel cloth.

Washing. Wash acrylic with a mild soap or detergent and lukewarm water. Use a clean, soft cloth or a sponge and as much solution as possible. Rinse well. Dry by blotting with a damp cloth. Do not use window cleaning fluids, scouring compounds, gritty cloths, gasoline, or strong solvents such as alcohol, acetone, carbon tetrachloride, etc. To remove tar, grease, paint, etc. use kerosene.

Polishing. There are polishes made for polishing acrylic. A periodic waxing with automobile paste wax (not a cleaner-wax combination) will protect the surface and maintain lustre. Apply a thin coating of wax with a soft cloth; buff lightly with cotton flannel. After waxing, wipe with a clean, damp cloth to remove static charges which will attract dust particles. Do not use household spray waxes, as many of these contain agents harmful to the surface.

Scratch Removal. Minor surface scratches can be visibly removed by sanding out the scratch with 400–600 grit wet or dry sandpaper and buffing with a clean muslin wheel dressed with fine-grit buffing compound.

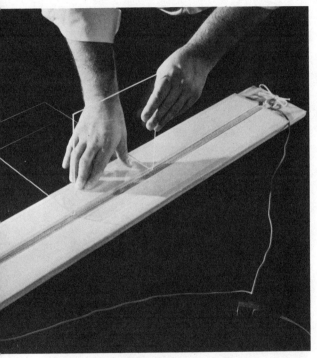

Fig. 12. To bend sheet acrylic, first remove protective paper and mark bend line with a china marker. Place on fixture with bend line centered on the element. Allow material to heat thoroughly (until it softens in the line area), then bend to the desired angle and hold until the plastic cools.

DAVENPORT DESK

5

DAVENPORT DESK

A Davenport desk is a small desk with origins in early 19th century England. The prototype is believed to have been a shipboard desk ordered by a Captain Davenport from the cabinetmaking firm of Gillow and Sons. It was a very popular style of desk in the early and middle Victorian years.

Although there was considerable variety in the design of Davenport desks, all had drawers in the side (one or both sides), rather than in front. The writing surface was usually a hinged compartment lid, but some desks had pull-out writing surfaces. The desks tended to be elaborately decorated. Ours is made of cherry, with Carpathian elm burl-veneer panels. The panel trim is walnut.

Many of the early Davenport desks were fiendishly ingenious, with secret compartments, swing-out drawers, and compartments with small drawers and pigeon holes that rose above the desk top when a catch was released.

The dimensioning of this desk started with a modern hanging file. The lower double drawers will each accommodate these useful files. You could quite properly have drawers on one side only, with dummy drawer fronts on the other side, or a combination of drawers that run the full width of the desk with some that don't. Dummy drawer fronts can be made up that are attached to the drawer rails so you could easily reverse the side with the drawers when the desk is moved to a different location.

Opportunities are endless for tailoring this desk to your exact needs. Plans are given for an interior compartment with drawers and pigeon holes if you want them in your desk; materials for the compartment, however, have not been included in the cutting list.

You will need about 35 board feet of $3/4''$ cherry lumber for the desk. Begin construction by planning how you will get all the parts out of your lumber. When you blank the parts, leave some extra allowance on lengths for squaring and fitting. (Dimensions are given assuming nominally $3/4''$-thick wood; when you surface-sand the wood, it usually ends up less than $3/4''$ thick.)

DRAWER CASE

Begin construction with the front and back frames of the drawer case. Rabbet top rails, bottom rails, and stiles to receive the veneered plywood panels. Assemble the frames with dowels. Four drawer-frame assemblies are required. They

EXPLODED VIEW

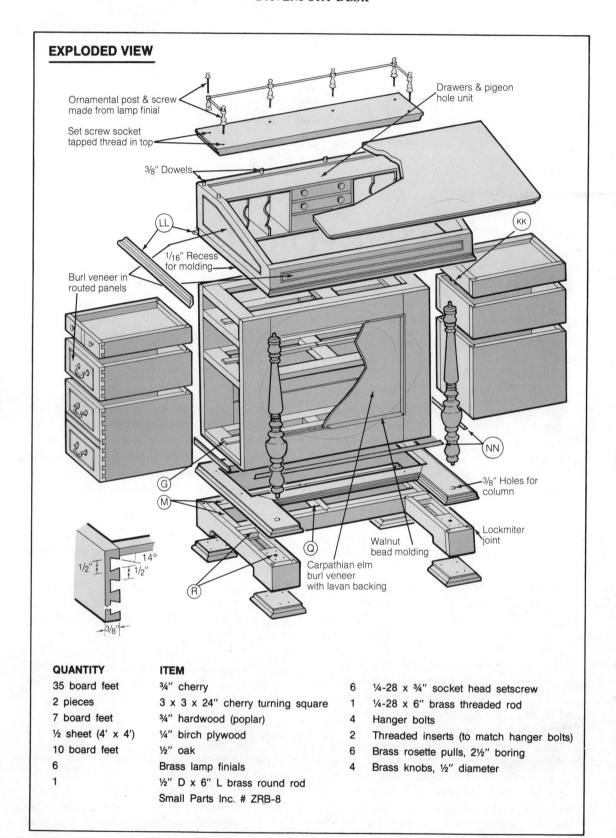

Ornamental post & screw made from lamp finial

Set screw socket tapped thread in top

3/8" Dowels

LL

1/16" Recess for molding

Burl veneer in routed panels

Drawers & pigeon hole unit

KK

NN

3/8" Holes for column

Lockmiter joint

Walnut bead molding

Carpathian elm burl veneer with lavan backing

G

M

Q

R

14°

1/2"

1/2"

3/8"

QUANTITY	ITEM		
35 board feet	¾" cherry	6	¼-28 x ¾" socket head setscrew
2 pieces	3 x 3 x 24" cherry turning square	1	¼-28 x 6" brass threaded rod
7 board feet	¾" hardwood (poplar)	4	Hanger bolts
½ sheet (4' x 4')	¼" birch plywood	2	Threaded inserts (to match hanger bolts)
10 board feet	½" oak	6	Brass rosette pulls, 2½" boring
6	Brass lamp finials	4	Brass knobs, ½" diameter
1	½" D x 6" L brass round rod		
	Small Parts Inc. # ZRB-8		

CUTTING LIST

KEY	PART NAME	QTY.	MATERIAL	DIMENSIONS
A	Top Rail	2	¾" cherry	3⅜ x 19"
B	Bottom Rail	2	¾" cherry	3⅝ x 19"
C	Stile	4	¾" cherry	4⅜ x 21¼"
D	Drawer Rail	8	¾" cherry	2 x 10½"
E	Drawer runner	8	¾" hardwood	1¼ x 23½"
F	Drawer Back Rail	4	¾" hardwood	3 x 8"
G	Drawer Guide	6	¾" hardwood	1⅛ x 12½"
H	Base Side	2	¾" cherry	2¾ x 22"
I	Base Inside Piece	2	¾" cherry	2¾ x 9¼"
J	Base Front	2	¾" cherry	2¾ x 4"
K	Base Back	1	¾" cherry	2¾ x 28"
L	Base Cross Brace	1	¾" cherry	1⅞ x 27"
M	Base Cleat	6	¾" hardwood	1¼ x 12"
N	Base Top	2	¾" cherry	4⅞ x 23"
O	Base Back Trim	1	¾" cherry	1¾ x 29"
P	Base Front Trim	1	¾" cherry	1¾ x 24"
Q	Base Brace	1	¾" hardwood	1⅞ x 12"
R	Base Glue Blocks	3	¾" hardwood	3 x 3" (split one)
S	Foot	4	¾" cherry	4⅞ x 4⅞"
T	Box Side	2	¾" cherry	7½ x 21"
U	Box Front	1	¾" cherry	4 x 27"
V	Box Back	1	¾" cherry	7½ x 27"
W	Box Top	1	¾" cherry	6⁷⁄₁₆ x 27⅞"
X	Box Lid	1	¾" cherry	16⅝ x 27⅞"
Y	Box Bottom	1	¾" cherry	20 x 24"
Z	Panel	2	¼" plywood	15 x 19"
AA	Drawer Front	6	¾" cherry	5³⁄₁₆ x 10⅜"
BB	Lower Drawer Side	4	½" oak	11 x 13"
CC	Lower Drawer Back	2	½" oak	11 x 10⅜"
DD	False Rail	2	¾" cherry	¾ x 10⅜"
EE	Middle Drawer Side	4	½" oak	5³⁄₁₆ x 13"
FF	Middle Drawer Back	2	½" oak	5³⁄₁₆ x 10⅜"
GG	Top Drawer Front	2	¾" cherry	1¾ x 10⅜"
HH	Top Drawer Side	4	½" oak	2 x 13"
II	Top Drawer Back	2	½" oak	2 x 10⅜"
JJ	Drawer Bottom	6	¼" birch ply	9⅞ x 12¾"
KK	Drawer Runner	6	½" hardwood	2¼ x 13"
LL	Box Side Molding	2	¾" cherry	½ x 23"
MM	Box Front, Back Molding	2	¾" cherry	½ x 29"
NN	Base Cove Molding	3	¼ cherry	¹⁵⁄₁₆ x 28"
OO	Column	2	Cherry	3 x 3 x 24"

FRONT AND SIDE VIEWS

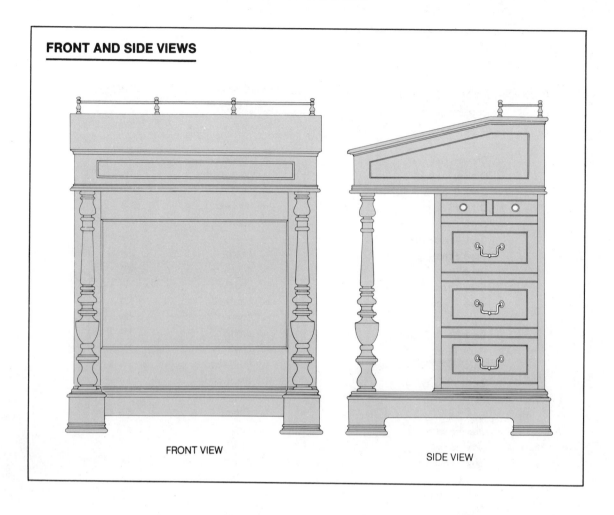

FRONT VIEW

SIDE VIEW

Fig. 1. Drilling the dowel holes in rails and guides requires accuracy. Best way is in a horizontal boring setup, as shown here. Always work with the same mating sides of the workpieces as the reference surface. This way, if you accidentally drill a hole slightly off the center-line, the parts are offset instead of twisted when you dowel them together, which is a lot easier to correct.

Fig. 2. Before gluing, completely assemble the case dry to be sure all joints are true. Shown is the top drawer frame being glued and aligned to one of the sides with a pair of shop-made right-angle gluing jigs, and double-checked with a carpenter's square. As each successive frame is added, it will be aligned by having the unglued side dry-doweled to the other side of the case.

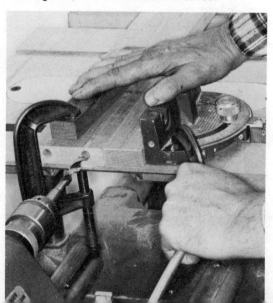

DRAWER CASE

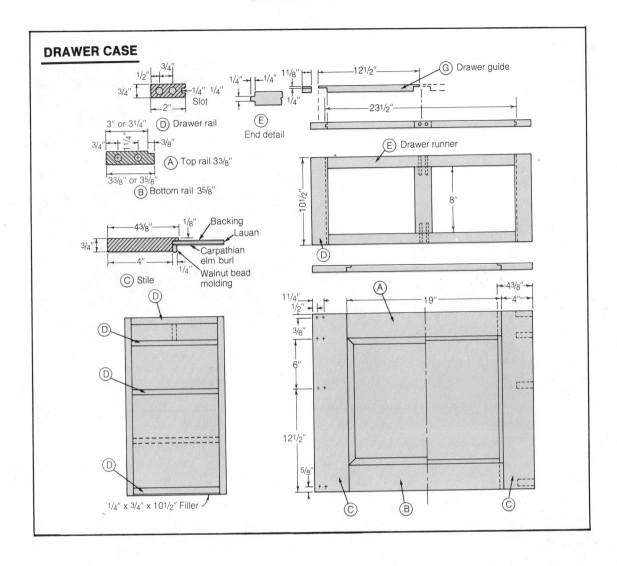

Fig. 3. Final step in assembling the drawer case is gluing on second side. As this involves 16 dowels, I suggest asking help. Apply glue to all side holes and insert dowels all the way before putting any glue in the frame holes.

are identical except that the top one does not have drawer guides. Rails and guides can be doweled, rather than mortise and tenoned, as shown in Fig. 1. The back drawer rail is doweled in place after the rails and guides are assembled.

When laying out double-hole locations, note that the bottom drawer-frame assembly is spaced up 1/4" from the bottom of the case and the space is to be filled with a filler block. This was done to keep the face of the bottom-drawer rails clear of the base cove molding.

The center-drawer guides are positioned with a gap between them for inserting a piece of plywood to serve as a drawer stop. Shims can be added to the face of the plywood for exact drawer positioning.

BASE FRAME

The ends of the parts for the base frame and the sides, and the ends of the front and back of the box, should all be formed at one time. Both the base and the box use identical lock miter joints. I prefer this joint to a splined miter (a plain miter would not be strong enough for the desk) as it is far easier to clamp. Alignment of the joint is positive and you only have to clamp from one side. Follow the steps shown in Figs. 4 and 5 to make the joints, but first make test cuts in pieces of scrap the same thickness as your stock.

After forming the lock miter joints, cut the grooves in the inside of the box sides, front and back, for the bottom panel, and in the base frame parts for glue blocks and cleats.

Rabbet and dado the base frame parts and do a trail assembly, then glue (Fig. 6). Do not assemble the box at this time.

All of the moldings for the base and box should be formed at one time with one setup. For safety in handling, I glued the box trim strips and

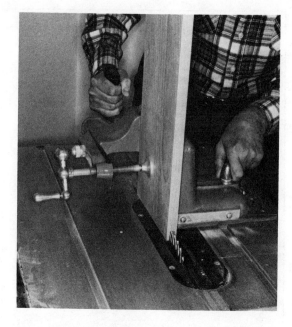

Fig. 4. To make a lock miter joint, first cut a dado in the end of the board. A Rockwell tenoning jig is invaluable for holding workpieces securely.

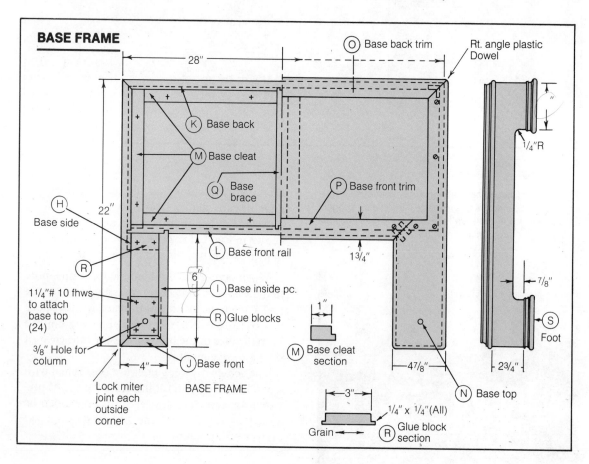

Fig. 5. Next, cut off the inside stub tenon. For precise cuts on small workpieces, it's hard to beat this Dremel table saw.

Fig. 6. Gluing up the base frame. The lock miter joints are easy to assemble; alignment is positive, and clamping is required in one direction only.

the base back and front strips back-to-back to waste pine. Follow the sequence shown in Figs. 8–10 to form the molding.

Miter the base top parts and assemble them with reinforcing dowels (Fig. 11). Use the base frame as a jig to get the parts cut correctly. When glued, drill all screw holes for attachment to the base-frame cleats. Next, position the base top on the inverted drawer case, and drill for screws.

BOX

Before the box is assembled make jigs and rout out the recesses in the sides, front, and back for the veneered panels. These recesses should be $5/16''$ deep. The bottom panel is made narrower than the front-to-back opening and glued only at the front to allow expansion and contraction with changes in humidity. With normal humidity change, the top can be doweled to the sides and back.

To assemble the box, glue the bottom panel to the box front, then glue up all corner joints immediately. After the box is glued, rabbet around all sides to receive the molding, which can be mitered and glued to the box. The rabbet

Fig. 7. Cleats are used to attach the base top to the base. The cleats are tenoned into the base frame after being first clamped to the drawer case and drilled for attaching the base top to the drawer case.

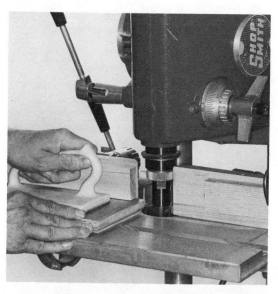

Fig. 8. First step in making the molding is to cut a rabbet in the board edge, thus doing away with waste prior to routing. Fingerboards hold the box top against the fence for making the cut.

Fig. 9. The undercut cove part of the desk molding is best done on a shaper as the right cove bit is not easy to locate. Do the shaping in several light, slow passes, end-grain first.

Fig. 10. The squared edge of the cove part of the molding was cleaned out with a slotting cutter with the router set up in a shaping table.

Fig. 11. Mitered joints between base tops and base front trim are reinforced with two dowels. Dowel holes must be drilled through the base trim as the dowels have to be driven into the joints after assembly.

MOLDING

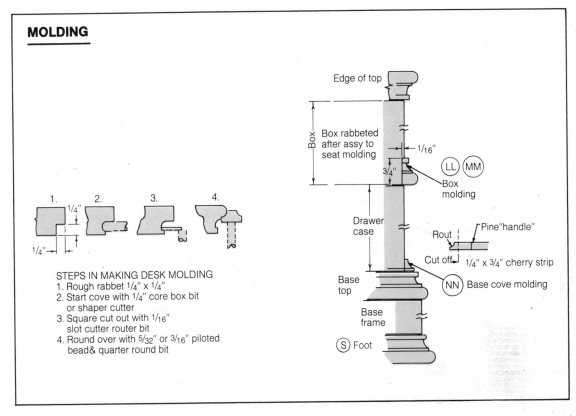

STEPS IN MAKING DESK MOLDING
1. Rough rabbet 1/4" x 1/4"
2. Start cove with 1/4" core box bit
   or shaper cutter
3. Square cut out with 1/16"
   slot cutter router bit
4. Round over with 5/32" or 3/16" piloted
   bead& quarter round bit

Edge of top

Box rabbeted
after assy to
seat molding

1/16"

3/4"

(LL) (MM)

Box
molding

Drawer
case

Rout

Pine"handle"

Cut off

1/4" x 3/4" cherry strip

Base
top

(NN) Base cove molding

Base
frame

(S) Foot

BOX

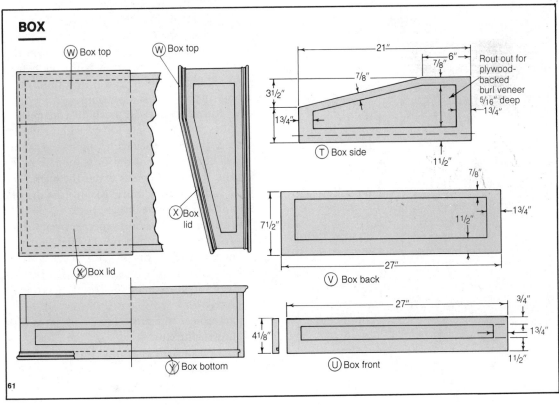

(W) Box top

(W) Box top

(X) Box
lid

(X) Box lid

(Y) Box bottom

21"

6"

7/8"

Rout out for
plywood-
backed
burl veneer
5/16" deep

7/8"

31/2"

13/4"

13/4"

(T) Box side

11/2"

7/8"

13/4"

71/2"

11/2"

27"

(V) Box back

27"

3/4"

41/8"

13/4"

(U) Box front

11/2"

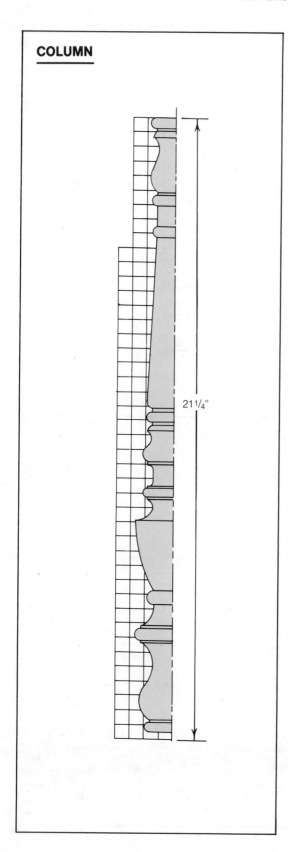

COLUMN

21¼"

provides a better looking joint, and allows more thickness to be left on the molding for safer ripping from the blank.

COLUMNS

Turn the two columns following the pattern. The top of the column is fitted with a short hanger bolt that threads into a steel threaded insert in the bottom of the box. A longer hanger bolt in the bottom of the column passes through clearance holes in the base top and glue block and is secured with a washer and nut.

DRAWERS

The two large drawer fronts are given the appearance of being two drawers. The fronts and dummy rails are glued up with dowels. Before gluing, rout a $1/16''$ by $1/16''$ rabbet in the drawer fronts as shown, to enhance the two-drawer appearance. If either of the big drawers is going to contain a hanging file, notch the sides for the support rails before you assemble the drawers. The drawer fronts are routed out to a depth of $5/16''$ to receive the Carpathian elm burl panel (Fig. 12). The panel should be glued into the drawer after routing the dovetails and before drawer assembly. We used a thin walnut bead molding ripped from scrap wood.

The drawers otherwise are built conventionally. Sides, and front, are joined with router-jig dovetails, sides and back with tongue-and rabbet joints. The drawer bottom is slotted into the sides and front, but passes under the back. The runner is doweled or mortised into the drawer front and nailed to the drawer back.

The Carpathian elm burl veneer proved to be a real problem as it would not lay flat and was extremely brittle. It was difficult to cut without breaking, and impossible to clamp flat to true the edges for book-matching the large drawer case panels.

To get veneer to lie flat, I had to treat it with the following mixture:

3 parts plastic (urea) resin glue (powder)
4 parts cold water
2 parts glycerine (drug store)
1 part denatured alcohol

DRAWERS

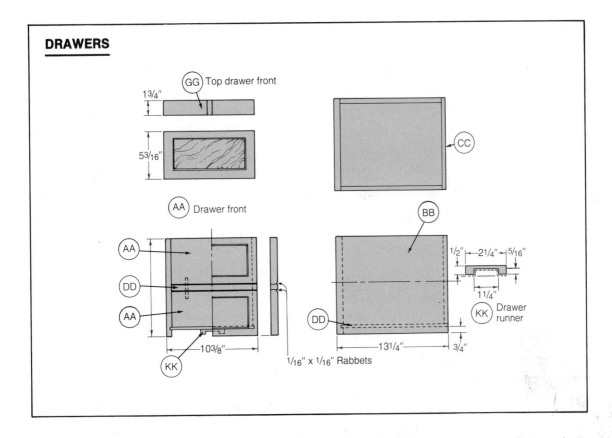

Fig. 12. Routing out recesses for burl veneer panels. Jigs are required to guide the router when routing out the 5/16"-deep recesses in the box sides and drawer fronts. Material must be left in the middle of the recess to support the router. This waste is routed out last.

Fig. 13. Carpathian elm burl veneer is brittle, and seldom flat enough to cut accurately by any means. Before use, soak the veneer in a mixture of dilute plastic resin glue and glycerine and let dry several days while flattened under weights.

Fig. 14. Fixture to hold veneer for edge dressing. To dress veneer edges for butt joints, clamp the stacked veneer between boards and sand it on a disk or belt sander.

Measurements are by volume. The plastic resin glue must be fresh; the powder goes bad in the can. Mix the powder and water, add the other two ingredients. The diluted glue sizes the veneer to add strength, the glycerine provides flexibility. The alcohol speeds drying. Soak the veneer in the solution for two minutes, drain dry, wipe the surfaces and put the veneer between sheets of aluminum foil, stack between boards and weight the pile to flatten. Drying will take several days. The veneer will come out flat, flexible, and easy to cut.

Quarter-inch lauan plywood was used for the large drawer-case panels, and the backside was veneered with low-cost veneer to balance out any warp. Veneer for the small panels inset in the drawers and box were glued to $1/8$" plywood. No veneer was added to the backs as these panels will be glued into the drawers. All of the veneered panels were trimmed with walnut bead molding.

The box is attached to the drawer case with brass screws through the box bottom into the top drawer rails.

GALLERY

The gallery was made using inexpensive brass table lamp finials for posts. Drill the finials from the bottom to $1/16$" from the top with a #43 drill, then tap the hole for 4-40 threads. Cut off the tops of the finials as shown and dress the cut edges. Turn the rail post sections from $1/2$" brass rod, and drill for $1/8$"-diameter brass rod rails, and a clearance hole for a 4-40 threaded rod. Attach the post to the top by threading a $1/4$-28 x $3/4$" socket-head setscrew into the wood and thread the finial onto the rod. Cut $1/8$" rod for the rails and insert in post rail sections. Secure these sections to the finals with the dinial tips and 4–40 threaded rod.

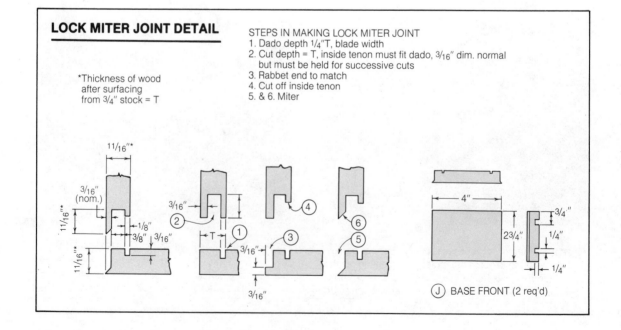

LOCK MITER JOINT DETAIL

STEPS IN MAKING LOCK MITER JOINT
1. Dado depth $1/4$"T, blade width
2. Cut depth = T, inside tenon must fit dado, $3/16$" dim. normal but must be held for successive cuts
3. Rabbet end to match
4. Cut off inside tenon
5. & 6. Miter

*Thickness of wood after surfacing from $3/4$" stock = T

(J) BASE FRONT (2 req'd)

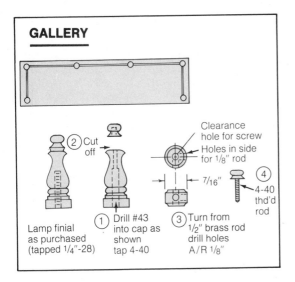

GALLERY

② Cut off

Lamp finial as purchased (tapped 1/4"-28)

① Drill #43 into cap as shown tap 4-40

Clearance hole for screw
Holes in side for 1/8" rod

7/16"

④ 4-40 thd'd rod

③ Turn from 1/2" brass rod drill holes A/R 1/8"

FINISHING

The wood can either be stained, or allowed to darken naturally with age. We stained. We used fruitwood stain on the cherry, walnut stain on the walnut, and a light-colored oak stain on the Carpathian elm burl. All the parts can be stained and varnished completely before assembly, which makes the task a lot easier. The top coat consisted of two coats of UGL's ZAR Quick Dry polyurethane coating lightly sanded between coats to knock off any dust particles, followed by three coats of their Gloss ZAR with more thorough sanding between coats. All coats were applied with foam brushes, whic lay on a thinner and smoother coat than you will get with a hair or nylon brush.

Fig. 15. Assembling the desk carcase. The desk was built in modules—base frame, base top, drawer case, and box. The base frame and base top are first drilled for screws, then separated. Base top is then attached to the drawer case, and the base frame reattached to the base top.

Fig. 16. Attach the box to the drawer case with brass wood screws—brass, because the screws at the front of drawer case will show inside the box. After box top and lid have been mortised for hinges, the top is attached to the box with dowels.

6

BLANKET CHEST

This handsome knotty-pine blanket chest features traditional Early American frame-and panel construction and is lined with aromatic red cedar. A layer of 6 mile polyethylene between the pine and the cedar seals in the aroma.

The blanket chest is not a difficult project but don't plan on doing it over a weekend. There is a lot of work. Take one step at a time, and you should end up with a piece of furniture you cna be really proud of.

Knoty-pine lumber, sometimes called antique white pine, should not be confused with lumberyard common shelving, which usually has large, unsound (and unattractive) knots and is prone to warp. Knotty-pine is obtainable from hardwood lumber dealers.

FRAME

Begin construction by planning the cutting of $3/4''$ or $13/16''$ knoty-pine stock to get the most attractive knot and grain arrangements for the panels, then cut all parts for the frame to dimension.

Hand-cut dovetails are used on the corners for strength and appearance. These can be cut with a saber saw (Fig. 1). To keep construction simple, other frame joints are spline-reinforced butt joints (Fig. 2). That may seem complicated, but it isn't. The joints are assembled dry and clamped as simple butt joints; then a slot is plunge-routed on the inside surface at each joint for a $1/4'' \times 1/4''$ spline. The spline provides spositve alignment for the joint when it is glued, in addition to strengthening the basically weak butt joint. (Although this joint will not be as strong as either a mortise-and-tenon joint or a dowel joint, once the aromatic cedar liner is nailed in place the chest will be exceptionally strong.)

When all your corner dovetail joints have been cut and fitted, glue the frames together. Now sand panel openings in frames and the whole exterior.

Blank $1/2''$ plywood for the bottom; place the glued-up frame on the bottom and mark the inside edge. Staple 6-mil polyethylene sheeting to the bottom, leaving $4''$ all around to fold up on the sides.

EXPLODED VIEW

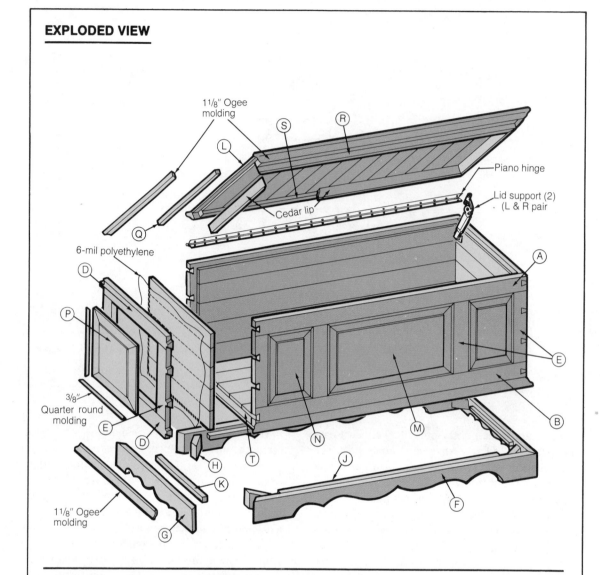

1 1/8" Ogee molding

S

R

L

Cedar lip

Piano hinge

Lid support (2) (L & R pair

6-mil polyethylene

Q

D

A

P

3/8" Quarter round molding

E

E

B

D

T

N

M

H

J

1 1/8" Ogee molding

K

F

G

MATERIALS LIST

QUANTITY	ITEM
34 board feet	$\frac{13}{16}$" knotty pine
8 board feet	3/8" knotty pine, or 1 pc. 1/4"
	Knotty pine plywood, 20" x 48"
1 bundle (40 sq. ft.)	Tongue and groove 3/8" aromatic red cedar
1 piece	1/2" plywood, 20" x 48"
24 feet	1 1/8" ogee molding
38 feet	3/8" quarter round molding
48 inches	Piano hinge, drilled for screws
40 square feet	6-mil polyethylene
1 pair	Lid supports: left hand # 100-039
	Right hand #100-038 Woodworker's
	Supply of New Mexico

FRONT AND SIDE VIEWS

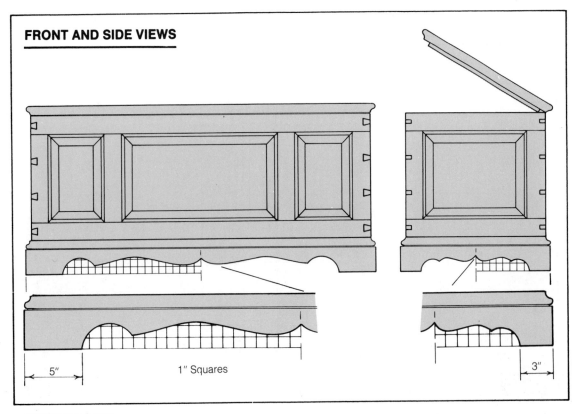

5"

1" Squares

3"

CUTTING LIST

KEY	PARTS NAME	QTY.	MATERIAL	DIMENISIONS
A	Top Rail	2	knotty pine	¾ x 2½ x 48"
B	Bottom Rail	2	knotty pine	¾ x 3½ x 48"
C	End Top Rail	2	knotty pine	¾ x 2½ x 20"
D	End Bottom Rail	2	knotty pine	¾ x 3½ x 20"
E	Post	12	knotty pine	¾ x 2½ x 12"
F	Base	2	knotty pine	¾ x 3 ½ x 49⅝"
G	End Base	2	knotty pine	¾ x 3½ x 21⅝"
H	Glue Block	4	knotty pine	¾ x 3 x 3"
J	Cleat	2	knotty pine	¾ x 1 x 43"
K	Cleat	2	knotty pine	¾ x 1 x 15"
L	Lid Panel	1	knotty pine	⅜ x 20 x 48"
M	Center Raised Panel	2	knotty pine	¾ x 11⅞ x 21⅞"
N	Side Raised Panel	4	knotty pine	¾ x 11⅞ x 7⅞"
P	End Raised Panel	2	knotty pine	¾ x 11⅞ x 14⅞"
Q	End Lid Frame	2	knotty pine	¹³⁄₁₆ x ¹³⁄₁₆ x 20"
R	Front Lid Frame	1	knotty pine	⁷⁄₁₆ x ¹³⁄₁₆ x 48"
S	Back Lid Frame	1	knotty pine	⁵⁄₁₆ x ¹³⁄₁₆ x 48"
T	Bottom	1	Plywood	½ x 20 x 48"

DOVETAIL DETAIL

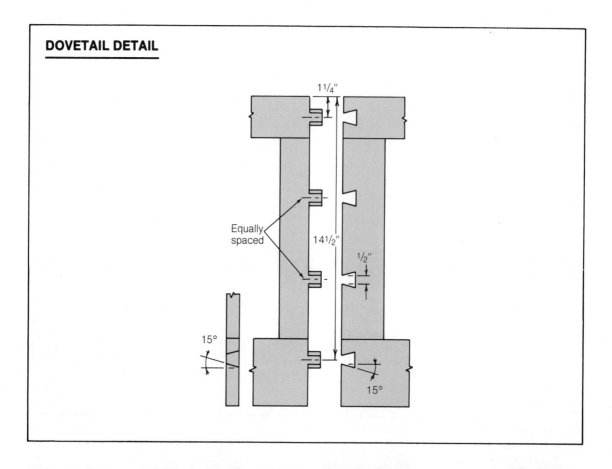

Equally spaced

1¼"

14½"

½"

15°

15°

Fig. 1. Dovetail pins and tails can be cut with a sabre saw and fine-toothed blade at slow speed. Clean up the tails with a chisel and file, then fit the pins to the tails.

Fig. 2. Each frame butt joint is reinforced on the inside with a spline fitted into a plunge-routed slot. Spline also provides positive alignment for gluing.

CEDAR LINING

Go through your bundle of tongue-and-groove cedar and select eight pieces long enough to span the front and back frame center openings so that each piece so used can be nailed at each end (Fig. 3). Also, sort out some good ones for the lid. Use short pieces for the bottom, where they will be the least visible. Set aside a long piece for making the lid lip.

Apply cedar lining to the area of the bottom inside the line you previously marked, using ¾" finishing nails. Butt the grooved edge of the first plank just inside the back edge line and drive nails through the edge of the plank where they will be covered by the side planking. Nail the rest of the planking through the tongues. Nail heads should be either hidden or countersunk.

After the bottom is lined, attach the frame to the bottom with flathead wood screws or drywall screws.

Staple polyethlene to the inside of the side frame and line them with cedar. Trim the top plank so that its top edge is exactly ¼" from the top of the frame.

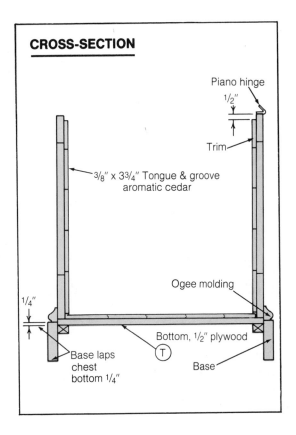

CROSS-SECTION

Piano hinge

½"

Trim

⅜" x 3¾" Tongue & groove aromatic cedar

Ogee molding

¼"

Bottom, ½" plywood

T

Base laps chest bottom ¼"

Base

Fig. 3. T&G cedar lining must be selected so that each piece can be nailed to the front and back chest frames. Use angled nails through the tongues.

BASE

Blank the four sides of the base and miter the ends, then saw the scrollwork decoration. Before assembling the base, sand the scrollwork. Reinforce the glued-mitered corners with glued and screwed corner blocks. Attach cleats to the base blocks with glue and screws; then attach the base to the chest bottom with screws only.

PANELS

Glue up blanks for the eight panels and trim each for a ⅛" loose fit in a frame opening. Panel raising can be done several ways—router, shaper, table saw, radial-arm saw. Or you can use a planer accessory for a radial saw or drill press, or do it by hand with saw and chisel. I usually do my panel raising with my radial-arm-saw planer accessory. The panel-raising dimensions given are not critical.

The panels are held in the frame openings

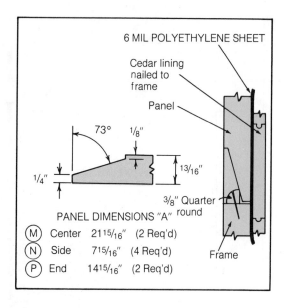

PANEL DIMENSIONS "A"

(M) Center 21¹⁵/₁₆″ (2 Req'd)
(N) Side   7¹⁵/₁₆″ (4 Req'd)
(P) End   14¹⁵/₁₆″ (2 Req'd)

Fig. 4. Raised panels are sandwiched between the cedar lining and nailed-on quarter-round moldings.

against the cedar lining by ³/₈″ quarter-round molding mitered and nailed in place (Fig. 4). No glue has to be used.

TOP

Edge-glue ³/₈″ knotty-pine lumber for the top, or glue up ¹³/₁₆″ lumber and have it planed to ³/₈″ on a wide belt sander, which can be found at most commercial woodworking shops today.

The lid material should not be left ³/₄″ thick because the weight will make the lid excessively heavy.

Glue ¹³/₁₆″ x ¹³/₁₆″ lid frames across the ends of the lid panel, then lay down 6-mil polyethlyene sheeting and nail cedar lining in place. The T & G cedar must go front-to-back, not-end-to-end, as the lid must be strong enough to sit on.

Check to see that the inside dimensions of the lid frame exactly match the inside dimensions of

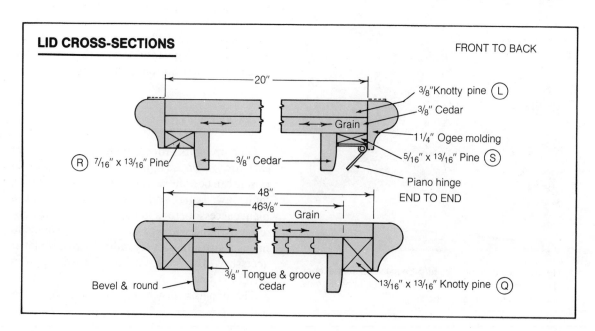

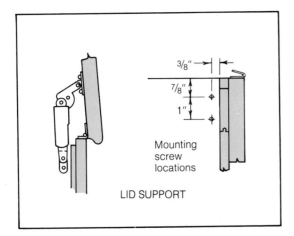

3/8"

7/8"

1"

Mounting
screw
locations

LID SUPPORT

the chest frame. A near-perfect match is required for a good seal when the chest is closed. Disassemble, and glue and screw the front and back frames between the two lid end frames.

Miter, glue and nail ogee molding around the edge. Finish-sand the lower edge of the top, and temporarily join the lid to the chest with the piano hinge. Fit the cedar lip that will project into the chest $1/2''$ when the lid is closed. The exposed outer side of this lip should be beveled slightly. The underside of the top edge can be covered with a felt or foam gasket, if desired.

After completing this sanding of the chest, apply a pigment stain and varnish finish to the knotty pine. No finish of any kind should be applied to the cedar lining. Re-hinge the lid and attach safety lid supports following the manufacturer's mounting instructions.

Fig. 5. A pair of lid supports are used to prevent injury from accidental closing. The proper supports will hold the lid at any position.

7

NANCY'S CHAIR

My daughter Nancy was quite tiny at the age of two and no chair we could buy for her was small enough for her to sit in without first climbing up onto it. We found a chair for her in a country antique shop, restored it, and refinished it. The chair had a certain charm and was always admired.

Twenty years later we decided to build some chairs as presents for our friends' children, and decided to use Nancy's captain's chair as a starting point. A few changes were desired: the arm would not be angled quite so far back, and the legs would be a little farther apart—both changes for improved stability.

The seat is 1³/₄″ pine; the arm is glued up from pieces of the same pine; the legs, spindles, and stretchers are maple.

The first step was to take all the dimensions off the old chair and figure out the angles required for drilling the holes in the seat, arm, and legs. Sighting on the leg from the front and side with a protractor gave side and front views of the seat angles. These were then converted to polar coordinates with simple trigonometry.

I cut a 12″-by-12″ waferboard panel as a seat bottom templet. (The seat blank also has to have the same dimensisons.) Then I transferred the

Fig. 1. New captain's chair (right) is slightly modified version of original antique. Some of the rake was taken out of the arm and spindles were beefed up, but overall dimensions were not changed.

locations of the measured leg holes to the blank and drilled the holes at angles as calculated with a ¹/₂″ drill (Fig. 2). Dowels cut to leg length were inserted and checked for appearance.

A second waferboard panel serves as a seat top templet for locating the arm post and spindle

FRONT AND SIDE VIEWS

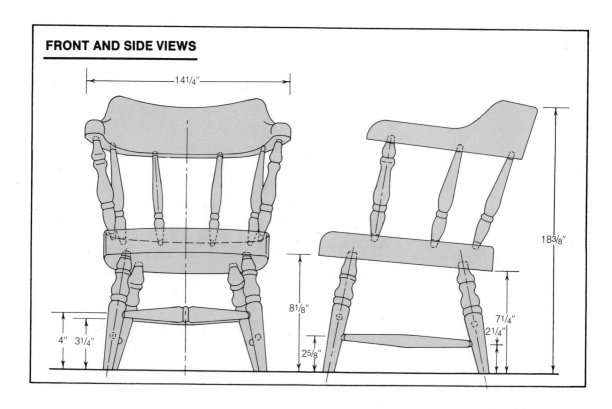

MATERIALS LIST

QUANTITY	DESCRIPTION
3 square feet	¾ clear pine
1 square foot	¾ maple
1 square foot	¾ maple
	Engraved brass nameplate

CUTTING LIST

KEY	QTY.	PART NAME	MATERIAL	DIMENSIONS
A	1	Seat	pine	¾ x 12 x 1¾″
B	2	Arm	pine	1¾ x 4 x 10⅜″
C	1	Arm Center	pine	1¾ x 7 x 3¼″
D	1	Back	pine	1¾ x 5½ x 13½″
E	1	Front Stretcher	maple	1⅛ x 1⅛ x 11¾″
F	1	Back Stretcher	maple	⅞ x ⅞ x 10¾″
G	2	Side Strecher	maple	⅞ x ⅞ x 11½″
H	4	Leg	maple	1⅜ x 1⅜ x 11½″
J	2	Arm Post	maple	1¼ x 1¼ x 10½″
K	4	Spindle	maple	1 x 1 10¼″

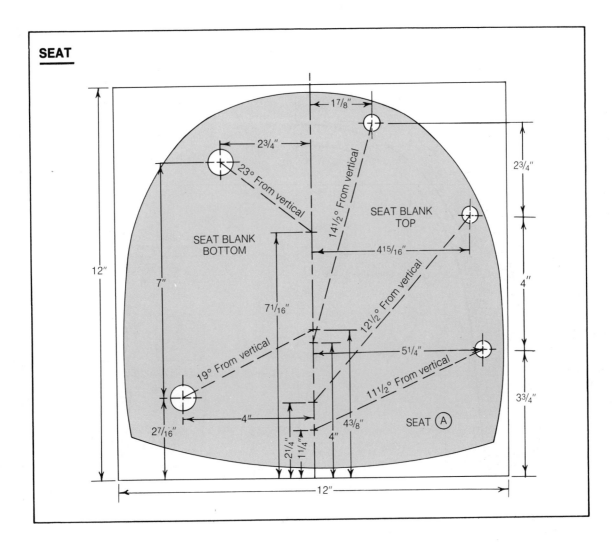

SEAT

SEAT BLANK TOP

SEAT BLANK BOTTOM

SEAT (A)

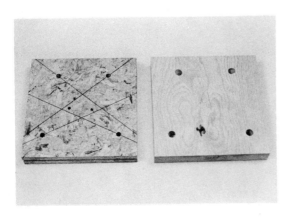

Fig. 2. Waferboard seat-drilling templet (left) and seat blank after being drilled for legs. To maintain proper hole spacing, 3/4"-thick leg and spindle seat templets must be shimmed 1/4" to equal thickness of 13/4" seat blank.

holes (Fig. 3). Fastened together with screws and a 1/4" spacer, the two templets became a complete seat templet. I made a similar templet to locate the upper ends of the arm posts and spindles in the arm. With the three templets and a collection of dowels, a mockup of the chair can be assembled to see how the various angles work out.

The seat should be made from a single piece of pine if possible, with the grain running front-to-back. Leave the seat blank square until all the holes have been drilled. Exactly how you glue up the arm depends on the rest of your stock of 1 3/4" pine. For maximum strength, all the gluing should be side-grain to side-grain.

The lower arm blank must have reference edges the same as the previously made drilling jig so that hole locations can be easily transfered. If

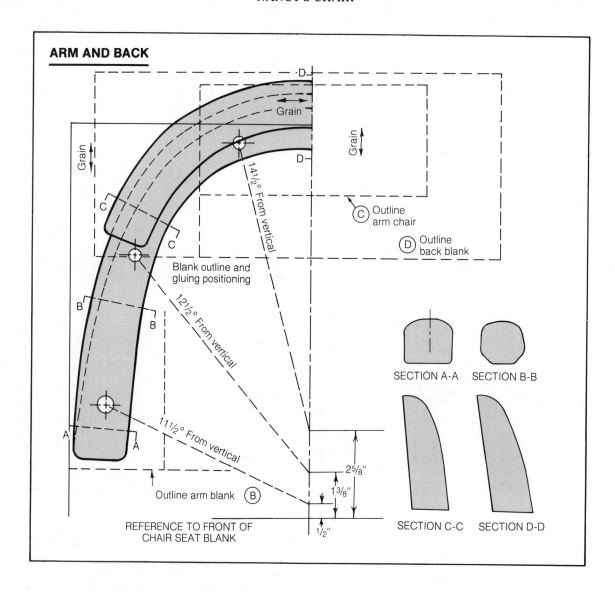

ARM AND BACK

Grain

Grain

14 1/2° From vertical

Outline
arm chair

Outline
back blank

Blank outline and
gluing positioning

12 1/2° From vertical

Grain

11 1/2° From vertical

2 5/8"

1 3/8"

Outline arm blank (B)

1/2"

REFERENCE TO FRONT OF
CHAIR SEAT BLANK

SECTION A-A   SECTION B-B

SECTION C-C   SECTION D-D

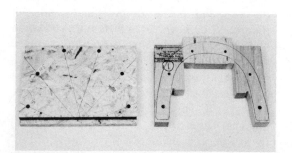

Fig. 3. Drilling templet for seat spindle and arm blank. How you piece up the arm depends on your supply of 1 3/4" pine. For joint strength, arrange pieces so gluing is side-grain to side-grain. Corner dimensions of blank and templet must be identical.

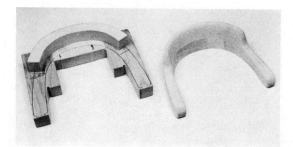

Fig. 4. Chair back is made in two pieces: glued-up arm and one-piece back. Grain of pieces is at right angles for maximum strength.

possible, the back should be cut from a single piece of pine, for appearance (Fig. 4).

As templets have been made and checked, it is a simple matter to drill accurate leg, arm post, and spindle holes in the seat and arm. Tilt the head of the drill or the table to the specified angle and insert a dowel in the chuck with the other end in the hole in the templet (Fig. 5). Rotate the templet on the table so that the slope of the angle as marked on the seat or arm blank is at a right angle to the tilt of the table or head. Clamp locating blocks to the table so the templet can be removed and the blank (or blanks if you are making more than one chair) can be accurately positioned for drilling. Replace the dowel with a Forstner bit, set the depth stop, and drill holes (Figs. 6–8).

After the seat has been drilled on both sides, scoop out the top for comfort (Fig. 9), saw to outline, round over the front edge and sand (Fig. 10).

Fig. 5. Setup for drilling holes for legs in seat. A dowel inserted in hole templet is used to set up for drilling leg holes in seat blank. Templet, which is 3/4" thick, must be shimmed to 1 3/4" to avoid lateral shift of leg positions.

Fig. 6. To drill leg hole in seat, replace 1/2" dowel with 3/4" Forstner bit in chuck. The still-squared seat blank can be accurately drilled. This procedure works especially well if your are making more than one chair.

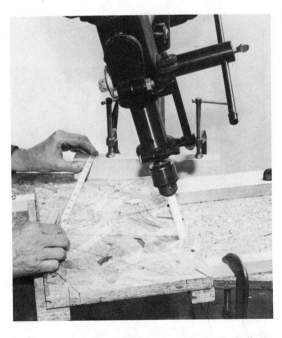

Fig. 7. Setup for drilling spindle hole in back is similar to that used for leg holes except it was done on a radial drill press. Dowel is used to set angle and locate back templet against stop blocks.

Fig. 8. Forstner bit replaces dowel and back replaces templet for drilling.

Fig. 9. For comfort, the seat should be hollowed slightly. The first step is to rough out the hollow with gouges.

Fig. 10. Roughing the seat is followed by aggressive sanding with a portable disc sander.

Make a cardboard pattern to align the upper
and lower arm pieces for gluing. Some waste can
be removed by bandsawing, but I found the fas-
test and most foolproof way to contour the arm
was to use a 60-grit belt on a bench sander and
just have at it aggressively (Fig. 11). Work by eye
and by feel. When it appears to be almost to
shape, switch to an 80 grit, and then 120 grit.
Finish with a pad sander and 180 abrasive paper.
If you are going to have a name plate on the
chair, cut the recess for it now (Fig. 12).

As there was a lot of turning to be done in
making four chairs—fifty-six pieces to be
exact—I bought a Sears #24909 Diameter Sizing
Guide and modified it for use on my Shopsmith
(Fig. 13). I also bought a set (#24911) of additional indicators.

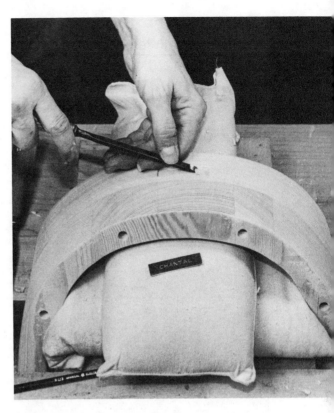

Fig. 12.   Chair back was supported on sacks of lead shot
while recess for the nameplate was carved. This was to
prevent marring soft pine.

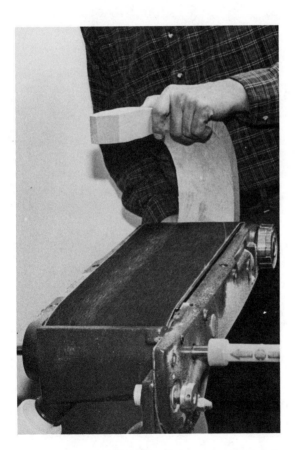

Fig. 11.   Sand assembled back blank on a stationary belt
sander, starting with 60-grit abrasive, ending with 120-
grit. Shape by eye and feel.

Fig. 12A.   Each chair was personalized with a brass
engraved nameplate. Custom-engraved nameplates can
be purchased in shopping centers.

STRETCHERS AND SPINDLES

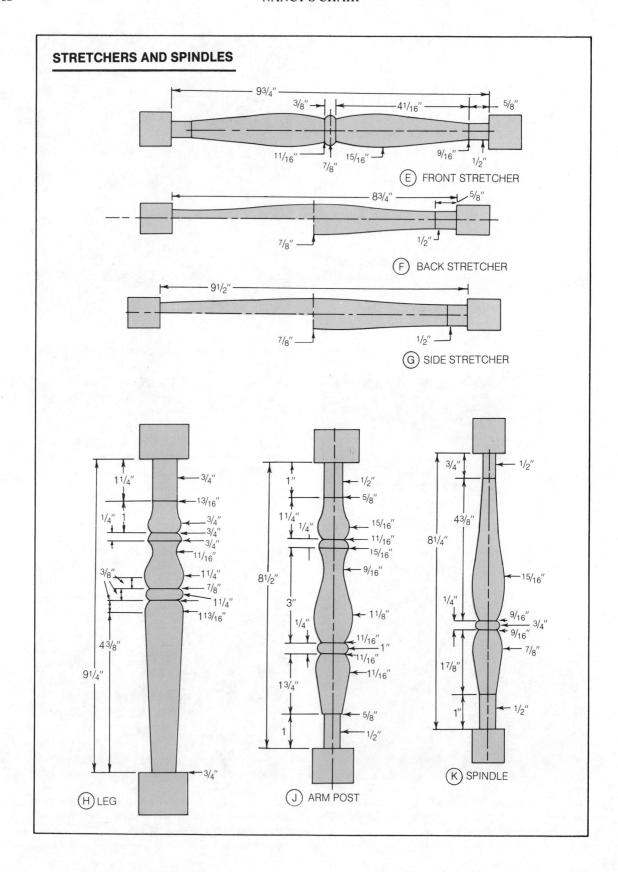

Ⓔ FRONT STRETCHER

Ⓕ BACK STRETCHER

Ⓖ SIDE STRETCHER

Ⓗ LEG

Ⓙ ARM POST

Ⓚ SPINDLE

Fig. 13. Turning the spindles was speeded by using a modified Sears Diameter Sizing Gauge, modified for use on my shopsmith. Fingers on one end of the rod locate end diameters .

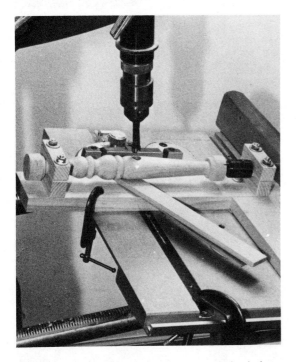

Fig. 14. Drilling front and back stretcher holes in legs requires a careful setup for accuracy. The fixture positions the leg and prevents it from turning under the drill; the scrap of wood under the leg prevents deflection.

As the guide comes, it has too much play for accurate close-diameter repetitive gauging. I made two-dozen $1/16$"-thick spacer washers of sheet phenolic (circuit board) plastic. I got ten clamp-type shaft collars from Small Parts. Inc. (#SCA-10) to use with the washers and friction spacers supplied with the guide to shim and position the indicators in position along the shaft and lock them in place. Don't use setscrew shaft collars because the setscrews will chew up the soft brass shaft tubing.

For each of the turnings, two sets of indicators were set up on the reversible (end-to-end) shaft. The first set locates the ends of the turning and indicates maximum diameters. With the shaft reversed in its mounting, the second set of indicators locates V-grooves (they are depthed by eye), and locates and indicates minor diameters, Caliper measurements were required only for sizing the tenons.

All parts of the chair should be finished before assembly. All the legs and stretchers have to be assembled and glued in one shot. Assemble these parts dry first to make sure everything fits and that none of the leg tenons or stretchers is too

Fig. 15. Clamping legs and stretchers for gluing requires planning and care. Leg spread is controlled by the four clamps on the bench; the side-to-side squareness of the seat and front-to-back slant of the seat is controlled by one or two cauls clamped across the seat. If joints are well-fitting, use white glue; if not, yellow glue.

Fig. 16. After legs and strechers are glued, cut off legs and face the ends. A bench belt sander with temporary table to support the other legs does it nicely.

Fig. 17. Gluing spindles in stages. First, the arm posts, then the forward spindles. Then glue all six to the back.

long. You shouldn't have to force the joints together. The spread of the legs must be controlled either with four pipe or bar clamps, or by blocks of wood C-clamped to your bench (Fig. 15). The left-to-right and front-to-back tilt of the seat must also be controlled in the clamping. This can be accomplished with one or two cauls clamping the seat to the bench.

If joints are well fitting, use white glue because it will give you a little more clamp closing time than yellow glue. For loose-fitting joints, use filled epoxy cement.

The spindles and arm posts are best glued a few at a time. This is not difficult to manage because there is some flexibility in the spindles. Again, assemble seat, arm posts, spindles, and arm without glue first to make sure everything will go together. Begin by gluing the arm posts to the seat. Use the four spindles and the arm as a jig. Glue the two forward spindles, then the two back spindles to the seat using the arm as a jig. Last, glue everything to the arm. Use cauls across the top of the arm to prevent the arm from tilting sideways (Fig. 17).

8

CHIPPENDALE FRETWORK MIRROR

Mirrors traditionally called "fretwork" have the fretwork at both top and bottom. They are also called Chippendale fretwork mirrors, although he was never known to have made them. The mirrors were made between 1720 and the early 1800s, and there was little change in the design over the period.

A common feature of the mirror was a narrow, gilded molding next to the glass. The better mirrors had beveled glass, but as the glass was thin, the bevel was very flat. The frames were usually mahogany or walnut, sometimes just facing on pine.

American-made mirrors were more likely to have curved, angled, or molded top corners. British-manufactured mirrors had square-topped corners. The Queen Anne-style molded corners lasted here fifty years after the end of the Queen Anne period in England.

These mirrors tended to be small—smaller than today's Chippendale fretwork mirrors—as glass was expensive, and the English luxury tax was high.

The fretwork at the top and bottom could be either identical (but inverted) or different. A gilded eagle or pheasant was a popular decoration in a cutout at the top; shells and other decorations were also used. If a bird was used, it usually appeared to be flying through the opening.

Instead of carving an eagle or some other decoration for two planned mirrors, I looked around to see what could be found ready-made. I purchased an eagle-decorated picture hook and a

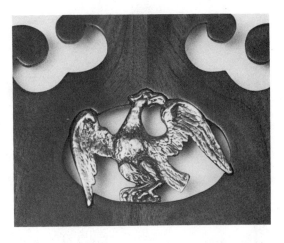

Fig. 1. Instead of carving your own, search for a ready-made eagle that can serve as an attractive decoration for the mirror.

CORNER PATTERN

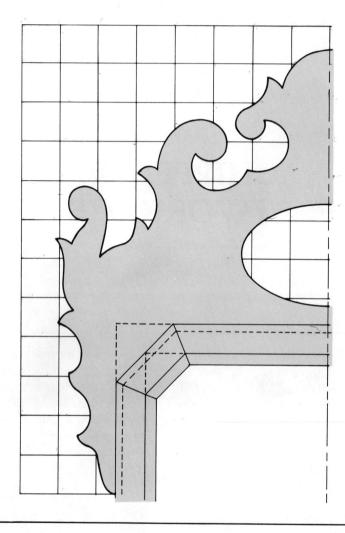

MATERIALS LIST   *(Note: For one mirror)*

QUANTITY	DESCRIPTION
2 pieces, each 2 square feet	In-flitch veneer—mahogany walnut burl. (In-flitch means the pieces were sawn from the log one after the other sothe grain and figures match.)
4 square feet	¼" birch veneer plywood or equivalent
30 inches	1 x 2 mahogany or walnut
30 inches	1 x 2 clear pine
1	Brass eagle #R51-101 picture hook or #HA54-079 decoration; Ball and Ball, Exton Pa.
Kit	Gold Leaf: Art supply stores

CORNER PATTERN

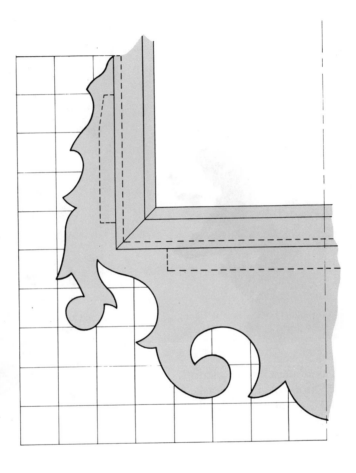

FRAME SECTION

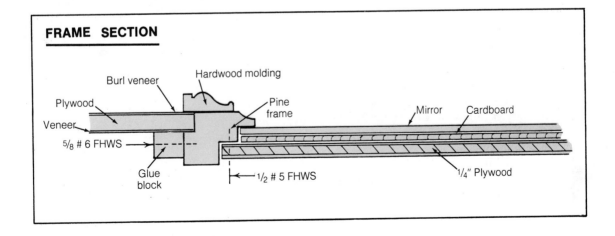

Fig. 2. Eagle at left is a picture hook (strap unbent); eagle at right is available from a catalog firm as a household accessory.

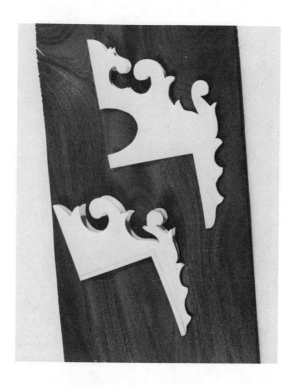

Fig. 3. Locate folded fretwood patterns on two matched pieces of burl veneer for most pleasing grain and figure appearance.

brass eagle classified as a "household accessory" from Ball and Ball, of Exton, PA (Fig. 1). I asked that the hook be unbent, which made it easier to cut off the strap. The eagles were laid on the fretwork patterns for two mirrors (Fig. 2). The holes were dimensioned to fit the eagles.

THE FRETWORK

The time-consuming part of making the mirror is sawing and sanding the fretwork, and setting up to mold the frame parts (see Figs. 3–7).

Centerline-matched walnut and mahogany crotch veneers were glued to ¼″ birch plywood. Veneer was also glued to the back of the plywood to prevent it from warping. After sanding the tape from the veneer, centerlines were matched up and the blanks were screwed together face to face with the screws in scrap areas (Fig. 5). During sawing and edge sanding, this protected the face edge from damage.

Sawing was done with a 30 tpi blade. I used a sander/grinder to clean up the edges, with a 100 grit belt split to ⅓ inch for the concave surfaces (Fig. 6).

Fig. 4. Tape veneer joint with special thin kraft tape made for the purpose. Put tape strips across the joint first, then along the joint. Clamp scrap wood over joint while adhesive dries.

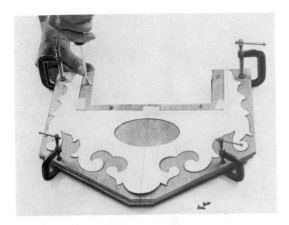

Fig. 5. Setup for sawing veneered plywood. To protect veneers, screw plywood blanks together with veneers face to face.

Fig. 6. After sawing to outline, sand the edges of the two pieces (still screwed together) on a band sander. Split the belt in thirds to get into tight inside curves.

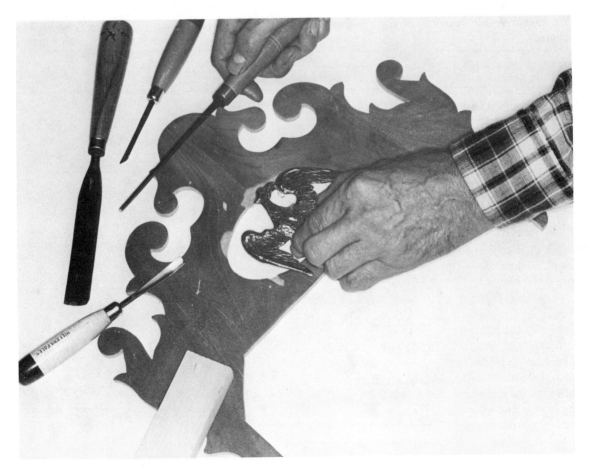

Fig. 7. Carve away wood from around the oval opening to seat the decoration. Drill small holes in brass and wood for escutcheon. Bend over pins on back to secure eagle; it can be removed for polishing.

THE FRAME

How you go about molding the frame depends on the tools and materials at hand. In the tradition of Yankee ingenuity, using the best materials where they would show, I made the frame of pine with a facing of molded hardwood.

Making the mirror framing in two parts had additional advantages. First, the gilding and the stain/filler/varnish finishing do not have to be done to mating edges. The routing and sawing to get the required sections is easier, and the dadoes (or rabbets) for the ornaments can be made to fit more accurately (see Figs. 8–12)

The parts for the frame should be molded as 17″ blanks. When these have been shaped, miter the ends. The stopped slots that receive the fretwork can be cut after frame assembly. The frame behind the fretwork is rectangular, with the corners reinforced with splines. Only the part of the frame visible in front of the fretwork is angled.

Fig. 8. Profile of pine frame was routed and sawed on back-to-back blank. Rabbet for fretwork ornament was cut in center of blank, cove molding formed on shaper.

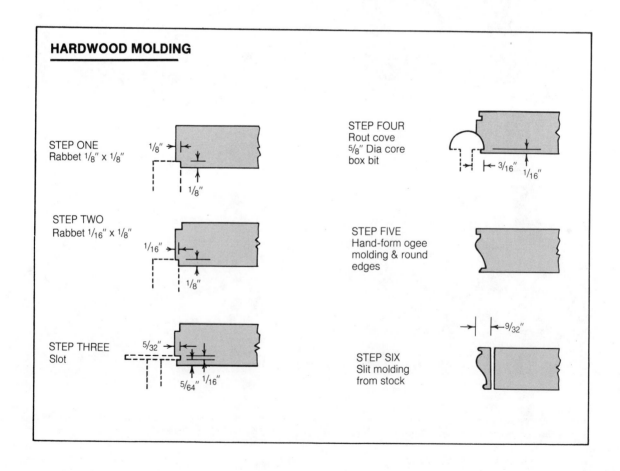

HARDWOOD MOLDING

STEP ONE
Rabbet 1/8″ x 1/8″

1/8″

1/8″

STEP TWO
Rabbet 1/16″ x 1/8″

1/16″

1/8″

STEP THREE
Slot

5/32″

5/64″   1/16″

STEP FOUR
Rout cove
5/8″ Dia core
box bit

3/16″   1/16″

STEP FIVE
Hand-form ogee
molding & round
edges

9/32″

STEP SIX
Slit molding
from stock

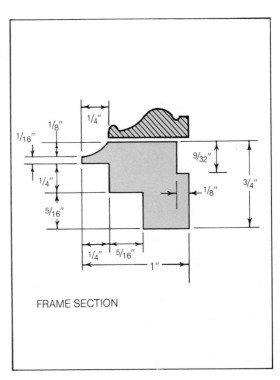

FRAME SECTION

Fig. 9. Double rabbet for glass and back panel was sawed on table saw.

HOW TO ROUT AND CUT FRAME

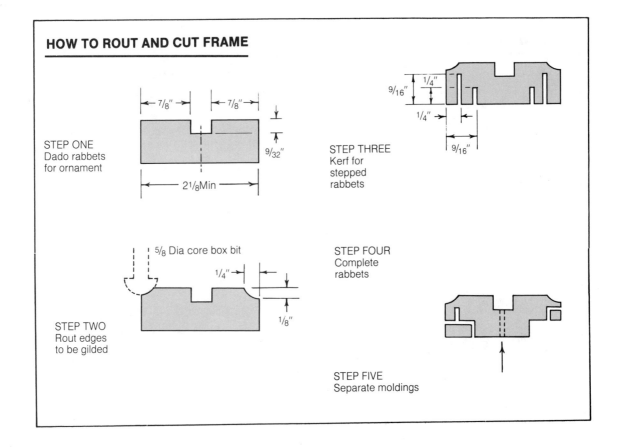

STEP ONE
Dado rabbets
for ornament

STEP TWO
Rout edges
to be gilded

⁵/₈ Dia core box bit

STEP THREE
Kerf for
stepped
rabbets

STEP FOUR
Complete
rabbets

STEP FIVE
Separate moldings

Fig. 10. Miter joints of the pine frame were reinforced with 1/16″-thick feather splines. Here, slot is being sawed for spline.

Fig. 11. Top corners of the pine frame are angle-mitered. First, make saw cuts on each side of mitered joint; then chisel away waste and fit angled pine piece.

Fig. 12. Veneer strip glued across frame holds sides in positions while fitting and gluing angle-mitered top corners.

Strips of veneer are also used to bed these joints while being glued. Trim and sand off veneer when glue is dry.

GILDING

Sand thoroughly, and fill any surface indentations with wood filler, such as ZAR Wood Patch. Seal the wood with two coats of orange or white shellac diluted with two parts alcohol. Sand lightly between coats with used 220-grit or finer paper. Be careful not to cut through edges. If you think you have, apply a third coat.

Apply a coat of dull-red or burnt-sienna acrylic paint, thinned with medium. Any defects in the wood surface—particularly at glued joints missed in the sanding will now be very visible and should be repaired before proceeding with two more thin coats of the acrylic paint. Sand with 220 or finer paper. Instead of acrylic paint, a basecoat prepared for use with gold leaf can be used.

Apply a coat of gold leaf size to the wood. This coat should be very thin, but without any holldays. The size adheres the gold leaf to the surface; if size is missing, there will be a hole in the gold.

The size can be applied with a small, soft brush or a piece of velveteen. Adhesive sizes usually change color when they dry—typically, from milky to clear.

When the size is dry, apply the gold leaf.

There are two kinds of gold leaf: real and imitation. The real is frightfully expensive; use imitation.

This gold leaf comes in books of 25 sheets, about 5 inches square, with the leaves separated by paper.

Work in an area with no cross ventilation. The slightest breeze will blow the leaf away.

Cut strips wider than the molding to be gilded. Using scissors, cut the leaf and the interleaving sheet of paper at the same time.

Lay on the leaf in overlapping strips. As the leaf doesn't stretch, patch gaps with fragments. Crumple leaf to fill low areas or valleys.

When the surface is completely covered with leaf, gently rub the surface with a small brush which will press the leaf down and pull away overlaps. If any bare spots appear, just patch them.

If leaf won't adhere to a bare spot, apply size, let dry and apply leaf.

When the surface is completely covered, burnish with a ball of cotton or a soft cloth.

Real gold leaf does not require a protective coat when you are done. Imitation leaf does. Use either clear acrylic medium, or satin sealer sold with the gold leaf.

The mahogany was finished with stain, filler, and satin polyurethane varnish. The pine was also stained to reduce chance visibility.

THE GLASS MIRROR

If you want to do the mirror right, the glass should be beveled. Draw a pattern for the glass showing the bevel, including the mitered bevels at the upper corners. Take it to a good glass house which has had some experience with custom beveling. When the glass mirror is ready, take your frame along to be sure it fits. The glass will cost $35 to $40.

9

HEPPLEWHITE DESK

This handsome rolltop desk is designed in the style of George Hepplewhite, a master furniture maker of the 18th century. Not much is known about him except that he was a cabinetmaker. He is recognized today as one of the four greatest furniture designers. The simple and clean lines of his style have always remained popular. Characteristics of his furniture are slender, straight legs with tapered spade feet, or tapered legs without feet. Mahogany was his favored wood.

The use of decorative inlays or fancy veneers would be most appropriate for dressing up this desk. The desk is finished in dark-brown mahogany with authentic reproduction drawer pulls and knobs. This desk can be an attractive addition to any home.

When I built this desk, I had a very limited and somewhat strange collection of power tools in my home shop. All wood was cut close to dimension on a 16″ Rockwell Scroll Saw—it was the only power saw I had. Wood was jointed, squared, and brought to dimension on a 12″ bench-mounted disc sander. All mortises and tenons, etc. were formed with a router. A drill press and a pad sander (not a good one, either) completed the list of power tools.

What all this means is, you can build complete furniture without a shop full of tools. It may take longer, and you will have to do some operations very inefficiently, but you can do it. It took forever to saw the rolltop slats, but I made them.

EXPLODED VIEW

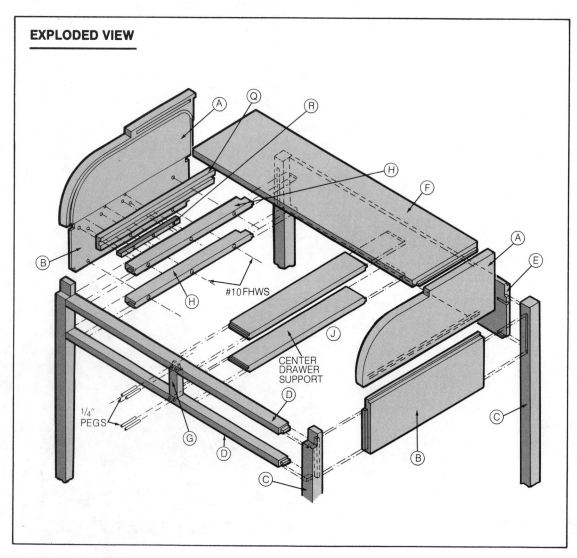

MATERIALS LIST

QUANTITY	DESCRIPTION	SOURCE
20 board feet	$\frac{13}{16}$" mahogany	
3 board feet	$1\frac{1}{16}$" mahogany	
10 board feet	¼" mahogany	
4 board feet	$\frac{11}{16}$" poplar	
3 board feet	½" poplar	
4 ft. x 4 ft.	¼" birch plywood	
1 sq. ft.	⅛" birch plywood	
32" x 14"	¼" tempered hardboard	
18" x 36"	Medium-weight canvas	
4	#D-37 drawers pulls (2 ¾" centers)	Ball & Ball
2	#G-18 knobs (¾")	Ball & Ball
2	#G-18 knobs (⅝")	Ball & Ball
2	$\frac{13}{16}$" flush pulls	Hardware store

CUTTING LIST

KEY	QTY.	PART NAME	MATERIAL	BLANK DIMENSIONS
A	2	Upper Side	mahogany	1 x 7½ x 20″
B	2	Lower side	mahogany	¾ x 6¾ x 18″
C	4	Leg	mahogany	1¾ x 1¾ x 31″
D	2	Front Rail	mahogany	¾ x1½ x 34″
E	1	Back	mahogany	¾ x 6¾ x 34″
F	1	Top	mahogany	¾ x 10 x 34 ¾″
G	1	Center Stile	mahogany	¾ x 1⅛ x 5″
H	4	Drawer Support	poplar	¾ x 1¾ x 18¼″
J	2	Ctr. Drawer Support	poplar	¾ x 3⅛ x 18¼″
K	2	Side Drawer Guide	poplar	¾ x 1¼ x 17″
L	1	Center Drawer Guide	poplar	1⅛x 1¼ x 17¾″
M	1	Writing Board Panel	mahogany	¾ x 18¼ x 31⅛″
N	1	WB Front Frame	mahogany	1⅛ x 1⁷⁄₁₆ x 36⅝″
P	2	WB Side Frame	mahogany	1⅛ x 1¹³⁄₃₂ x 18″
Q	2	WB Support	mahogany	¾ x 1½ x 17″
R	2	WB Tenon	maple	½ x ⅝ x 9″
S	2	Upper Side Molding	mahogany	¾ x 20″ (board edge)
T	2	Lower Side Molding	mahogany	¼ x 20″ (board edge)
U	2	Drawer Front	mahogany	¾ x 3⁷⁄₁₆ x 15⅞″
V	4	Drawer Side	poplar	½ x 3⁷⁄₁₆ x 18½″
W	2	Drawer Back	poplar	⅜ x 2¹³⁄₁₆ x 15½″
X	2	Drawer Bottom	birch ply	¼ x 15½ x 18½″
Y	16	Rolltop Slat	mahogany	⁷⁄₁₆ x ¾ x 34¹¹⁄₁₆″
Z	1	Rolltop Lead Strip	mahogany	⅜ x 1 x 34¹¹⁄₁₆″
AA	2	Top, Bottom	mahogany	¼ x 7¾ x 33¾″
BB	2	Side	mahogany	¼ x 7¾ x 5¾″*
CC	2	Center Partition	mahogany	¼ x 7¾ x 5½″*
DD	6	Partition	mahogany	¼ x 7¾ x 5½″*
EE	1	Shelf	mahogany	¼ x 7¾ x 9¾″*
FF	1	Stile	mahogany	¼ x 7¾ x 2″*
GG	2	Attachment Block	poplar	½ x 1¹⁵⁄₁₆ x 4 ⁹⁄₁₆″
HH	1	Compartment Back	birch ply	¼ x 5¾ x 33¾″
JJ	2	Drawer Front	mahogany	½ x 1¹³⁄₁₆ x 4 ⁹⁄₁₆″
KK	4	Drawer Side	mahogany	¼ x 1¹³⁄₁₆ x 7½″
LL	2	Drawer Back	mahogany	½ x 1¹³⁄₁₆ x 4 ⁵⁄₁₆″
MM	2	Drawer Bottom	birch ply	⅛ x 4⁵⁄₁₆ x 7¼″
NN	1	Desk Back	birch ply	¼ x 7 x 35¼″

CUTAWAY VIEW

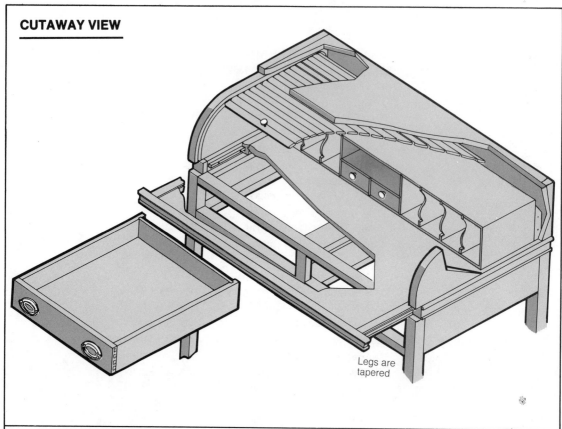

Legs are
tapered

FRONT AND SIDE VIEWS

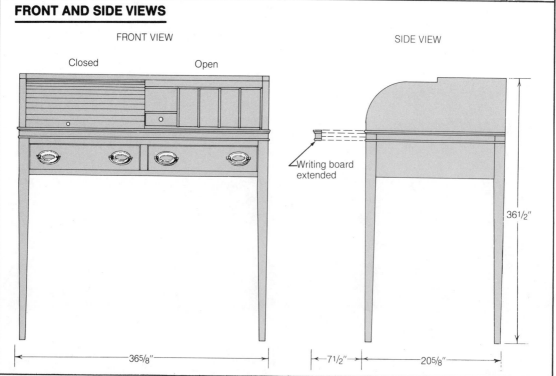

FRONT VIEW

SIDE VIEW

Closed

Open

Writing board
extended

36½″

36⅝″

7½″

20⅝″

SIDES

Begin construction with the sides. Rout the track in the upper sides before you blank the sides from stock. Make a routing templet. The templet shown (Fig. 1) is designed to guide the edge of a 5³⁄₄″-diameter router baseplate. Cut the

routing templet ¹⁄₄″ tempered hardboard or plywood.

Make a paper pattern for the upper side and trace left and right onto wood. Align templet with outline and clamp securely. The edge marks on the templet align with the bottom edge of the

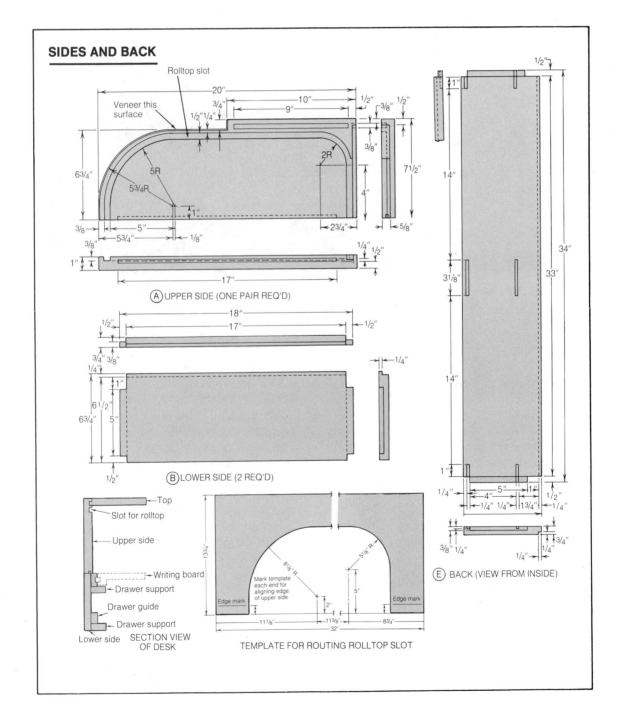

SIDES AND BACK

Ⓐ UPPER SIDE (ONE PAIR REQ'D)

Ⓑ LOWER SIDE (2 REQ'D)

Ⓔ BACK (VIEW FROM INSIDE)

SECTION VIEW OF DESK

TEMPLATE FOR ROUTING ROLLTOP SLOT

Fig. 1. Routing track in upper side with a templet. Rout the two matching tracks before cutting the upper side blanks from the board. Bags of lead shot, instead of clamps, hold down corners of templet

upper side piece. Route the slot with a $1/2''$ straight bit. Flip the templet over to rout the slot in the other side.

Rout mortises in the upper sides for the top and for the lower side, and rabbet for the back panel. Sand curved and top front edges. It's optional, but I veneered the curved edge of the upper sides for appearance— I didn't want so much end-grain showing so prominently.

Blank the lower sides and form tenons. Sand the inside surface and glue upper and lower sides together. Now sand the outside surfaces, and sand the rolltop tracks.

LEGS

The legs should be made next. The front legs are a left and right pair, the rear legs are identical. Plane or saw $1\frac{3}{4}''$ stock. Draw centerlines on two adjacent surfaces of each leg, then lay out the leg tapers and mortises. Chisel mortises to $1/2''$ depth. Saw leg tapers to just outside dimension lines, then sand to finish dimension. Cut off legs to exact dimension, top and bottom. Notch the tops of the front legs for the writing board and mark the center of the bottom of each leg.

Fit legs to desk sides. Be sure legs fit exactly vertical. Check with a carpenter's square between the bottom surface of the lower side and leg. The center mark on each leg should be $3/4''$ out from square. Do not glue at this time.

Blank the front rails, back, top, and center dtile, and cut mortises and form tenons. Now fit the legs to the front rails and the back (Fig. 2), checking for alignment. Fit the center stile between the front rails.

Clamp desk sides, front rails, back and top together without glue and check alignment (Fig. 3). Disassemble, and finish-sand all interior surfaces.

LEGS

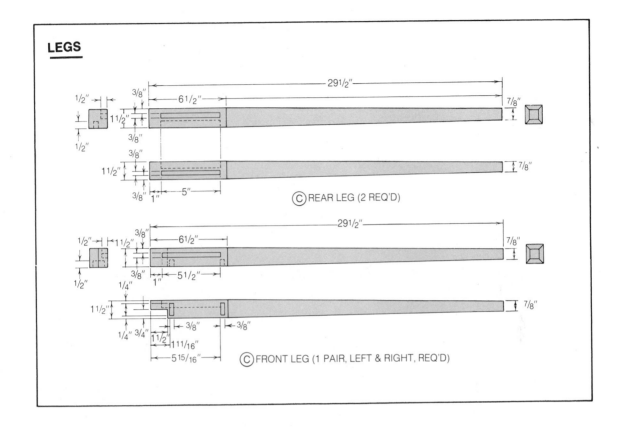

Ⓒ REAR LEG (2 REQ'D)

Ⓒ FRONT LEG (1 PAIR, LEFT & RIGHT, REQ'D)

Fig. 2. Mortise-and-tenon joints for gluing leg-and-rail assembly to the side.

Glue the center stile between the front rails, using the front legs as a clamping jig to assure alignment. When dry, glue the front rails to the front legs, and the back between the rear legs. Check alignment before the glue dries.

DRAWER SUPPORTS

The drawer supports are integral parts of the corner joints. They are designed to provide additional rigidity. Blank all of the drawer supports, shape tenons, drill and countersink. Clamp all parts of the desk together again and check the fit of the drawer supports. Now drill pilot holes through the drawer supports into the sides for $1\frac{1}{4}''$ #10 flathead woodscrews.

Unclamp one end of desk, apply glue to the drawer supports, reassemble and clamp desk to align drawer support; screw and clamp drawer supports to the side. Immediately unclamp desk

WRITING BOARD

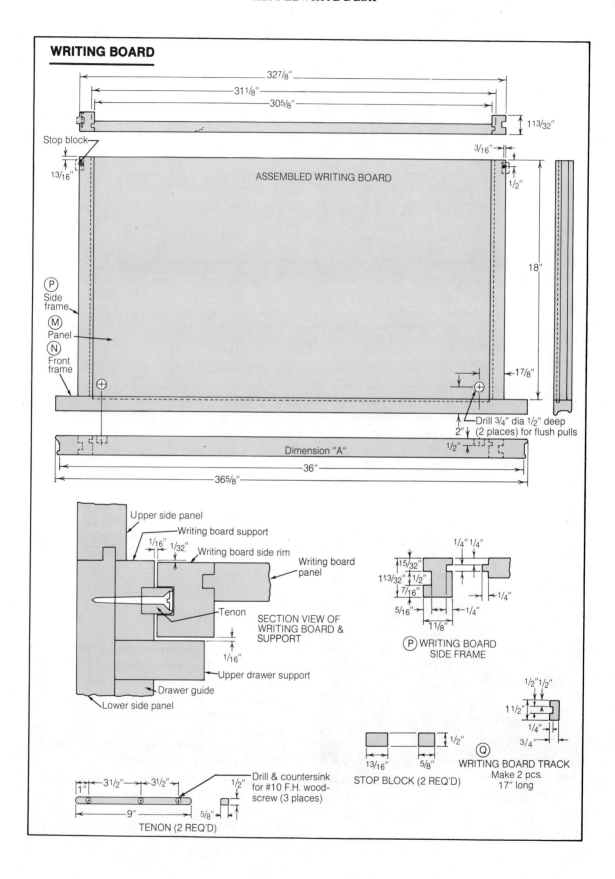

ASSEMBLED WRITING BOARD

32 7/8"
31 1/8"
30 5/8"
1 13/32"
3/16"
1/2"
18"
1 7/8"

Stop block
13/16"

Ⓟ Side frame
Ⓜ Panel
Ⓝ Front frame

Drill 3/4" dia 1/2" deep (2 places) for flush pulls
2"   1/2"

Dimension "A"
36"
36 5/8"

Upper side panel
Writing board support
1/16" 1/32"
Writing board side rim
Writing board panel
Tenon
SECTION VIEW OF WRITING BOARD & SUPPORT
1/16"
Upper drawer support
Drawer guide
Lower side panel

1/4" 1/4"
15/32"
1 13/32" 1/2"
7/16"
5/16"   1/4"
1 1/8"   1/4"
Ⓟ WRITING BOARD SIDE FRAME

1/2" 1/2"
1 1/2"
1/4"
3/4"
Ⓠ WRITING BOARD TRACK
Make 2 pcs.
17" long

1/2"
13/16" 5/8"
STOP BLOCK (2 REQ'D)

Drill & countersink for #10 F.H. wood-screw (3 places)
1/2"
3 1/2" 3 1/2"
1"
9"   5/8"
TENON (2 REQ'D)

DESK DRAWER

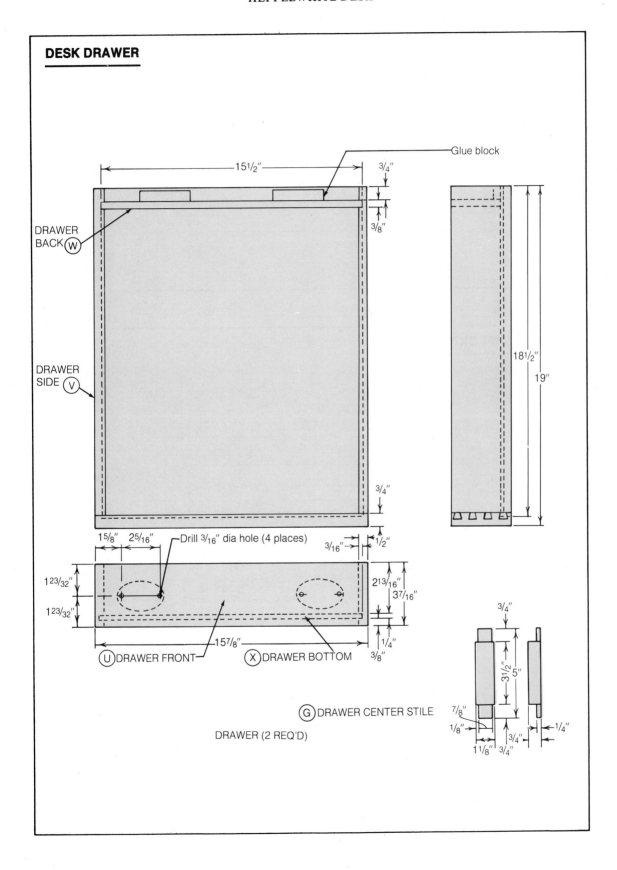

Glue block

15¹/₂″

³/₄″

³/₈″

DRAWER BACK (W)

DRAWER SIDE (V)

³/₄″

18¹/₂″

19″

1⁵/₈″   2⁵/₁₆″   Drill ³/₁₆″ dia hole (4 places)

³/₁₆″   ¹/₂″

1²³/₃₂″

2¹³/₁₆″
3⁷/₁₆″

1²³/₃₂″

15⁷/₈″

¹/₄″

³/₈″

(U) DRAWER FRONT   (X) DRAWER BOTTOM

(G) DRAWER CENTER STILE

DRAWER (2 REQ'D)

³/₄″

31/2″   5″

7/8″

1/8″   ¹/₄″

1¹/₈″   ³/₄″   ³/₄″

RAILS

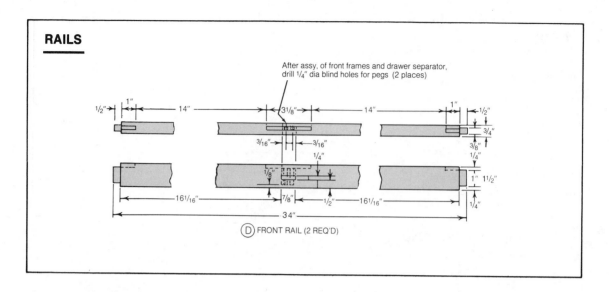

After assy. of front frames and drawer separator,
drill 1/4" dia blind holes for pegs (2 places)

(D) FRONT RAIL (2 REQ'D)

DRAWER SUPPORTS

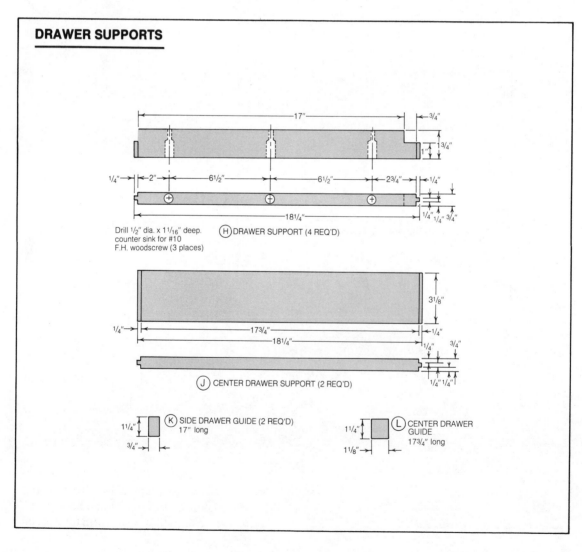

Drill 1/2" dia. x 1 1/16" deep.
counter sink for #10
F.H. woodscrew (3 places)

(H) DRAWER SUPPORT (4 REQ'D)

(J) CENTER DRAWER SUPPORT (2 REQ'D)

(K) SIDE DRAWER GUIDE (2 REQ'D)
17" long

(L) CENTER DRAWER
GUIDE
17 3/4" long

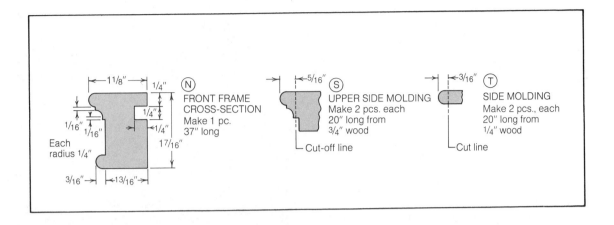

FRONT FRAME CROSS-SECTION
Make 1 pc. 37" long

UPPER SIDE MOLDING
Make 2 pcs. each 20" long from 3/4" wood

SIDE MOLDING
Make 2 pcs., each 20" long from 1/4" wood

Fig. 3. Carcase is assembled—one joint at a time, if possible—with other parts clamped dry to ensure alignment.

Fig. 4. Maple tenon is screwed into the support, which fits behind the top of the leg.

and remove the side assembly. When the glue is dry, repeat for one other end.

DESK CARCASE: FINAL ASSEMBLY

For each step in this assembly procedure, the whole desk is clamped together to serve as a gluing jig.

1. Glue one side to the front leg and rail assembly.

2. Glue the top to the same side.

3. Glue the other side to the top and the front leg and rail assembly.

4. Glue both center drawer supports to the front rails.

5. Glue the back to both sides and to both center drawer supports.

Blank the drawer guides; sand, and glue in place. The center guide is pieced-up from 3/4" and 1/2" stock. Blank and fit the plywood back panel.

Blank the writing surface and form tongues on

the front and sides. Rout the front frame molding (including the ends) and rip the front frame from stock. Rout the groove in the front frame; rout grooves in side frame stock, rip side frames from stock.

Note: Dimension *A* must exactly match desk case width. Glue the frames to the writing surface panel.

Drill $3/4$"-diameter holes $1/2$" deep for the two flush pulls. Blank stop blocks (they prevent the board from being pulled all the way out), clamp blocks to board and drill through for a 1" #6 FH screw. Remove.

Blank and rout writing-board supports and maple tenons. (Maple is needed for strength.) Drill and countersink the tenons for $1 1/2$" #10 woodscrews. Screw tenons and supports in place (Fig. 4). Do not glue. Slide writing board into desk. There should be a minimum of $1/16$" looseness.

Rout and sand the upper and lower desk moldings. The moldings are attached with glue and small finishing nails. Drill slightly undersize pilot holes in the moldings for the nails to prevent splitting.

Fig. 5. Assemble compartment from the inside out. Note the carefully squared L-shaped clamping blocks at either side. These blocks assure that the compartment is clamped square initially.

COMPARTMENT

The compartment is built in two parts: the pigeon holes and the supporting back.

Caution: Check the thickness of your $1/4$" mahogany. If it is less than $1/4$" thick as it may be if purchased as "$1/4$ inch," correct the width of your dadoes accordingly.

The grain on the partitions runs vertically. Edge-glue boards to get the $7 1/2$" width for all parts. Sand blanks before cutting out individual parts. Before assembly, finish-sand the curved edge of the six partitions and drill and countersink the holes for the $3/4$" #6 FH screws. Trial-assemble the pigeon holes without glue to be sure everything fits (Fig. 5).

Steps in Compartment Assembly

1. Glue the shelf between the center partitions.
2. Glue the center partitions and stile to the bottom.
3. Glue the partitions to the bottom, three at a time.

4. Glue the top to all eight partitions in one shot.
5. Glue ends, one at a time.

Blank the plywood compartment back panel and the support blocks. Drill and countersink the blocks for $1 1/4$" #6FH woodscrews. Glue and nail back to blocks. (The back is attached to the pigeonholes after finishing).

DRAWERS

Blank parts for large drawers, rout dovetail joints, trim parts to height, rout slots for bottom and back. Sand all inside sufaces and assemble. When forming the parts for the small compartment drawers, do as much routing as possible before cutting off individual pieces. Sand and assemble.

ROLLTOP

This is actually the easiest part of the desk to build. Select a straight-grained blank for the slats. To form the slats, face both edges of the

COMPARTMENT

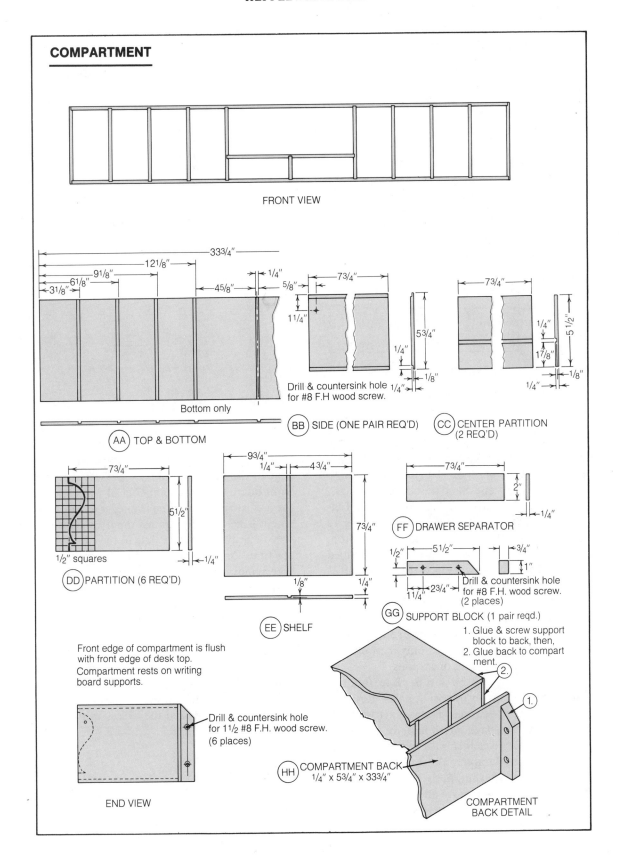

FRONT VIEW

33³/₄"

12¹/₈"

9¹/₈"

6¹/₈"

3¹/₈"

4⁵/₈"

¹/₄"

5/8"

Bottom only

AA TOP & BOTTOM

7³/₄"

1¹/₄"

¹/₄"

¹/₈"

Drill & countersink hole for #8 F.H wood screw.

BB SIDE (ONE PAIR REQ'D)

7³/₄"

5³/₄"

¹/₄"

1⁷/₈"

¹/₄"

¹/₈"

5 ¹/₂"

CC CENTER PARTITION (2 REQ'D)

7³/₄"

5¹/₂"

¹/₄"

¹/₂" squares

DD PARTITION (6 REQ'D)

9³/₄"

¹/₄"

4³/₄"

7³/₄"

¹/₈"

¹/₄"

EE SHELF

7³/₄"

2"

¹/₄"

FF DRAWER SEPARATOR

¹/₂"

5¹/₂"

³/₄"

1"

1¹/₄"

2³/₄"

Drill & countersink hole for #8 F.H. wood screw. (2 places)

GG SUPPORT BLOCK (1 pair reqd.)

Front edge of compartment is flush with front edge of desk top. Compartment rests on writing board supports.

Drill & countersink hole for 1¹/₂ #8 F.H. wood screw. (6 places)

END VIEW

1. Glue & screw support block to back, then,
2. Glue back to compart ment.

2.

1.

HH COMPARTMENT BACK
¹/₄" x 5³/₄" x 33³/₄"

COMPARTMENT BACK DETAIL

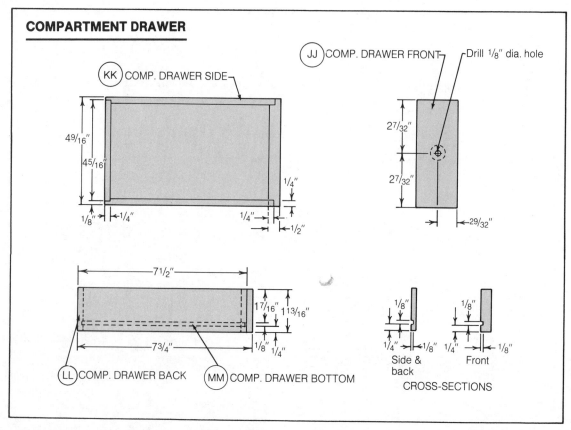

COMPARTMENT DRAWER

KK COMP. DRAWER SIDE

JJ COMP. DRAWER FRONT — Drill ⅛″ dia. hole

49/16″   45/16″

1/8″   1/4″   1/4″   1/2″   1/4″

2⁷/₃₂″   2⁷/₃₂″   29/32″

7½″   1⁷/₁₆″   1¹³/₁₆″   7¾″   ⅛″   ¼″

LL COMP. DRAWER BACK   MM COMP. DRAWER BOTTOM

1/8″   1/8″   1/4″   1/8″   1/4″   1/8″

Side & back   Front

CROSS-SECTIONS

blank, shape rounded front of slat, finish sand, then rip off a ⁷/₁₆″-thick slat. Repeat, until 16 slats have been made. Sand the backs of the slats.

Blank the lead strip, and tenon the ends. Finish and wax all rolltop slats before gluing to canvas. Assemble a frame for gluing the rolltop. The frame shown consists of members clamped to a 36″-wide flush door (Fig. 6). Be sure the sides and the front cleats of the frame are square.

To avoid confusion and mistakes, C-clamps holding the frame together have their handles *down*. The C-clamps holding the rolltop in the fixture have their handles *up*: only these clamps are moved during gluing operations.

Start by arranging the slats in place, face up. Put warped strips in opposing pairs. Restrain them with lattice wood clamped across both ends. Clamp the back board in place and draw the slats snugly together with two bar clamps. Adjust the bar clamps so the lead strip and the last slat are parallel and mark both side boards for reference. Now remove all the "handles up" C-clamps and you are ready to start gluing.

Cut out a piece of canvas 32½″ by 18″ and tape

the canvas to the door over wax paper. The front edge of the canvas should be ¼″ away from the front board. Apply a light coat of white glue to the lead strip, lay it in the frame, and clamp. Be sure it is held tightly against the front board.

Now begin gluing the slats to the canvas, two at a time. Place all the slats in the frame, in order, then remove the two next to the lead strip.

Apply glue to these two slats, put them in place on the canvas, lightly clamp the lattice hold-down strips and back board and draw the slats together with bar clamps until the last slat is at the reference marks at both ends. Now clamp the two glued strips to the canvas under a long caul (Fig. 7). When the glue is dry, repeat for the next two slats. When finished, check between the slats for glue, and trim the excess canvas from the last slat.

FINISHING

This desk was finished with brown mahogany NGR stain, paste filler, and lacquer. Today, I would use a topcoat of varnish because brush

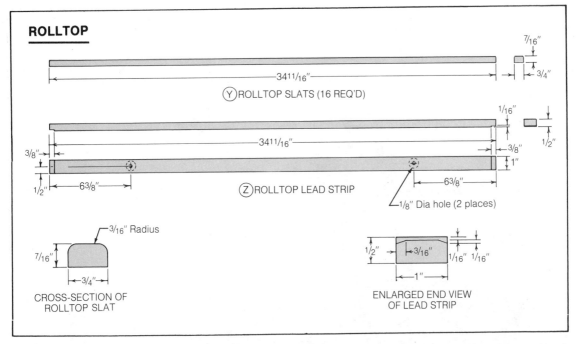

ROLLTOP

3411/16″ — Y ROLLTOP SLATS (16 REQ'D) — 7/16″ — 3/4″

3411/16″ — Z ROLLTOP LEAD STRIP — 3/8″ — 3/8″ — 1″ — 1/16″ — 1/2″

1/8″ Dia hole (2 places)

CROSS-SECTION OF ROLLTOP SLAT — 3/16″ Radius — 7/16″ — 3/4″

ENLARGED END VIEW OF LEAD STRIP — 1/2″ — 3/16″ — 1/16″ 1/16″ — 1″

applied varnishes have improved tremendously since 1971. See Chapter 21 for complete finishing details.

FINAL ASSEMBLY

Insert the large drawers in the desk. Cut and glue felt-faced blocks to the inside back of the desk at each drawer corner so the drawers will close just flush with the desk frame. Install drawer pulls.

Press $13/16″$ flush pulls into the $3/4″$ holes in the writing board. This can be easily done with two wood blocks and a C-clamp. Slide the writing

Fig. 6. Jig for assembling rolltop. A 36″-wide flush door serves as a base board. Glue slats to canvas two at a time.

board into the desk; from rear of desk attach stop blocks to the writing board with screws.

Assemble the compartment pigeon holes and its back with glue and small nails. Insert the compartment into the desk from the rear. The front edge of the compartment is flush with edge of the desk top. Check for $1/32″$ clearance between one compartment and writing board; if insufficient, shim up the compartment with scraps of veneer. Now drill through compartment-mounting screw holes into the desk sides and insert screws.

Wax the track with paste wax and run the rolltop into the track from the back of the desk. It should slide easily past the compartment without interference; if not, remove the compartment and bevel the top edge of the back. The rolltop should operate smoothly. (Be careful when pushing it open; without knobs or the back on desk in place, it can come flying out!)

Install knobs on rolltop and position it open with $1/4″$ of the first slat visible. Cut two blocks from scrap and mount them in the track in the back of the desk to limit rolltop travel to this position. Glue felt strips on the inside of the back panel to protect the rolltop finish. Nail the back panel in place and glue $3/8″$ circles of felt under each end of the lead strip to prevent marring the

10

CONTEMPORARY COFFEE TABLE

An Oriental design, boldly figured oak, and prewoven cane are brought together in an attractive and useful coffee table that will fit right in with today's decor. White oak is preferred over red oak, but if you have to use red oak, be careful to select light-colored wood.

ENDS

Start with the ends. Surface $5/4$ oak to $1\frac{1}{16}''$. Blank the top and bottom ends in back-to-back pairs for easier handling when shaping or routing the stopped mortises. Cut two blanks 6" wide for the corner and center posts, one blank for each end.

Shape or rout the mortises in the top and bottom ends and chisel the stopped ends of the mortises square (Fig. 1). Face the mortised surface of the parts square.

Form tenons on the post blanks (Fig. 2) and rip the posts from the blanks. Rip posts $1/16''$ overwidth. Shoulder the tenons on the center posts on their center-facing sides and finish-sand these surfaces as well as the center surfaces of the

top and bottom rails. It is easier to sand now than after assembly.

Glue and clamp the ends. Be sure the center posts are correctly positioned to produce a 3"-wide opening at the center (the caned openings are undersized for routing). The outer edges of the corner posts should be 18" apart.

Touch sand the surfaces to provide a smooth working surface, and build a fixture for routing the cane openings. The fixture for routing the outside openings can guide the router by a bushing, but depth-of-cut limitations will require an edge-guiding fixture for the inside cutouts for the caned frames.

Rout the stopped mortises for the tenoned ends of the top. This mortise has to be stopped well back from the edges of the ends to preserve strength in the ends.

Complete construction of the ends by a rediusing the corners and breaking all edges. Then rout the openings for the came frame, using the fixture (Figs. 3–7).

Blank the two bases and form the bottom edges. Put a radius on the ends and break edges. counterbore and drill pilot holes for screws to attach the bases to the ends.

EXPLODED VIEW

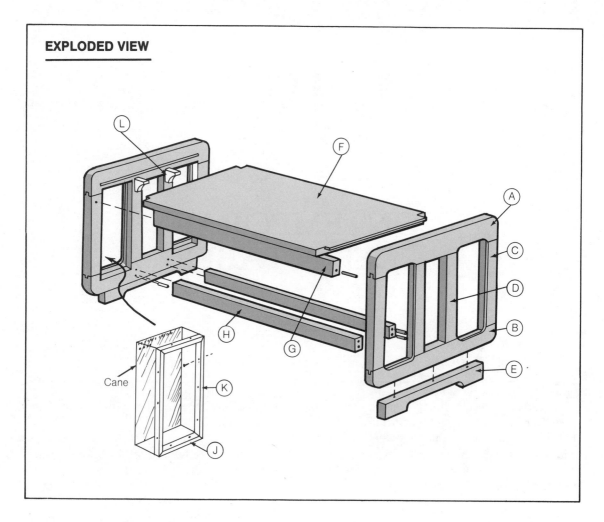

Cane

POSTS AND ENDS

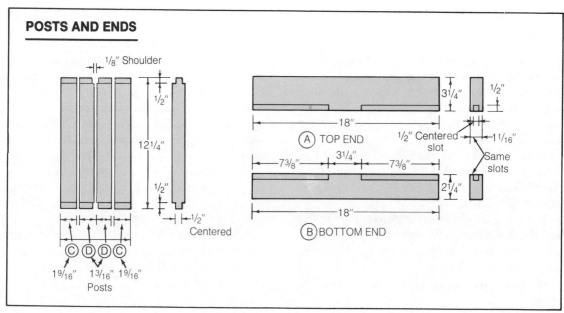

1/8" Shoulder

1/2"

12 1/4"

1/2"

1/2"
Centered

C D D C

1 9/16"   1 3/16"   1 9/16"
Posts

3 1/4"

1/2"

18"

(A) TOP END

1/2" Centered slot

1 1/16"

Same slots

7 3/8"   3 1/4"   7 3/8"

2 1/4"

18"

(B) BOTTOM END

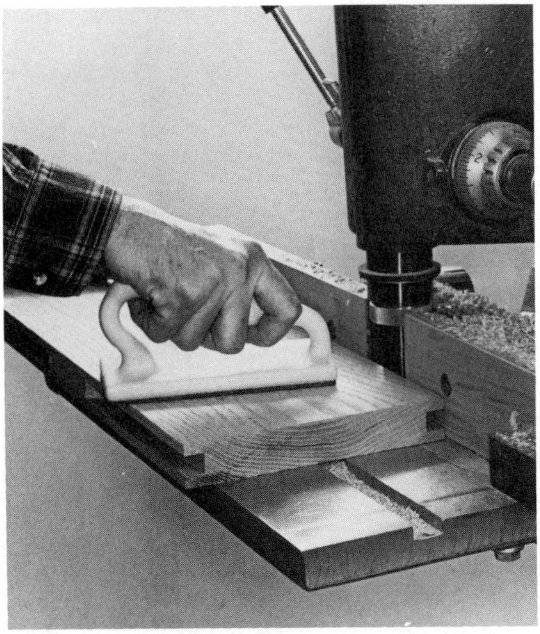

Fig. 1. With the top and bottom ends blanked in back-to-back pairs, shape the stopped mortises.

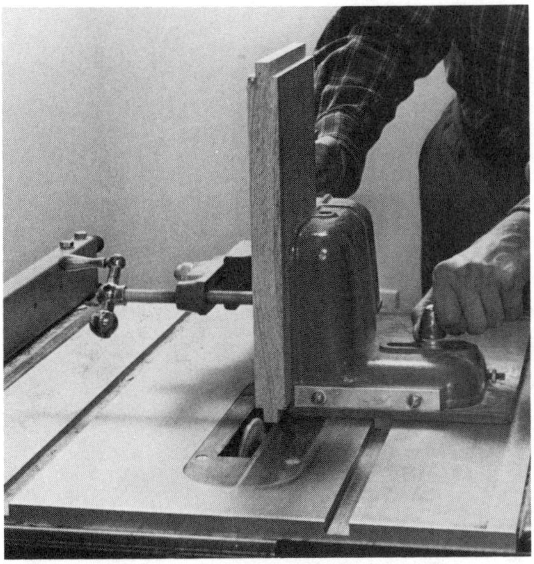

Fig. 2. Form the tenons on the corner and center posts of each end with the parts combined in common blanks. This speeds the job, reduces splintering waste, and assure that the parts are the same length.

MATERIALS LIST

QUANTITY	DESCRIPTION
4 board feet	¾ white oak (1⅛″)
8 board feet	¾ white oak (¾″) (length in multiples of 3′)
1 piece 18″ x 36″	Prewoven cane

CUTTING LIST

KEY	QTY.	PART NAME	MATERIAL	BLANK DIMENSIONS
A	2	Top End	1⅛″ oak	3¼ x 18″
B	2	Bottom End	1⅛″ oak	2¼ x 18″
C	4	Corner Post	1⅛″ oak	1⁹⁄₁₆ x 12¼ ″
D	4	Center Post	1⅛″ oak	1³⁄₁₆ x 12¼ ″
E	2	Base	1⅛″ oak	⅞ x 1½ x 15½″
F	1	Top	¾″ oak	17⅞ x 33⅞″
G	2	Apron	¾″ oak	1¾ x 32⅞″
H	2	Long Rail	¾″ oak	1¾ x 32⅞″
J	8	Cane Frame Rail	¾″ oak	⅜ x 5⅜″
K	8	Cane Frame Stile	¾″ oak	⅜ x 13¼″
L	Bracket	¾″ oak	2 x 2″	

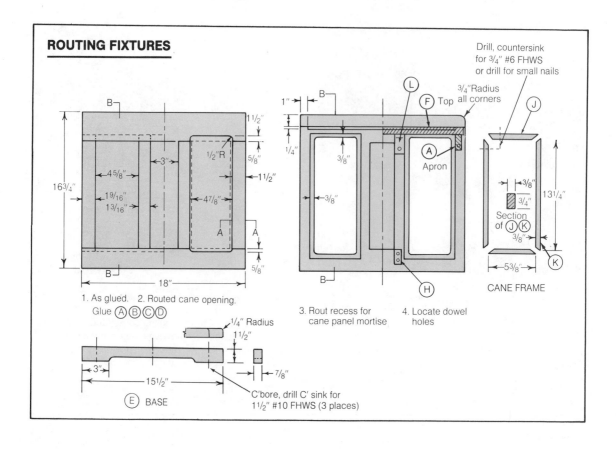

ROUTING FIXTURES

Drill, countersink for 3/4" #6 FHWS or drill for small nails

3/4"Radius Top all corners

Apron

CANE FRAME

1. As glued.   2. Routed cane opening.
Glue Ⓐ Ⓑ Ⓒ Ⓓ

3. Rout recess for cane panel mortise

4. Locate dowel holes

Section of Ⓙ Ⓚ

1/4" Radius

C'bore, drill C' sink for 1 1/2" #10 FHWS (3 places)

Ⓔ BASE

Fig. 3.   Place table end on fixture base.

Fig. 4.   Place fixture frame #1 on table end.

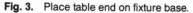

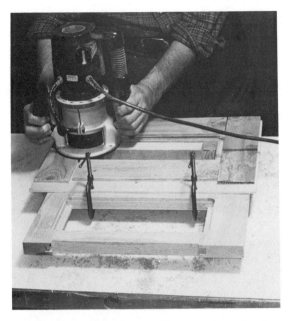

Fig. 5. Clamp all parts together and rout opening for cane insert. A bushing is used to guide the router because of rounded corners.

Fig. 6. Remove table end from fixture. Add 1/8″ hardboard shim under the center boss on fixture base. Replace table end on fixture with inside surface up and clamp fixture frame #2 on table end.

Fig. 7. Rout inside of recess in the table end for installation of the cane insert. The special fixture guides the router by edge of its base. This is necessary to get the 13/16″ depth of cut.

ROUTING FIXTURES

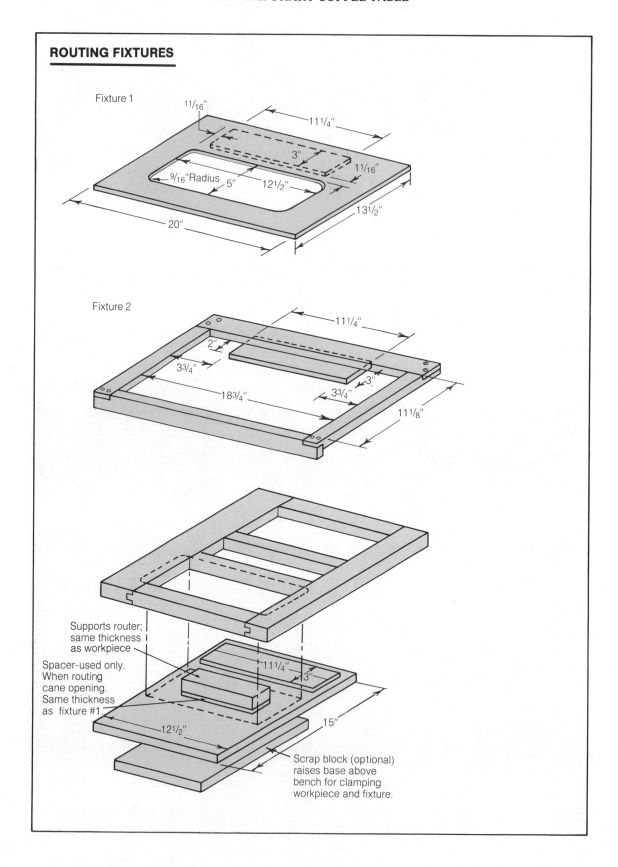

Fixture 1

$1^1/_{16}''$

$11^1/_4''$

$3''$

$1^1/_{16}''$

$^9/_{16}''$Radius $5''$ $12^1/_2''$

$13^1/_2''$

$20''$

Fixture 2

$11^1/_4''$

$2''$

$3^3/_4''$

$3''$

$18^3/_4''$ $3^3/_4''$

$11^1/_8''$

Supports router;
same thickness
as workpiece

Spacer-used only.
When routing
cane opening.
Same thickness
as fixture #1

$11^1/_4''$ $3''$

$12^1/_2''$ $15''$

Scrap block (optional)
raises base above
bench for clamping
workpiece and fixture.

TOP AND RAILS

Joint and edge-glue ³⁄₄″ boards for the top. When the glue is dry, sand the top smooth, checking with a straightedge. Trim the top to exact length, but leave overwidth until tenon routing has been done.

Rip ³⁄₄″ stock for the aprons and long rails, sand all sides, but leave overlength.

Form the tenons on the ends of the top, and shoulder them to fit into the end mortises. When the tenons have been completed, trim the aprons and long rails to matching length.

Drill ³⁄₈″ holes in the ends of the rails and aprons for dowels. Counterbore and drill pilot holes in the aprons for attachment to the top. Assemble the aprons and the top with screws only, no glue.

Now, fit the top to each end (Fig. 8) and transfer dowel-hole locations to the ends with

Fig. 9. For accurate dowel joints, use dowel centers to transfer dowel holes from aprons and long rails to the table ends.

dowel centers (Fig. 9). Drill mating dowel holes in the ends. Fit the long rails to the ends, and drill mating dowel holes.

Fig. 8. Assemble table with dowels and screws to be sure everything fits properly before final sanding and finishing. Finishing is completed before final assembly.

TABLETOP

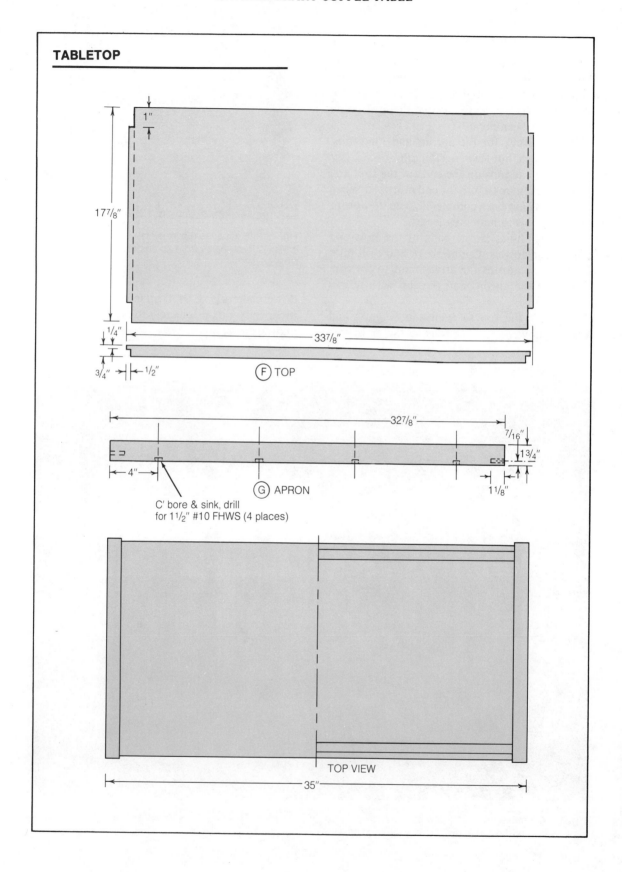

1"

17⁷/₈"

¹/₄"

33⁷/₈"

³/₄" ¹/₂"

Ⓕ TOP

32⁷/₈"

7/₁₆"

1³/₄"

4"

1¹/₈"

Ⓖ APRON

C' bore & sink, drill
for 1¹/₂" #10 FHWS (4 places)

TOP VIEW

35"

FRAMES

Rip the frame parts for the cane panels from
3/4" stock. After assembly, these frames can be
attached to the ends either with flathead screws
or with small nails. Drill and countersink pilot
holes for screws, or drill pilot holes for nails now,
before frame assembly. Miter the ends of the
frame parts and glue them together to make the
four frames. Do not install cane at this time.

Blank and sand four brackets; drill and countersink pilot holes for screws. With the table
assembled dry, attach the four brackets (Fig. 10).

Now disassemble the table and complete all
sanding and edge breaking. Finish up with 150-
grit paper.

FINISHING

In finishing the table, I wanted to keep the
wood as light as possible, but at the same time

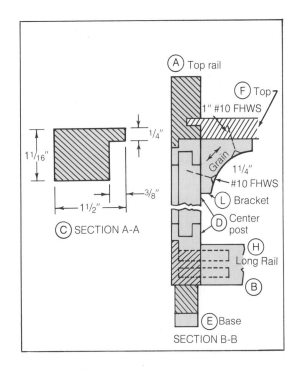

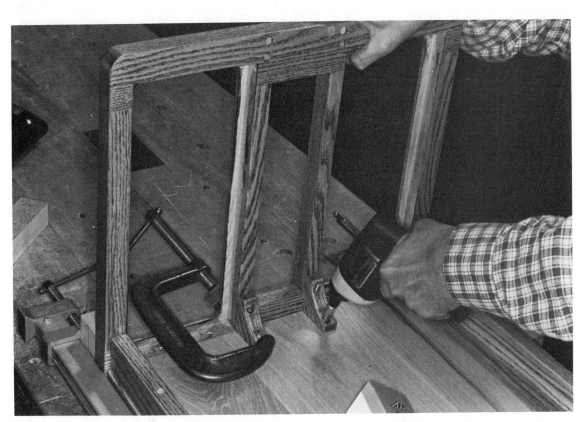

Fig. 10. Shop-made wood brackets under top reinforce dowel and mortise-and-tenon
joints. Bracket grain must run diagonally for maximum strength.

Fig. 11. Steps in finishing (from left): Two coats of quick-dry ZAR to seal surface from the stain; wipe-on ZAR pigmented stain to fill the pores; sanded stain; two coats satin ZAR polyurethane varnish.

accentuate the figure of the oak by filling the open pores with dark material. This was accomplished with the following finishing procedure. The tenons at the ends of the top must be masked, and you should be careful to keep finish materials out of dowel holes and off mating surfaces.

1. Apply two coats of UGL's Quick-dry ZAR polyurethane coating.

2. Wipe on a coating of ZAR Black Walnut stain and sealer, and allow the coating to dry over-night.

3. Sand the surface with 150-grit paper (Fig. 12) removing all of the stain except that which is in the pores.

4. Topcoat the surface with two coats of ZAR Satin polyurethane varnish, sanding lightly between coats.

CANE

The prewoven cane is glued to the front of the cane frames with white or yellow glue. Cut pieces of prewoven cane 1″ oversize all around. Dampen the cane enough to get it to lay flat and staple it by its edges to scrap plywood covered with wax paper. Do not soak the cane or use glycerine as you would to do a chair seat. Soaking fills the pores and prevents glue adhesion.

Position the frame on the cane for a symmetrical pattern of holes (Fig. 13). Have solid cane, hot holes at the edges for best appearance. Clamp scrap blocks to position the frame on the cane (Fig. 14); then apply glue to the frame and clamp it to the cane. Leave clamped overnight—the glue will dry slowly. When dry, trim excess cane with a utility knife and install the frames in the end openings.

Fig. 12. The stain, after drying overnight, must be sanded from the surface of the oak, leaving stain only in the open pores of the wood.

Fig. 13. Staple prewoven cane to plywood protected with wax paper, then clamp scrap wood to locate two adjacent frame sides so the frame doesn't move while you're gluing.

Fig. 14. Clamp frame to the cane with moderate pressure and leave overnight. The glue will dry slowly because of the moisture in the dampened cane.

ASSEMBLY

Disassembled, the table can be shipped Parcel Post or UPS, with only glue, two long clamps and a screwdriver needed for assembly in case you are building it for someone at a distance.

Begin assembly by gluing one end to the top. Check the clamped assembly carefully with a carpenter's square to be sure it is square. Next, glue and dowel the long rails to the same end with the other end assembled dry to act as a jig. Last, dowel and glue the second end to the table.

A Chinese lattice would be an appropriate alternate panel. Lattice should be scroll-sawed from ¼" birch plywood.

11

SHAKER SHELF

Shakers did not believe in ornamentation on their furniture. The beauty of their tables and chairs, cabinets and shelves was in their plain, functional simplicity. Woodworking was to the Shakers, like all work, a form of worship, to be approached with honesty and craftsmanship. A piece of furniture was to be perfect for its purpose.

The design of this shelf is not based on any particular Shaker piece, but it is in the Shaker tradition.

CONSTRUCTION

You'll need 14 feet of 1 x 6 select pine (an 8', and a 6' piece). The two pieces were taken to a cabinet shop to be abrasively planed—the 8-footer down to $7/16''$ and the 6-footer down to $3/8''$.

Blank the two sides to length, then clamp them back to back for routing the dadoes (for the three shelves) and the rabbet (for the bottom). Saw the front edges of the sides to rough outline on a scroll saw, then sand smooth.

Chisel hinge mortises (Fig. 1) and drill holes for the screws. After finish-sanding the inside of both sides, set the pieces aside.

Next, blank the three shelves and bottom. When sawing the shelves to width, remember there are three different measurements. Bevel the front edges of the shelves to match the slant of the front edges of the sides. Sand both top and bottom of the shelves and the inside of the bottom.

The bottom section has a back panel, and a door stop. The back gives rigidity to the shelf unit, and the door stop ... does just that. Blank the two pieces of the door stop; sand; and glue them together.

Slot the hinge side of the door to receive lattice-wood inserts. This is done to provide cross-wood grain (instead of end-grain) for the hinge screws and help prevent them from pulling out of the wood. After the lattice is glued, the doors are cut to dimension and mortised for the hinges.

Have a trial assembly before gluing—it's best to know now and be able to correct bad fits than after you have started applying glue. Make sure all inside sections of the shelf are finish-sanded before you start gluing.

The first step is to glue the center post between the bottom and the first shelf. Use aliphatic resin (yellow) glue. Then glue this section to one of the sides (Fig. 2).

EXPLODED VIEW

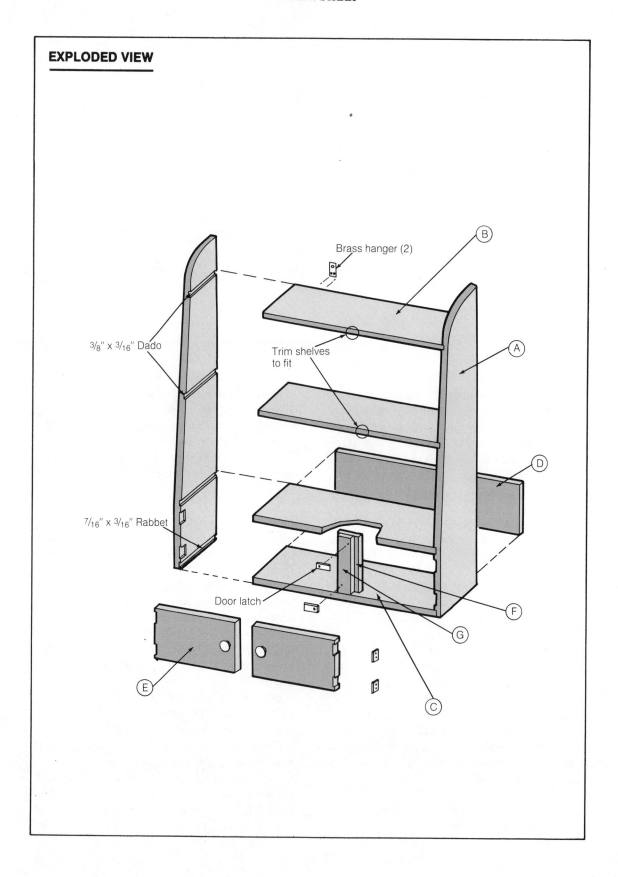

Brass hanger (2)

B

$3/8'' \times 3/16''$ Dado

A

Trim shelves
to fit

D

$7/16'' \times 3/16''$ Rabbet

Door latch

E

F

G

C

FRONT AND SIDE VIEWS

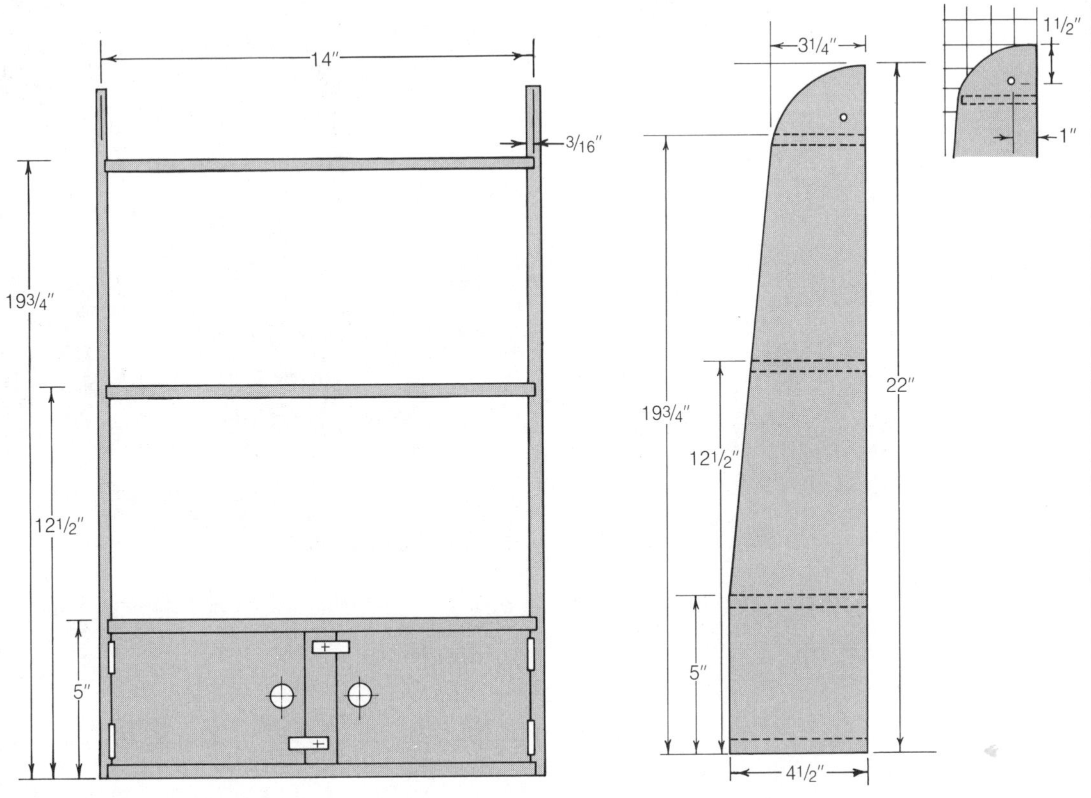

FRONT VIEW

SIDE VIEW

MATERIALS LIST

QUANTITY	DESCRIPTION
1 piece	1 x 8 select pine 14′ long
2 pairs	1¼ x 13/16" brass butt hinges
1 piece	1/16 x ⅝ x 3" brass

CUTTING LIST

KEY	PART NAME	QTY.	MATERIAL	DIMENSIONS
A	Side	2	7/16" pine	4½ x 22"
B	Shelf	3	⅜" pine	4½ x 14½"
C	Bottom	1	7/16" pine	4½ x 14½"
D	Back	1	7/16" pine	4 3/16 x 14⅛"
E	Door	2	7/16" pine	4⅛ x 6¼"
F	Door Stop	1	7/16" pine	1½ x 4 3/16"
G	Post	1	7/16" pine	1 x 4 3/16"

Fig. 1. Mortises must be chiseled accurately if the doors are to hang properly. After drilling holes for screws. Finish-sand the inside of both sides.

Fig. 2. First, glue the center post between the bottom and the first shelf. Then, as shown here, glue those parts to one of the sides.

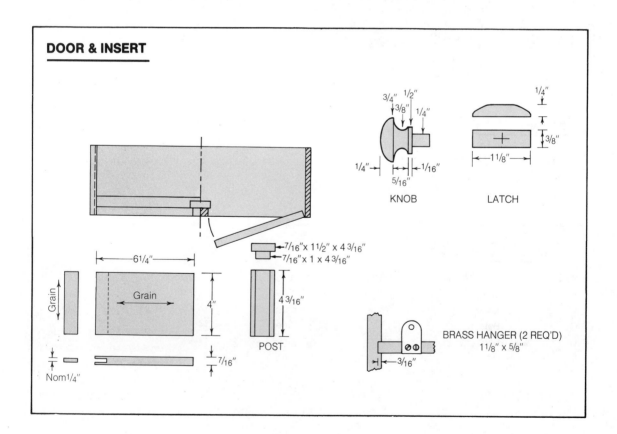

DOOR & INSERT

KNOB

LATCH

7/16" x 1 1/2" x 4 3/16"
7/16" x 1 x 4 3/16"

61/4"

Grain

Grain

4"

4 3/16"

POST

7/16"

Nom 1/4"

BRASS HANGER (2 REQ'D)
1 1/8" x 5/8"

3/16"

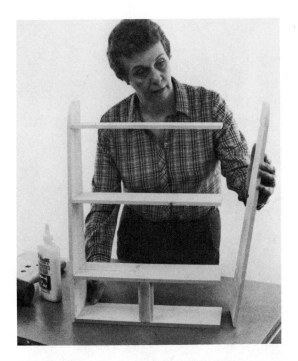

Fig. 3. After gluing the second and third shelf to one side, glue on the other side. Then attach the back piece of the bottom section.

Fig. 4. Glue lattice-wood insert in the doors to give side-grain rather than weaker end-grain holding power to the hinge screws.

Before walking away from the job (while it cures), make sure the parts are at right angles to each other. If not, adjust your clamping. Use the second side (without glue) to keep the shelves positioned.

Do not remove any excess glue oozing out of the joints. Excess glue can be cleaned up later with a chisel when it is partially dry. If the glue is removed while wet it smears, and you'll have a lot of sanding to do before finishing.

The second and third shelves are then glued to the side. Next the second side is glued on (Fig. 3). Blank the back piece of the bottom section, sand the inside and check for fit. Glue and nail in place. Now finish-sand the outside of the shelf unit and doors.

Make the latches from 1/4" x 3/8" pine. Shape with a knife and sand. Drill for 1/2" #4 roundhead screws.

Following the Shaker tradition, the knobs are turned with tenons and the tenons glued into the holes drilled in the door.

Minwax #221 Ipswich Pine, glaze and Constantine's Wood Glo varnish were used to finish the shelf.

HANGING

The Shakers would hang a small shelf like this from a peg rail by short leather thongs. We have included these thongs, but have added two brass hangers to the top shelf so the unit can be hung from nails. The shelf could also be hung by two screws through the back of the bottom compartment.

12

JEWELRY BOX

A musical jewelry box is a gift you can make for someone special. It is personal, and will be treasured for may years. The decoration can be individualized— her initials, a favorite flower or tune.

The music box shown here was designed for a friend who moved from Pennsylvania to New Mexico. The dogwood inlay is to remain her of all the dogwood in spring at Valley Forge near where she lived, and the inlay border shows a southwestern motif. Hawaiian koa wood was used for the frame and Carpathian elm burl for the panels to add richness to the design.

This jewelry box is also an opportunity to display your skill and to use rare and expensive woods in easy-on-the-budget small quantities. The box is not difficult to build, but you do have to be very careful about dimensions and fits. (The seemingly complicated dimensioning is caused by the fact that $1/4''$ plywood is no longer $1/4''$ thick, but only $7/32''$).

I have built four of these jewelry boxes. The basic shape of the box remained the same, but the methods of construction changed. At first, parts were cut and fitted individually, a time-consuming process. Now, I make identical cuts on different parts at one time, or I use a jig to produce identical parts. The time spent setting up is saved many times over by the fast, accurate assembly it produces.

Begin construction by blanking the lid and base-frame parts. Blank the lid parts back-to-back and saw out the rabbet for the top panel. If you use a Dremel saw for this, the waste can be used for some of the shelf or floor edging. Separate the parts, miter, and glue up the lid and base frames.

The reason for doing these parts first is to establish the dimensions of the box, which is $1''$ less than the outside dimensions of the lid and base. If these are off the nominal dimensions, the box dimensions should be adjusted accordingly.

The profiles of the lid and base frames are the same except reversed. Both should be routed at the same time.

To avoid splintering at the corners when routing a mitered frame, rout half of the first side (Fig. 1), then proceed around the frame counterclockwise, finishing by completing the first side.

Blank the corner posts in a single long piece and cut the rabbet. Cut the posts to length and groove the back posts to receive the back subpanel, which is $1/8''$ plywood. Using a separate internal back panel allows the whole frame to be

EXPLODED VIEW

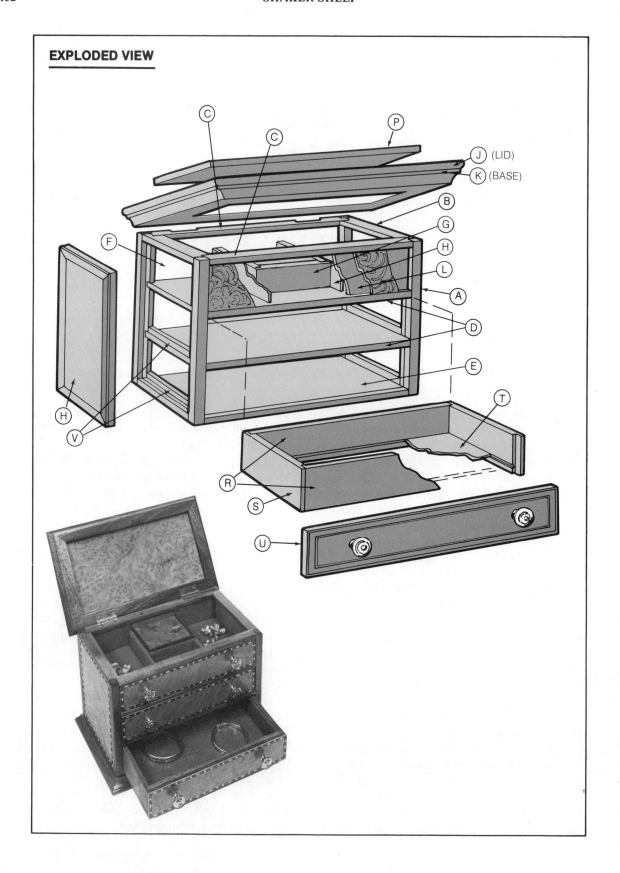

MATERIALS LIST

QUANTITY	DESCRIPTION
5 square feet	Carpathian elm burl veneer
2 board feet	3/4″ koa lumber
4 square feet	1/4″ birch plywood
3 square feet	1/8″ birch plywood
1 board foot	1/4″ mahogany or poplar
1	Floral inlay, Constantine #1W9 or equivalent
18 feet	1/4″ inlay border, Woodworkers' Store #A8043 or equivalent
1	Musical movement, single tune
1 pair	1½″ brass narrow butt hinges
1	Miniature box hinge (any)
6	Brass knobs, ½″ diameter #2525B, Mason & Sullivan
1 piece	Brass sheet, .016 x ½″ x 2½″
1 hide	Russell's Oasis #20 bright scarlet dyed goatskin, 4th quality, 3.5 square feet (minium size) from TALAS.

CUTTING LIST

KEY	QTY.	PART NAME	MATERIAL	DIMENSIONS
A	4	Corner Post	koa	$3/4 \times 9/16 \times 11/16''$
B	2	Side Corner Frame	koa	$1/4 \times 11/16 \times 6\frac{1}{4}''$
C	2	Front, Back Box Frame	koa	$1/4 \times 11/16 \times 10\frac{1}{4}''$
D	2	Shelf	birch ply	$9/32 \times 6\frac{1}{8} \times 11\frac{1}{4}''$
E	1	Floor	birch ply	$9/32 \times 6 \times 11''$
F	1	Back Structural Panel	birch ply	$1/8 \times 6\frac{7}{16} \times 10\frac{1}{2}''$
G	1	Movewment Box Panel	birch ply	$1/4 \times 1\frac{1}{4} \times 9\frac{1}{2}''$
H	1	Partition Panel	birch ply	$1/8 \times 1\frac{1}{4} \times 11''$
J-1	1	Lid Frame	koa	$3/4 \times 1\frac{1}{8} \times 12\frac{1}{4}''$
J-2	1	Lid Frame	koa	$3/4 \times 1\frac{1}{8} \times 7\frac{1}{4}''$
K-1	1	Base Frame	koa	$3/4 \times 1 \times 12\frac{1}{4}''$
K-2	1	Base Frame	koa	$3/4 \times 1\frac{1}{8} \times 7\frac{1}{4}''$
L	1	Front Panel	birch ply	$1/4 \times 2 \times 10\frac{15}{16}''$
M	2	Side Panel	birch ply	$1/4 \times 5\frac{3}{8} \times 6\frac{1}{4}''$
N	1	Back Panel	birch ply	$1/4 \times 6\frac{1}{4} \times 10\frac{3}{8}''$
P	1	Lid Panel	birch ply	$1/4 \times 6 \times 10\frac{1}{2}''$
Q	1	musical Mvt. Plate	birch ply	$1/8 \times 3 \times 3\frac{1}{2}''$
R	4	Draw Front BacK	poplar	$1/4 \times 1\frac{7}{8} \times 9\frac{15}{16}''$
S	4	Draw Side	poplar	$1/4 \times 1\frac{7}{8} \times 5\frac{3}{8}''$
T	2	Draw Bottom	birch ply	$1/8 \times 5\frac{1}{8} \times 9\frac{15}{16}''$
U	3	Draw Overlay	birch ply	$1/4 \times 1\frac{7}{8} \times 10\frac{15}{16}''$
V	4	Draw Guide	birch ply	$1/4 \times 3/8 \times 9\frac{3}{4}1''$

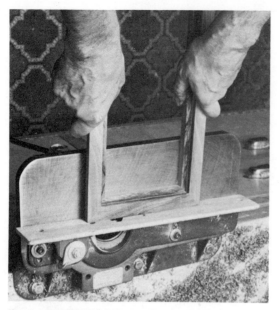

Fig. 1. Shaping the lid frame. To avoid splintering at the corners, rout half the first side, then proceed around the frame counterclockwise.

assembled before any work is done on the exposed side and back panels.

Using scrap cut to exact post height, set up the miter gauge of your table saw with stop blocks, as shown, and saw all notches. The posts are symetrical top to bottom.

The floor, the shelf blanks, and the top frame are all made initially to the same outside dimension so they can be clamped together. Then the posts can be notched simultaniously and accurately.

Blank the two shelves and the floor to the dimensions given and edge with koa as required. Cut parts for the top frame and assemble.

Clamp all four parts together and notch the corners. Separate and cut back the sides and back of the shelves. Also, make the cutout in the upper shelf for the musical movement compartment, which is open at the bottom for better sound. Drill holes in the upper shelf for screws.

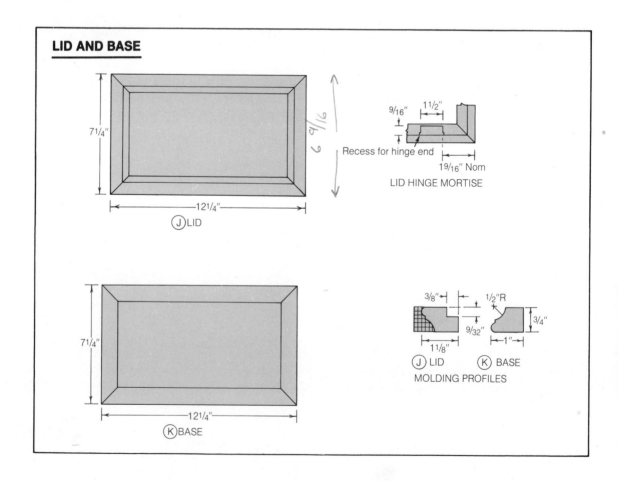

LID AND BASE

BOX FRAME

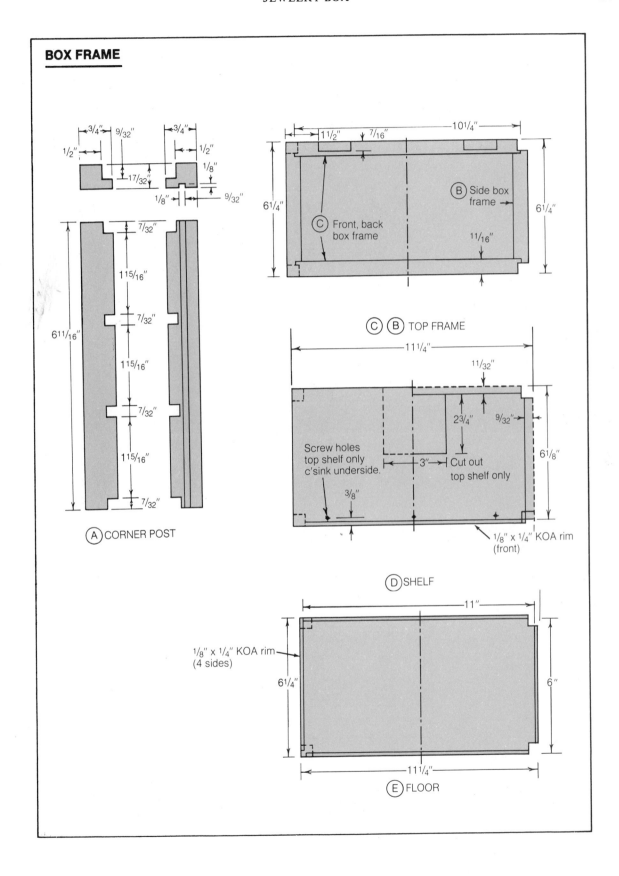

A CORNER POST

C B TOP FRAME

D SHELF

E FLOOR

DETAILS

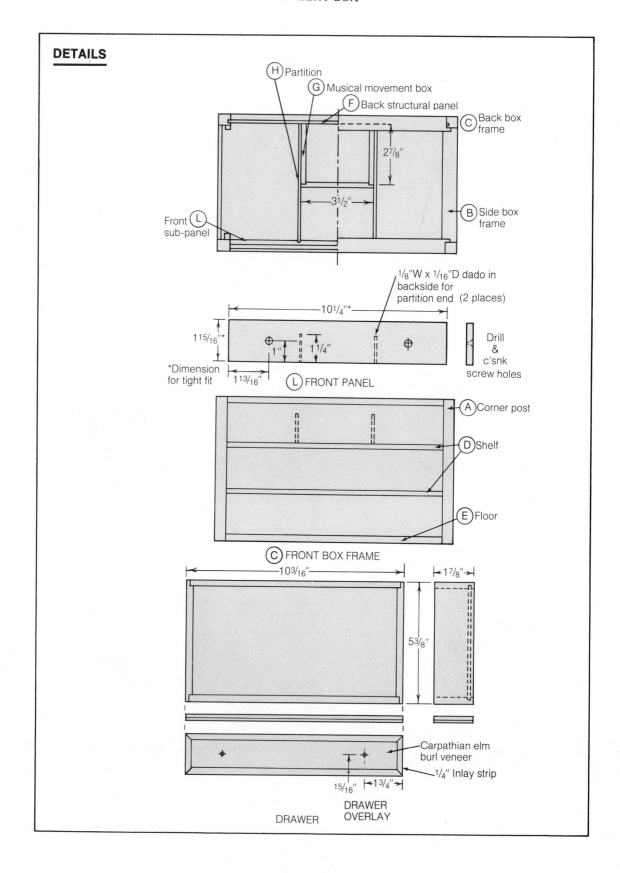

ASSEMBLING THE BOX

Start box assembly by gluing the back structural panel between the back posts using floor and the top frame for alignment (Fig. 2).

Blank the front panel, drill and countersink for knob screws, dado for partitions. Assemble the posts, top frame, and upper shelf dry and fit the front panel. Position the panel to allow septh for the false drawer front and glue and screw it to the upper shelf only (Fig. 3). Glue the upper shelf to the back posts and panel, using the rest of the box parts to ensure alignment. When dry, glue the lower shelf the same way.

Next glue the front posts to the two shelves, again with the floor and top frame assembled for alignment. Cut drawer guides and install them to the lower shelf now; it will be difficult to clamp them after the floor is added (see Fig. 4 for assembled box).

Glue on the floor and its drawer guides, but

Fig. 2. The floor, top frame, and front posts are assembled dry to serve as a jig to assure alignment of the back panel and the back posts.

Fig. 3. Gluing front panel to top shelf. Posts will be added to the jig before gluing. Washers strung under the two pieces of scrap wood bolted across the front of the top frame and top panel recess the front panel for the 1/4"-thick false drawer front.

Fig. 4. Assembled box, lid, and base frames. All framing should be completed before starting decorative panels.

not the top frame at this time. Blank the parts for the movement box anf glue them in the top compartment. Blank the partitions. Mortise the top frame and the lid frame for hinges.

VENEER WORK

Carpethian-elm burl veneer requires treatment to overcome its bittleness and get it to lay flat. In the condition it is received it cannot be sawed without chipping, or sawed or cut accurately with a knife. The necessary treatment is described in Chapter 5.

The floral inlay decorating the lid of the box was purchased and reworked. First, I wanted to get rid of the uninspiring walnut background, and secondly, the inlay as it came didn't fit the lid dimensions (Fig. 5).

The first step in reworking the inlay is to cut away the background. Trim away as much as

Fig. 5. Floral inlay (top) was purchased in a walnut background, which was inappropriate for the lid. The inlay was cut away from the background and most of it inserted in a different wood (bottom).

Fig. 6. Separating the inlay from the background. First, carefully slice away the large areas. To cut out the flowers and stems, make a series of slits, then split away the background in narrow strips.

you can in big pieces, then carefully cut away what is left next to the decoration (Fig. 6). The piece you cut away should always be smaller than the piece being left to avoid breakage. Scrape away any filler left on the parts.

Lay out the parts of the floral decoration as you want them and trace their outline with a sharp pencil as close to the inlay as you can keep it. Now locate the inlay border. Note that all of the parts of the original inlay were not used.

I stacked three oversize (1/2" all around) pieces of Carpathian-elm burl veneer (for three jewelry boxes) between low-cost veneer. I attached the cutting pattern to the face of the top piece of veneer with spray adhesive and put plain paper on the unerside of the bottom piece of veneer. I taped all five pieces of veneer securely at the edges.

I clamped an auxiliary table of 1/4" plywood on the scroll-saw table to provide support for the veneer to the edge of the blade, and to prevent losing small pieces cut off (Fig. 7.) The saw blade itself was used to saw a slot to the center of the plywood. The plywood should be as large as the scroll-saw table.

Use a fine blade—32 tpi is as coarse as you should go. Run your saw as slow as you can, feed slowly, stop and remove waste piece by piece so it doesn't jam up and break the veneer (Fig. 8). If there are small pieces of background veneer that will be surrounded by the inlay, cut them free first. When done, and before separating the veneer form the protective veneer, check the fit of the inlay parts.

Separate the veneers and place inlay parts in the cutouts taped side up. Tape the parts into the veneer using special thin veneering tape (Fig. 9, 10). Do not use masking tape—it is difficult to remove. When glueing and clamping the assembled inlay panel to the plywood core, use a piece

Fig. 7. The veneer sandwich must be supported to the edge of the blade. An auxiliary table of 1/4" ply, clamped to the saw table, does the job. Here, a slit is being cut to the center of the plywood.

Fig. 8. Backgrounds being sawn for three jewelry box lids simultaneously. Veneers are sandwiched and taped between inexpensive veneer.

Fig. 9. Carpathian elm burl background veneer is 1/40″ thick, the inlay 1/16″ thick. Fit the inlay into the background and tape in place.

Fig. 10. Taping inlay into new background. Wet tape thoroughly with a brush and press into place. Sometimes it helps to clamp it under a board and weight.

of resilient foam-core board as a pad to apply pressure to both the thick inlay and the thin veneer. Do not reuse foam-core board for another clamping.

PANELS

Cut oversize blanks for the side, back, lid, drawer front (3) and movement plate panels. Center the plywood blank for the lid panel on the untaped side of the inlaid veneer and trace the outline. apply carpenter's glue evenly and without gaps to the plywood and glue the untaped side of the veneer to the plywood. When dry, trim excess veneer from the plywood edge and glue burl veneer to the backside (it will be the visible lid interior surface).

Glue burl to the front of the rest of the panels, and when dry and trimmed, glue backing veneer (any kind) to the backs of the panels.

It would be a good idea to stack all of these panels and keep them clamped for a few days until the glue is thoroughly dry and the excess moisture has evened itself out in the wood. This will reduce any tendency to warp.

Scrape off any of the tape you can, then sand off the rest, and sand all the burl veneer until smooth and free of surface glue. Slight moistening will help get off the tape, and the same slight

Fig. 11. Sanded veneered panels are fitted into the frame without borders. Rabbets for border inlays are then routed using the panel edge as a guide.

moistening will make surface glue very visible. Use a pad sander for this, with the coarsest paper 150-grit. Remember, you have at most 1/28″ of veneer on the surface and you can go through it fast.

Fit the side, lid, and back panels in the box openings accurately and mark which way they go in. Bring the overlay-drawer fronts to dimen-

Fig. 12. Frames can be sanded cautiously on a belt sander with a dull 120-grit or finer belt. As all panels are set slightly below the surface of the frame, only the frames are sanded.

Fig. 13. Finish-sand frames and panels with small-orbit, high-speed pad sander to avoid visible scratches. Be careful to sand the whole surface evenly so you don't sand through accidently.

sion (1/8″ smaller each way than the opening) and veneer the edge with a dark veneer, such as walnut. Don't use koa veneer—it is impossibly brittle, and it doesn't match the solid wood.

Rout the edges of the panels and drawer fronts for the 1/4″ inlay banding. The inlay must fit exactly. If the rabbet is too wide, you can't clamp the inlay edge; if too narrow, you will be sanding off the white edge of the inlay. The depth of the rabbet should bring the inlay just barely higher than the sanded veneer.

Position the inlay banding to make the corners symmetrical and look good (Fig. 11). The corners on the different panels had to be matched in different patterns. Sand smooth.

The panels should go into the openings so that the face of the veneer is just below the frame surface; sand off backing veneer or shim as required. Glue in the panels. Glue in the box top frame, and sand the whole box and lid (Figs. 12, 13).

Trim the front and side edges of the movement plate with strips of koa wood and glue 1/8″ ply-

wood to the underside to fit into the movement compartment.

MUSICAL MOVEMENT

The jewelry box is designed to use a small single-tune Swiss or Japanese movement. The exact mounting arrangement will depend on the movement you select. A pushrod through the back top frame, held in place by the movement plate, actuates the movement whenever the lid is opened.

Blank parts for the two drawers, form joints, groove, drill and countersink holes for the pull screws, sand interior surfaces and assemble. Glue on the drawer fronts.

The jewelry box requires no stain and can be finished with either varnish or lacquer, you could pad on a finish for the ultimate in appearance.

Note: If you are dissatisfied with the colors of the inlay (the green seems to vary all over the place), colors can be touched up with colored

Fig. 14. This music box movement is installed on the underside of the lid. A brass pushrod engages hinge- mounted brass strap, depressing trip wire to prevent fly- wheel from rotating.

ink. Dilute the ink—a few drops in a teaspoon is usually too much. Test before applying with a small brush. Protect adjacent surfaces you don't want colored with shellac. The ink will raise grain; sand lightly with very worn 280-grit paper, then apply on a light coat of spray-can clear lacquer before finishing.

LINING

The first jewelry boxes I made were lined with red velvet. This box was lined with red leather. It can be done with a single skin of at least $3\frac{1}{2}$ square feet, but careful planning and layout is required to get out all the pieces (Fig. 15).

The leather is wrapped over chipboard panels which are used with a layer of felt and the turn- over glued (Fig.16). The back of each panel is covered with another piece of chipboard to pro- vide a flat surface for gluing to the drawer or box interior.

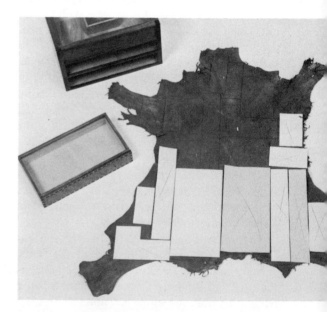

Fig. 15. One $3\frac{1}{2}$-square-foot skin provided sufficient leather to line the compartment and drawers, but careful cutting was required to get all the pieces and work around defects in the leather.

Fig. 16. Leather edges are folded over chipboard backing and fastened with white glue.

13

BANJO CLOCK

This half-scale Banjo Clock is an elegant gift that can be constructed in a single weekend. The clock is not a reproduction of any particular Howard or Eli Whitney model, but is a freely adapted version in the traditional style.

The mahogany clock has no complicated joints, and the round head can be made without a lathe. No special knowledge of clocks is required. The movement is a type called a "fit up." The movement is dropped in, and secured with a retainer of some sort.

A few years ago, fit-up movements were key-wound. Inexpensive thirty-hour models had to be wound daily, more costly eight-day models, once a week. Key-wound fit-up movements today are almost unobtainable, having been replaced by battery-driven quartz movements that run a year and keep far better time.

CONSTRUCTION

Before starting this project, buy your fit-up movement. You should not attempt to make the clock head without the movement on hand. They are supposed to have standard dimensions, but a slight change in some dimension might give you trouble.

Start construction with the round head. The head of the clock is made of three pieces of $13/16''$ stock. (If $3/4''$ stock is substituted, reduce the thickness of the box and neck from $2''$ to $1 7/8''$.) Cut and finish the inside diameters of each of the pieces before you laminate the layers.

Fig. 1. Chisel a flat on the bottom of the head to join the neck. This is easier than trying to form a mating curve on the top of the neck.

EXPLODED VIEW

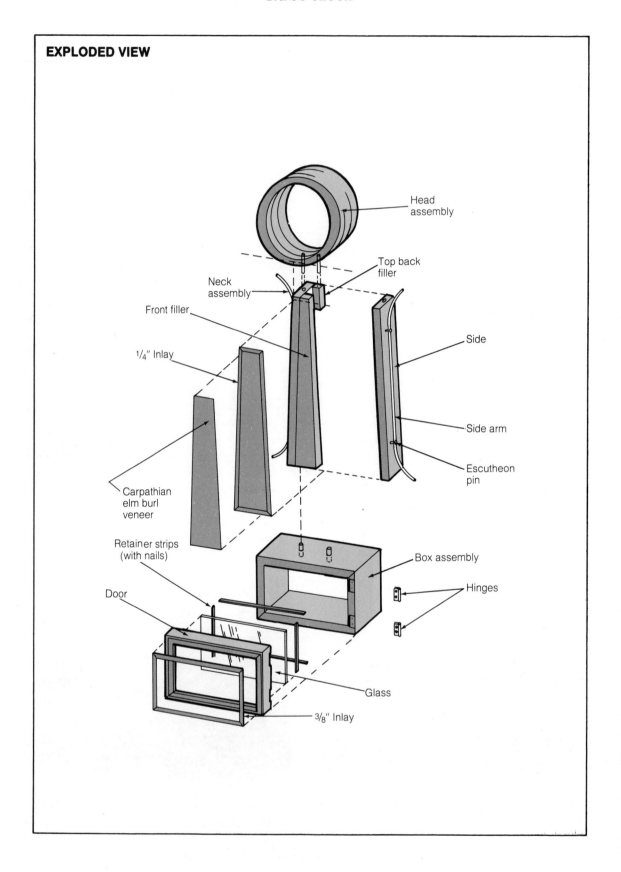

Lay out the three pieces on a single blank, and saber-saw the three holes. Finish the holes with a drum sander in a drill press. Saw the three pieces to an oversize outside diameter and glue together with the grain direction rotated 120 degrees between plies. When dry, sand the head to finished diameter. Chisel a flat on the bottom for joining the neck (Fig. 1) and drill a hole in the top for the finial.

Next, build the box and door. Rout one edge of ½" stock to form a blank for the door-frame parts. Make the front-surface rabbet for the inlay and the backside rabbet for the glass and decora-tion. Hand-sand the reed edge-molding. Now, before ripping the door-frame blank from the stock, glue the inlay to the door frame in one piece.

It is easier to rip the door frame and a blank for the box parts from the stock in one piece than to rip them separately, as the number of miter cuts to be made can be cut in half. After mitering, rip the door frames and box parts apart and glue up each assembly. When dry, rout or chisel the mortises for the hinges.

The neck is made in four pieces: two sides, front filler, and top back filler. Blank the pieces to dimension and assemble with glue. When dry, sand the front surface flat for the veneer and inlay. Drill the slanting hole in the top back filler block for the hanging nail.

With masking tape, tape a piece of 3" gummed kraft tape to your bench, gum side up. Place the completed neck on the tape and trace the outline. This is the outside edge of the veneer-and-inlay panel to be applied to the front of the neck, except that the panel must be ⅛" shorter to clear the bottom of the head. Cut and miter inlay strips to fit within this outline and attach to the

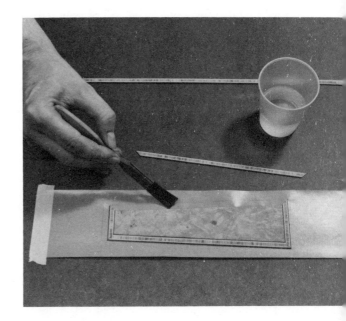

Fig. 2. Glue veneer and inlay strip for neck decorative panel to gummed kraft tape by wetting tape and pressing in place.

MATERIALS LIST

QUANTITY	DESCRIPTION
1 board foot	¹³⁄₁₆" mahogany
1 board foot	½" mahogany
1 piece (36")	Inlay, ¼" wide, Constantine B-49 or equivalent
1 piece (36")	Inlay, ⅜" wide, Constantine B-56 or equivalent
1 pair	Hinges, ¾" x 1¼₆" (Stanley #9449-A)
2 pieces	Brass rod, ⅛" diameter, 12" long
9	¾" 15 ga. brass escutcheon pins
1 piece	Carpathian elm burl veneer, 3" x 10"
1	Fit-up clock movement, complete with bezel, face, hands. #814001, S. LaRose, Inc. 2380 C25, Craft Products Co.
1	Eagle finial, #3242-C42, Craft Products Co.

tap by moistening the tape with water with a small brush and pressing the inlay in place (Fig. 2). Now cut and fit a piece of veneer inside the inlay and glue in place.

Remove the tape from the bench and apply glue to the exposed face of the inlay and veneer panel and glue to the front of the neck. When the glue is dry, scrape and sand off the kraft tape. Sand the surface carefully and evenly so you do not remove any more of the veneer than is absolutely necessary.

Drill holes in the head, neck, and box for the dowels (Fig. 3), and do a trial assembly.

Finish the parts of the clock before final assembly , Sand all parts smooth, dust. Apply a coat of varnish to the inlay and veneer only (Fig. 4), being careful to keep it off the mahogany. Stain and fill the mahogany, apply varnish to all surfaces.

The side arms are made from $1/8''$ round brass rod. Attach them to the clock with $3/4''$ brass

Fig. 3.   Dowels are used to reinforce the neck-to-box joint.

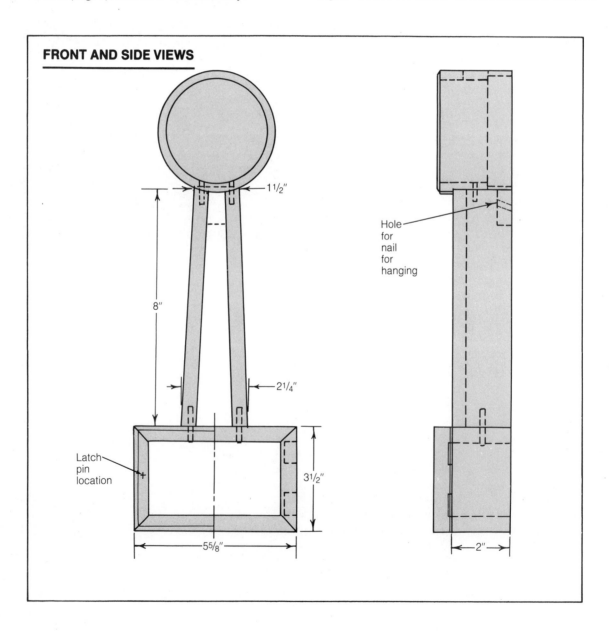

FRONT AND SIDE VIEWS

1½"

8"

2¼"

Latch pin location

5⅝"

3½"

Hole for nail for hanging

2"

DETAILS

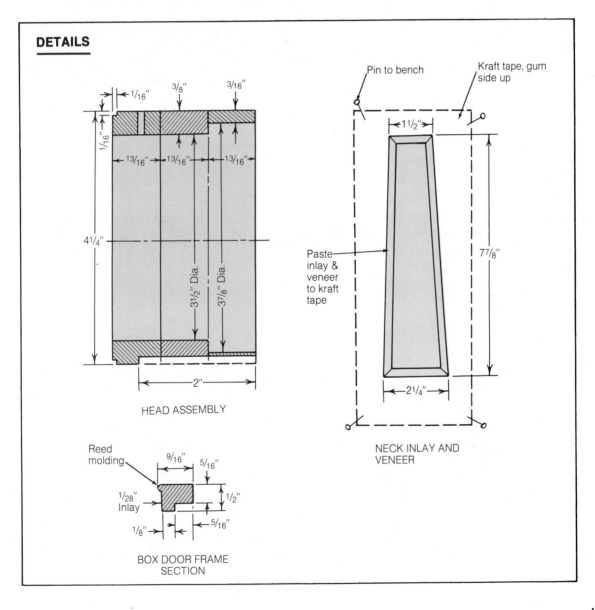

1/16" 3/8" 3/16"

1/16"

13/16" 13/16" 13/16"

4 1/4"

3 1/2" Dia.

3 7/8" Dia.

2"

HEAD ASSEMBLY

Reed molding

9/16" 5/16"

1/28" Inlay

1/2"

1/8" 5/16"

BOX DOOR FRAME
SECTION

Pin to bench

Kraft tape, gum side up

1 1/2"

Paste inlay & veneer to kraft tape

7 7/8"

2 1/4"

NECK INLAY AND
VENEER

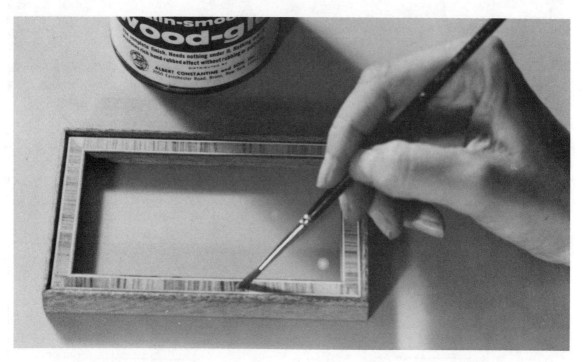

Fig. 4. Apply varnish to inlay and veneer trim on the door and neck but keep it off the mahogany. This coating pre- vents stain and filler from discoloring the inlay. Then stain and fill the mahogany, and varnish all surfaces.

Fig. 5. Drill four holes on each side for the escutcheon pins that attach the brass side arms.

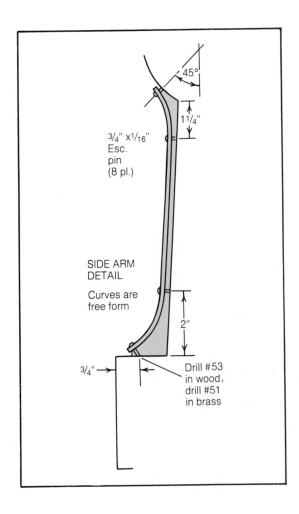

3/4" x 1/16"
Esc.
pin
(8 pl.)

45°

1 1/4"

SIDE ARM
DETAIL

Curves are
free form

2"

3/4"

Drill #53
in wood,
drill #51
in brass

escutcheon pins. Drill #51 holes for the pins (Fig. 5). Mount the rails to the neck first, then to the head and box.

Instead of the usual hook-and-eye latch to secure the door, I used a pin forced into the door that aligns with a hole in the side of the box.

There are several ways to decorate the door. Traditionally, a reverse painting on glass—a painting applied to the back of the glass— was used. To do the painting takes talent; to have it done is expensive. The next best choice is a gold decal made for the purpose, which can be obtained from antique clock-repair parts suppliers.

Other possibilities include a color photo of a favorite scene, a color postcard, or a piece of inlay work. A postcard or photo should be put behind a piece of single-thickness window glass.

Mounting the clock movement does not present any special problems. The bezel, face, and works come as an assembly and are inserted into the head from the front. (Mount the finial first, using 8-32 roundhead machine screws.) The rear retaining plate fits into the back of the head and is secured with nuts threaded on protruding studs.

All that remains is to attach the knobs, wind the spring or put in the battery, set the time, and hang the clock on a nail, or gift wrap it.

14

SHERATON BOOKCASE

This elegant bookcase was built ten years ago to hold paperbacks. Today, I use it for video tapes and computer games. It is a very simple project to build. Once the sides are cut out and dadoed for the shelves it just about falls together.

Blank the sides, shelves, and the top. Clamp the sides together, back edge to back edge, rout the stopped dadoes for the shelves, and form the tenons for the top and the floor. Unclamp and rout the dado for the 1/4" back panel. Note that this back panel is behind the shelves only and does not form the back of the drawer compartment.

Now clamp the two sides together and finish both front edges to dimension at the same time. Rout the tenons on the shelf ends, and rout the mortises in the top for the side tenons. Drill holes for pulls.

Rout the top edge molding, and the identical but inverted trim molding that will cover the edge of the floor. If your mahogany stock is limited, rip strips for the trim molding and glue them to a pine "handle" for routing. After the molding is formed and sanded, the trim can be ripped from the scrap pine. Rout the rabbet in

the back of the top for the back panel, and the two stopped dadoes for the side tenons.

Square up the turning stock for the legs, mark off for the long taper and bandsaw 1/16" over dimension. Then sand or plane the tapers to the finish dimension. Mark the shoulders of the

Fig. 1. Cutting tenon in leg to fit caster. Left, tapered leg with saw cuts forming the tenon. Center, the finished tenon after the tapers have been sawed. Right, caster fitted onto tenon.

PARTIALLY EXPLODED VIEW

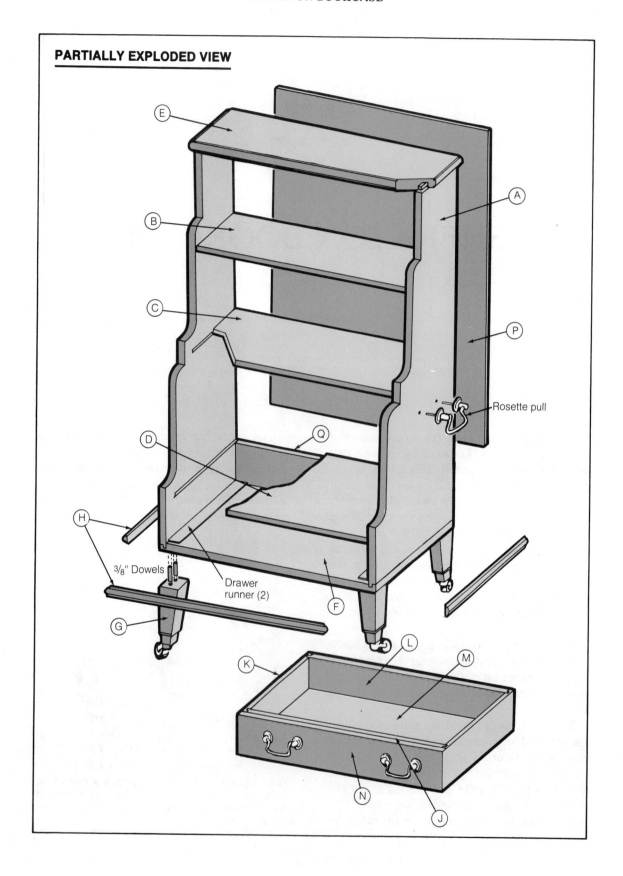

Rosette pull

3/8" Dowels

Drawer
runner (2)

socket tenon on all for sides and lay out the socket tenon tapers on the tapered sides of the legs. Now saw the shoulders (I used a Dozuki saw); then bandsaw the socket tapers (Fig. 1). Fit the tenons to the sockets of your swivel casters with a coarse file. Now complete the sanding of the legs before doweling them to the floor.

Cut the floor from $3/4''$ plywood and rout the dadoes for the sides (the lower back requires no dado). Align legs with the corners and drill $3/8''$ holes through the floor into the legs for dowels.

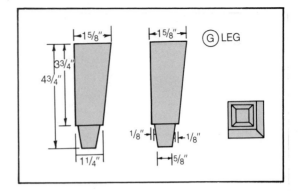

MATERIALS LIST

QUANTITY	DESCRIPTION
12 bd. ft.	½" mahogany lumber
1 pc.	¾" mahogany lumber, 6 x 23"
1 pc.	¼" mahogany plywodd, 21½ x 30"
2 ft.	1¾ x 1¾" mahogany turning square
1 pc.	⅛" plywood 10 x 20"
1 pc.	¾" plywood 11 x 22"
1 pc.	½" plywood 4 x 21"
2 bd. ft.	½" poplar
2	Brass rosette pulls, 2½" boring
2	Brass rosette pulls, 3" boring
4	Brass square socket casters, 1" inside top dimension

CUTTING LIST

KEY	QTY.	PART NAME	MATERIAL	BLANK DIMENSIONS
A	2	Side	mahogany	½ x 11 x 34⅜"
B	1	Upper Shelf	mahogany	½ x 6⅛ x 21⅜"
C	1	Middle Shelf	mahogany	½ x 7⅝ x 21⅜"
D	1	Lower Shelf	mahogany	½ x 10⅝ x 21⅜"
E	1	Top	mahogany	¾ x 6 x 23"
F	1	Floor	plywood	¾ x 11 x 22"
G	4	Leg	mahogany	1¹¹⁄₁₆ x 1¹¹⁄₁₆ x 4¾"
H	2	Trim Molding	mahogany	½ x ¾ x 24"
J	1	Drawer Front	pine	½ x 3¾ x 20¼"
K	2	Drawer Side	pine	½ x 3¾ x 9⅞"
L	1	Drawer Back	pine	½ x 3¼ x 20¼"
M	1	Drawer Bottom	plywood	⅛ x 9⁹⁄₁₆ x 20¼"
N	1	Drawer Overlay Front	mahogany	½ x 3¾ x 20⅞"
P	1	Back Panel	plywood	¼ x 21⅜ x 30¼"
Q	1	Lower Back Panel	plywood	½ x 4 x 21"

PATTERN FOR SIDE

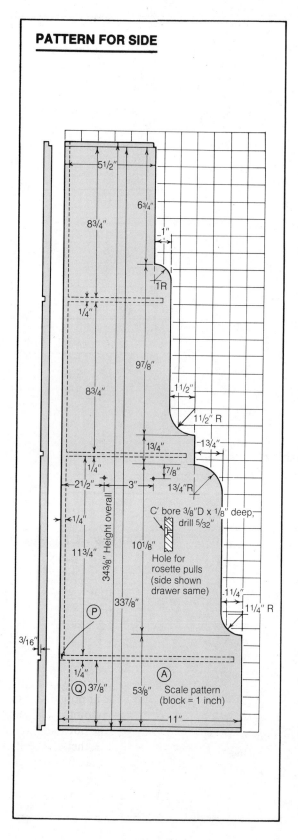

5½"

6¾"

8¾"

1"

1 R

¼"

9⅞"

8¾"

1½"

1½" R

13/4"

1¾"

¼"

⅞"

2½"

3"

1¾"R

¼"

C′ bore ⅜"D x ⅛" deep,
drill 5/32"

10⅛"

Hole for
rosette pulls
(side shown
drawer same)

11¾"

34⅜" Height overall

33⅞"

1¼"

1¼" R

3/16"

¼"

(P)

(Q) 3⅞"

(A)

5⅜"   Scale pattern
(block = 1 inch)

11"

(After you have the first hole drilled, insert a dowel in it for alignment while you drill the second hole).

Glue and dowel legs to the floor, then glue ¹/₁₆" x ³/₄" x 10" drawer runners in place. The purpose of the runners is to provide a smoother sliding surface for the drawer. Make runners from scrap hardwood.

Next, clamp the floor, sides, and lower shelf together and accurately fit the lower back panel into the back of the drawer compartment. The purpose of this piece is to square up the bookcase and prevent racking. With the carcase parts still clamped, glue and screw the lower back panel to the bookcase floor, then unclamp the sides and shelf before the glue sets.

Sand the shelves, and both the interior and exterior surfaces of the sides and top.

Glue and clamp the sides and the lower shelf to the floor and the lower back panel. Fit the top (dry) to be sure the sides are aligned. If possible, the carcase should be glued up laying on its back on a flat bench to prevent any twisting.

Fig. 2. Clamping the top of the bookcase to the sides. Blocks protect the surface and spread clamping force evenly across the work.

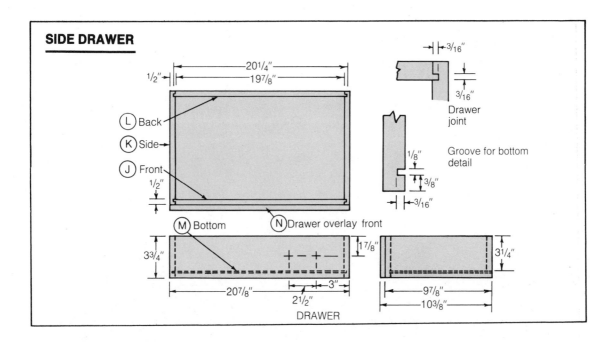

SIDE DRAWER

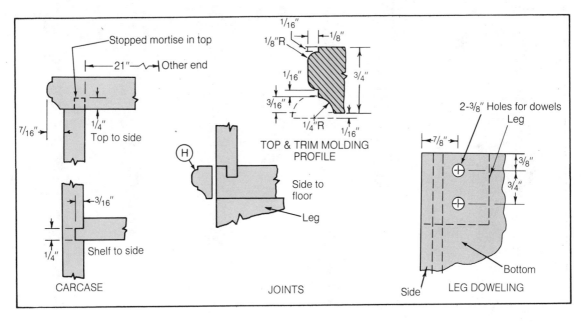

With the clamps still in place, remove the top, spring the sides outward slightly to avoid smearing glue and install the remaining two shelves (put the top back on for alignment). Last, glue and clamp the top to the sides (Fig. 2).

Miter the trim molding and glue and nail it to the edges of the floor. Cut the back panel to dimension, but do not nail it into the rabbet until after finishing has been completed.

The front panel of the drawer is mahogany, the rest of the parts can be pine or poplar. Form tenons and dadoes for the corner joints, and rout grooves in front and sides for the bottom. Sand all interior surfaces and assemble, then sand outside surfaces and attach the overlay front panel. Drill holes for the pulls.

The bookcase should receive a conventional stain, filler, and varnish finish.

15

COUNTRY CRAFTSMAN TABLE

The original of this little table has been in the family for several generations and was put to many uses over the years. The wood is maple, with bird's-eye maple veneer applied to the drawer front. The leg turning, on close examination, were found not to be turned at all, but hand-carved. My wife and daughter both liked the table, so when my daughter got her own apartment, I decided to make her a copy, as close to the original as possible, including hand-carving the leg "turnings."

While making the copy, I learned something about country woodworkers of a century ago, and that a lot of irregularities (let's not call them defects) in handmade furniture construction go completely unnoticed unless you look carefully and take dimensions. What this country craftsman needed, more than anything, was an accurate ruler.

The design appears to be about two notches above execution. The two drawer rails are nicely double-tenoned into the legs, but the back apron is a different length than the drawer rails, and the two sides are not the same length. The top is not square, and its out-of-squareness does not match the out-of-squareness of the frame below. The

drawer dovetails are handmade and laid out casually, but are neat and tight-fitting. The carved feet are nicely executed and finished off.

But somewhere into the carving of the tops of the legs our country woodworker must have suddenly realized he had made an error. One of the carved sections on one back leg top is $1/2''$ shorter than the other three. He never finished off any of the top carvings, but left them rough. I knew they were crude, but had never noticed one was short until I started taking off dimensions.

These are some of the things you can encounter with old handmade furniture. If you are going to make repairs or a copy, measure everything, and assume nothing is as it should be without checking.

Start construction of the table with the legs. Square up turning stock to finished dimension and lay out the "turnings." Carving the legs was not difficult, only tedious. The first one took the longest, as I experimented with different rasps and chisels. Stop cuts were made at the ends of the carving area to protect the square leg section as a first step. (The legs were similarly squared-off on the original; he probably did the same.) I used a Japanese Dozuki tenon saw for this. The

EXPLODED VIEW

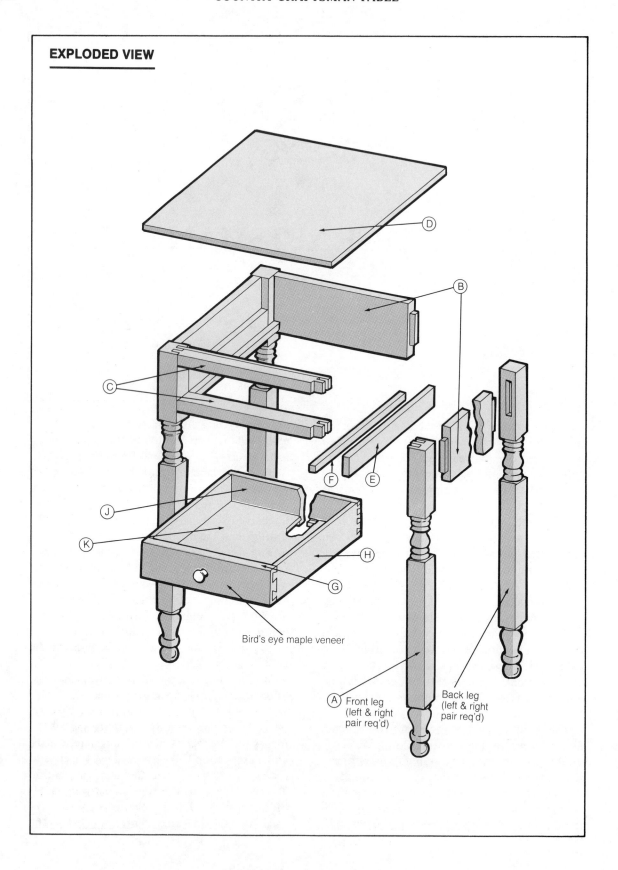

Bird's eye maple veneer

Ⓐ Front leg
(left & right
pair req'd)

Back leg
(left & right
pair req'd)

FRONT AND SIDE VIEWS

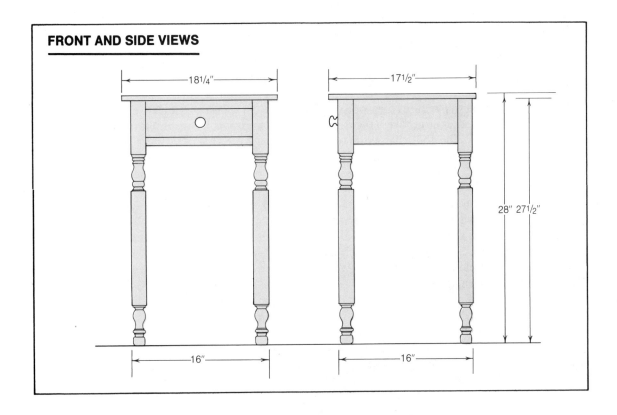

MATERIALS LIST

QUANTITY	DESCRIPTION
10 feet	2 x 2 maple turning aquare
4 board feet	1⅛" maple
4 board feet	¾" maple
4 board feet	¾"pine
1 square foot	bird's-eye maple veneer

CUTTING LIST

KEY	QTY.	PART NAME	MATERIAL	BLANK DIMENSIONS
A	4	Leg	maple	1¾ x 1¾ x 28"
B	3	Side	maple	⅞ x 5 x 13¾"
C	2	Drawer Rail	maple	⅞ x 1⅜ x 14¼"
D	1	Top	maple	9⁄16 x 17½ x 18¼"
E	2	Drawer Guide	pine	¾ x 2 x 12½
F	2	Drawer Runner	pine	⅝ x ⅝ x 12½"
G	1	Drawer Front	pine	¾ x 3⅛ x 12⅜"
H	1	Drawer Side	pine	½ x 3¹⁄16 x 13⅛"
J	1	Drawer Back	pine	½ x 2⅝ x 12⅜"
K	1	Drawer Bottom	pine	⅜ x 11⅝ x 12¾"

thin blade and fine teeth leave no teeth marks to chisel or sand away, and cutting on the pull stroke gives amazing control. I also used the Dozuki saw to score and locate all V-grooves in the carving.

The second carving step reduces the wood to a cylinder. Mark and score the grooves (Fig. 1, 2), then start chopping. The tool that ultimately worked best for me for almost all of the carving was an ancient $1\frac{1}{2}''$ chisel (Fig. 3). The big advantage of the tool was the ease with which it could be held and controlled.

If you are new at carving, take it slowly and cautiously at first. As a friend of mine said as he whittled an eagle from a block of wood with a hatchet, "You just chop away everything that doesn't look like an eagle."

Seriously, the hard work is getting the square section down to a cylinder. It goes easy from there. You could put the leg on a lathe and turn down to a cylinder and then hand carve from there. It would be cheating, but you'd save yourself the hardest two-thirds of the carving. Or you

could do the intitial roughing with a router or router crafter—anything to cut away the bulk of the wood fast.

Carve the legs to rough shape only. From there, the going will be faster and smoother with a file. At this stage don't use a Surform or rasp because it is too coarse. Start with a half-round bastard file (Fig. 4), finish shaping with finer half-round and rattail files. Finish up by sanding with a Sand-O-Flex hand drill attachment (Fig. 5).

To help keep the "turnings" circular, set up blocks with nail centers. Clamp them to your bench. High sides are quite easy to find this way, and laying out the carving will be more accurate. Also rough-carve all the legs before you start filing. Line them up, and do whatever additional carving you find necessary to get them all close together in appearance.

The rest of the construction is conventional. Apron and rail tenons were formed in the traditional way with saw and chisel. I drilled out the mortises on a drill press, then squared them with

Fig. 1. Punch centers on the top and bottom of the leg and set up clamped nail and block centers to mark the leg for carving. This allows quick identification of out-of-round carving. Pencil is positioned by V-groove in clamped block while leg is rotated.

Fig. 2. Score all V-grooves with a tenon saw before starting the carving. This also keeps the bottom of the groove from wandering as you carve.

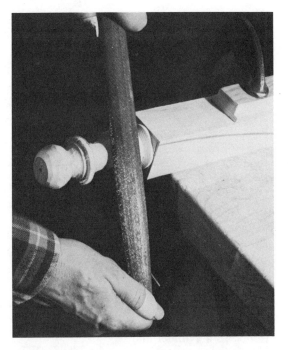

Fig. 3. For the actual carving I tried many chisels, but the best was an elderly 1½″ tool because it was easiest to hold and control.

Fig. 4. Most of the smoothing was done with a half-round bastard file. A rasp or Surform is much too coarse for this stage of the work.

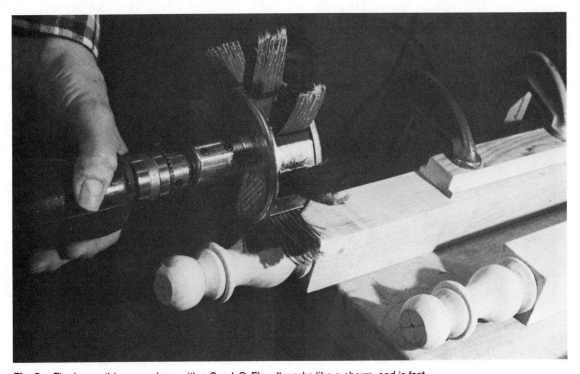

Fig. 5. Final smoothing was done with a Sand-O-Flex. It works like a charm, and is fast.

LEGS

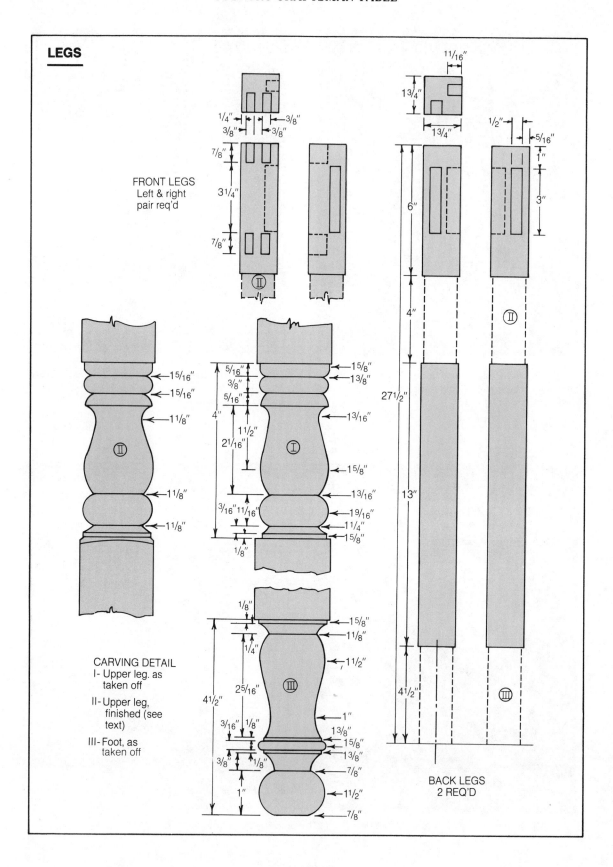

FRONT LEGS
Left & right
pair req'd

1/4"   3/8"
3/8"   3/8"

7/8"
3 1/4"
7/8"

Ⅱ

11/16"
1 3/4"
1 3/4"
1/2"
5/16"
1"
3"

6"

4"

Ⅱ

27 1/2"

13"

4 1/2"

BACK LEGS
2 REQ'D

1 5/16"
1 5/16"
1 1/8"

Ⅱ

1 1/8"
1 1/8"

5/16"
3/8"
5/16"
4"
11 1/2"
2 1/16"

1 5/8"
1 3/8"
1 3/16"

Ⅰ

1 5/8"
1 3/16"

3/16" 11/16"
1 9/16"
1 1/4"
1 5/8"
1/8"

CARVING DETAIL
I- Upper leg. as
taken off

II- Upper leg,
finished (see
text)

III- Foot, as
taken off

1/8"
1 5/8"
1 1/8"
1/4"
1 1/2"

2 5/16"

Ⅲ

4 1/2"

3/16" 1/8"
1"
1 3/8"
1 5/8"
1 3/8"
3/8" 1/8"
7/8"
1 1/2"

1"
7/8"

chisels (Figs. 6, 7). The mortises should be about $1/16''$ deeper than the tenon length. The table top and drawer bottom are glued up from solid wood as in the original.

The drawer dovetail joints, as in the original, are casually laid out and hand cut (Figs. 8, 9). The edges of the drawer bottom are beveled to fit into the $1/4''$ groove.

The drawer front is veneered with bird's-eye maple veneer as in the original. Drawer guides and runners are made of poplar, meeting the customary requirement of using whatever secondary wood is handiest.

Only three changes were made from the original table construction—two deliberately, and one without thinking. The drawer guides and runners were glued and screwed instead of nailed, and drawer stops were added. When I glued the veneer on the drawer front, I automatically glued veneer to the backside—accepted

Fig. 6. Mortises in legs were started by drilling a row of holes on a drill press using a brad-point bit. Mortises are cut slightly deeper than tenons for proper seating.

Fig. 7. Chiseling mortises for double-tenoned drawer rails. Extra stock was left on tops of legs until after mortises were cut so wood wouldn't split.

LEG AND FRAME ASSEMBLY

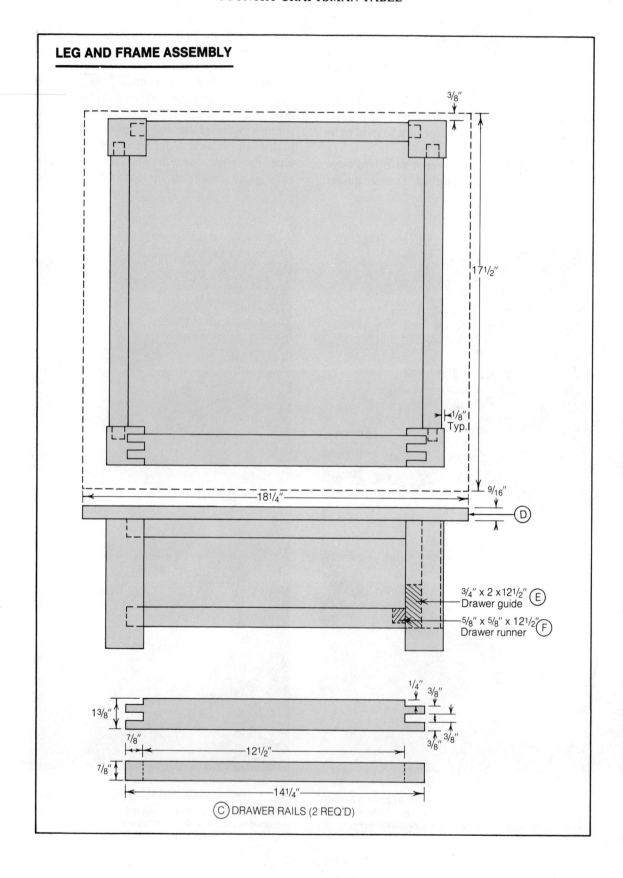

3/8"

17 1/2"

1/8"
Typ.

9/16"

18 1/4"

Ⓓ

3/4" x 2 x 12 1/2"
Drawer guide Ⓔ

5/8" x 5/8" x 12 1/2" Ⓕ
Drawer runner

1/4"   3/8"

1 3/8"

7/8"

3/8" 3/8"

12 1/2"

7/8"

14 1/4"

Ⓒ DRAWER RAILS (2 REQ'D)

Fig. 8. Chopping out the dovetail pins. I did the pin first, although the usual procedure is to do the tails first for easier fitting.

Fig. 9. Forming the dovetails. The sides of the tails were cut with the Dozuki tenon saw. Use a scribe or the knife blade to mark the tails for cutting.

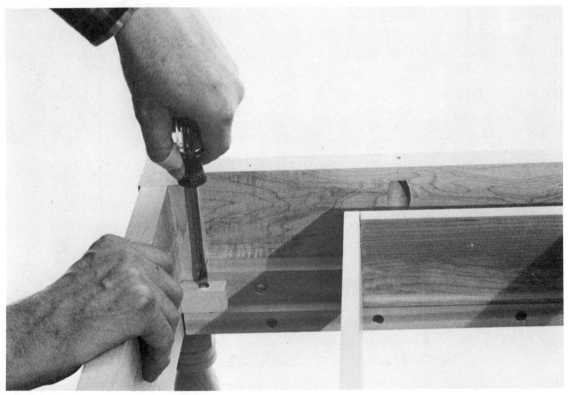

Fig. 10. Attaching the drawer guides. Two changes were made in the table copy: drawer guide rails and runners were attached with glue and screws instead of nails, and drawer stops were added.

DRAWER ASSEMBLY

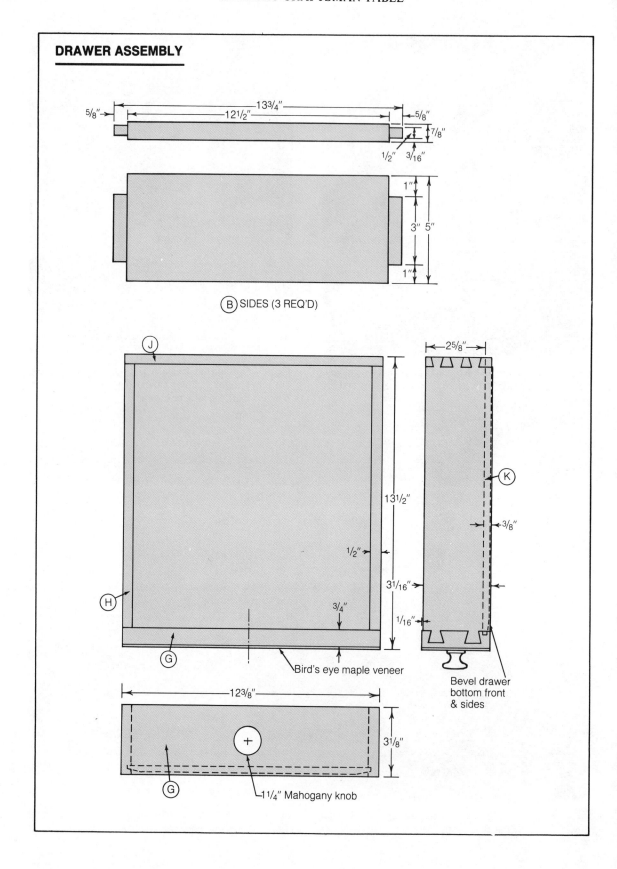

Ⓑ SIDES (3 REQ'D)

Bird's eye maple veneer

Bevel drawer bottom front & sides

1¼" Mahogany knob

Fig. 11. Clamping the glued drawer rail-front leg joints. To keep legs from rotating, clamp from both sides.

Fig. 12. For final assembly glue the side rails to the front legs. Note how clamping blocks are positioned so clamps apply force directly on centerline of joints.

good practice to prevent warping. The original had no veneer on the backside, and the drawer front hadn't warped in a century.

FINISHING

The original table presently has an almost warm-brown opaque stain and shellac finish. The original finish, or at least the earliest identif-iable finish, from traces found on the underside of the top, was white paint, removed a long, long time ago.

I used Constantine's Standard Maple NGR stain diluted 3 parts stain to 1 part clear thinner. For a top coat, we brushed on three coats of UGL Satin polyurethane varnish. The drawer interior was not stained, only varnished. As the mahogany knob on the drawer did not look to be original, a birch knob was substituted.

16

CANADIAN WALL SECRETARY

The original of this early 19th century Canadian wall secretary was made in pine and painted, but solid cherry was used for this version. As the cabinet was to be used in our kitchen, it was made $4/5$ scale. Full size, it would have been too big, but suitable for a living room.

The wall secretary has a lift-up, slant-top writing surface with ample room underneath for storing pencils, paper, and accessories. There are two fixed and two adjustable shelves with room for recipe books, plants, and a radio.

Cut stock for the two sides, top and bottom, and glue up these parts. The slanted tops of the side extensions should be finish-sanded before gluing, as this will be difficult to do later.

After these parts were glued up, I selected stock for the rest of the parts and took them to a local cabinet shop for abrasive planing on their 36"-wide belt sander. All the boards were sanded to thickness and finished with 150 grit. The sanding came under their minimum charge of $12—money well spent!

After assembly, rout the sides, cutting rabbets for the bottom, dadoes for the bottom and second shelf, and for the front panel. Drill $1/4$"-by-$1/2$"-deep holes for the shelf-support pegs. Use either a brad-point or Forstner bit for all the holes in the cabinet sides so the tip of the bit does not punch through the wood. Then, dado for the back panel. Locate the holes for the pegs that support the two adjustable shelves, and drill and chamfer the holes.

Blank the bottom, bottom shelf, and second shelf to width and length. Blank the front panel to length, but leave $1/4$" over width. Bevel the front edge of the bottom shelf $7^1/_2$ degrees and mortise for the hinges. Rabbet the bottom (for the back panel) and dado the bottom (for the front panel). Finish-sand edges.

Rout the decorative molding for the front of the desk compartment. Remember that the molding piece at the top of the panel is wider than the other three. Miter this piece of molding as shown and glue to the front panel. Bevel the top of the front panel 15 degrees.

The top and bottom are attached to the sides with doweled joints. Drill holes for the dowels in the sides and bottom (you can fit the top later if

EXPLODED VIEW

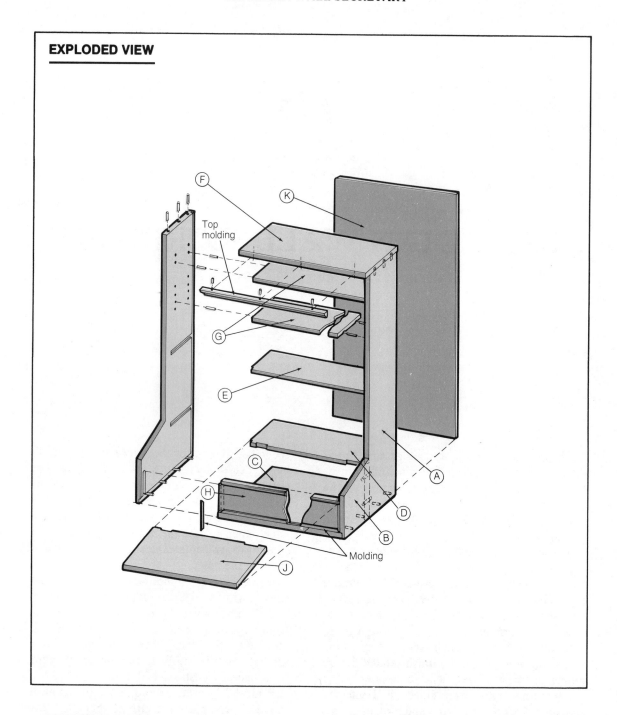

Top molding

Molding

MATERIALS LIST

QUANTITY	DESCRIPTION
14 board feet	¾" cherry
5 board feet or	¼" cherry or
1 piece 17 x 33"	¼" cherry veneer plywood

FRONT AND SIDE VIEWS

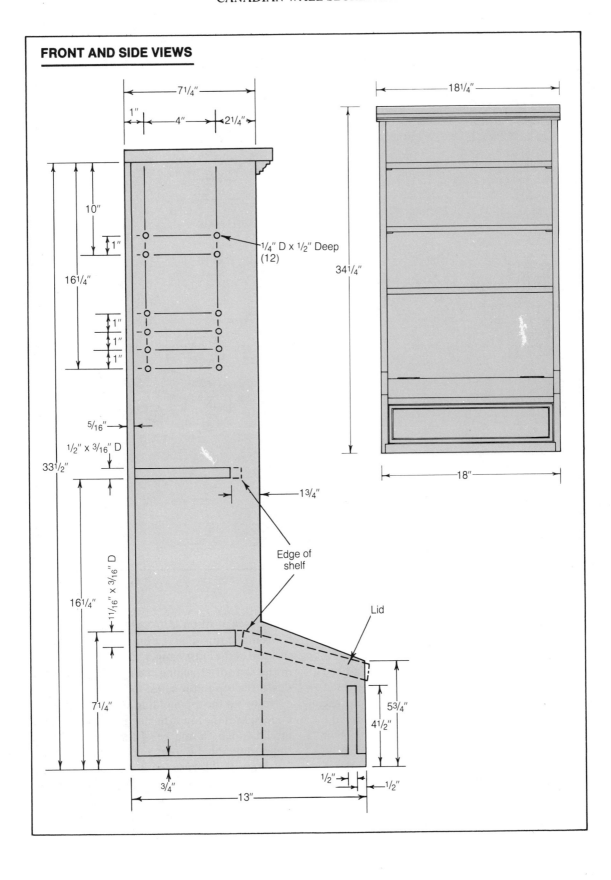

DETAILS

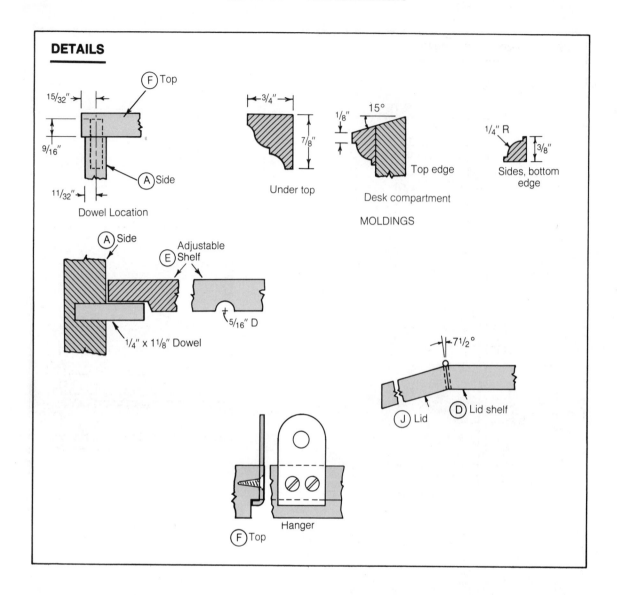

you want). Assemble the sides, bottom, two fixed shelves, and front panel dry and check for fit.

For the first gluing step, glue the two fixed shelves to one side. Use the other side (without glue) as a jig to position the shelves. Be sure the glued joints are square. Next glue and dowel the bottom to the same side, followed by the front panel (Fig. 2). Glue the second side. Finally, miter and glue in the remaining decorative molding.

Blank the top. There is a $1/8''$ overhang on each side, and $1''$ on the front. Rabbet the back of the top to receive the back panel. Block and clamp

the sides in position and locate the mating dowel holes in the top. Chisel a mortise in the back of the top for the brass hanger. Drill $1/4''$ dowel holes in the top for attaching the molding. Glue and dowel the top to the sides.

Now rout the top molding and attach it to the underside of the top with glue and dowels. Blank the lid to length and bevel the front and back edges (note the different angles, 15 degrees and $7\frac{1}{2}$ degrees). Mortise for the hinges. Blank the two adjustable shelves to length and width. Clamp them together bottom to bottom and drill (with a $5/16$ brad-point bit) the semicircular recesses for the support pegs.

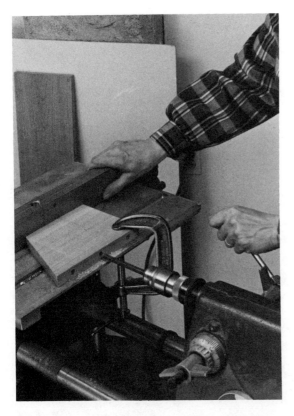

Fig. 1. Dowel holes were drilled with a Shopsmith in the horizontal position. Hole locations should be transfered with dowel centers.

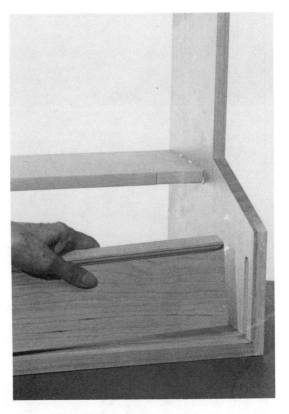

Fig. 2. Fitting the front panel to the glued-up side and bottom. The decorative trim molding on the top edge has already been glued to the front panel, and the combined surface has been beveled to match the slant of the lid.

You will need eight shelf-support pegs. Use $1/4''$ birch dowels cut to $1\,1/8''$. The pegs should fit snugly but not be forced into the holes.

Make the back panel from $1/4''$ cherry boards tongue-and-grooved, but not glued together. You could also use $1/4''$ cherry veneer plywood; or $1/4''$ luanan plywood with cherry veneer glued on one side and the least expensive veneer available on the back. Attach the panel to the bottom and second shelf with screws, and with screws or small nails around the edges. But do this after you complete the finishing.

The secretary was finished with Zar's Satin Stain #116 Cherry with three coats of Constantines Wood-Glo varnish.

HANGING

The weight of the secretary must be supported by the bottom shelf. This is accomplished by a screw or screws through the back panel, below the bottom shelf so they won't show. As the secretary is only 18″ wide, it is unlikely that you will be able to get screws into two studs, but the wall secretary can be attached to one stud if the hanger at the top is also fastened to the wall to keep the then otherwise top-heavy cabinet from tipping over sideways.

17

NEW MEXICAN WALL CABINET

The furniture of northern New Mexico—also called Taos furniture—combines Pueblo Indian, Spanish, Mexican, and country American influences. While this furniture probably inspired turn-of-the-century mission furniture, it has none of the planned massiveness of that style.

A trastero is a tall cabinet or cupboard, with a ventilated upper section and closed lower section. There are normally shelves behind the doors, but there also might be drawers. Trasteros could hold just about anything.

We had no room in our house for a full-size trastero so this cabinet—incorporating trastero features—was designed to hang in a family room over a sofa, to store and display souvenirs brought back from our travels.

The cabinet as constructed could stand on the floor. But, structurally, it was designed to hang on the wall. Further, it was designed to be partially taken apart for shipment.

The cabinet is 11″ deep; originally it was to be 12″, but that was thought to be too deep for hanging. You might want to make yours deeper.

Historically, a minimum of iron hardware was used in New Mexican furniture construction. Door hinges often were wood dowels. The usual frame joint was the through mortise-and-tenon. The tenon was always trimmed flush—it never protruded and the joints were locked with wood pegs. Native ponderosa pine was the principal wood used, with sharp points and edges rounded to avoid splintering.

Pine is a soft wood that requires a heavier construction for adequate joint and load-bearing strength, but it should never be heavier than necessary.

I did not hinge the doors. They are hung on pivots. These pivots are $1/8″$ stainless-steel rod turning in brass tubing pressed into the wood. If your doors are to be hung on these pivots, the doors have to be finished and hung before the cabinet is assembled.

CONSTRUCTION

Begin with the corner posts. Surface stock to $1^3/_4″$ x $1^3/_4″$ and lay out all of the mortises on the

EXPLODED VIEW

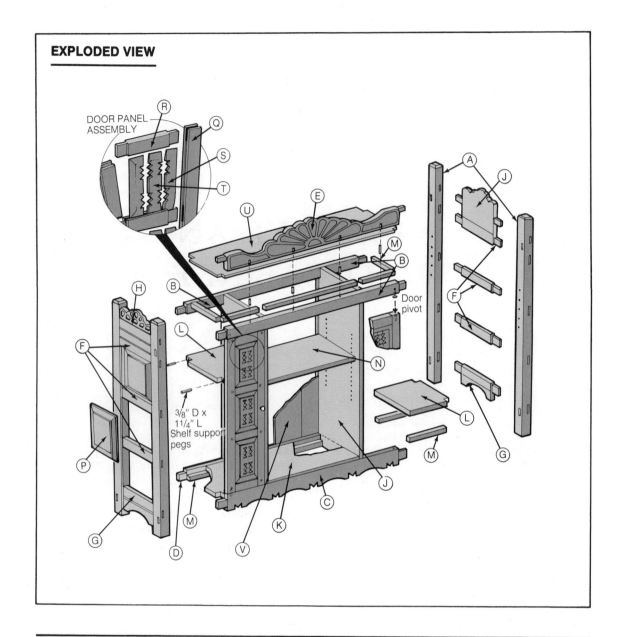

DOOR PANEL
ASSEMBLY

3/8" D x
11/4" L
Shelf support
pegs

Door
pivot

MATERIALS LIST

QUANTITY	DESCRIPTION
35 board feet	$\frac{13}{16}$" knotty pine
13 board feet	3/8" knotty pine
1 piece	1¾" 8" x 48" select pine
1 piece	1/8" dia. x 12" stainless steel round rod, #ZRX2-12"; Small Parts Inc.
1 piece.	5/32 od x .014" wall x 12" brass round telescoping tubing; #TTRB4-12", Small Parts Inc.
4 pieces	Swedish style shelf supports #D5711, The Woodworker's Store

four posts at the same time. Chop and clean out the mortises.

Blank the front and back rails, the end rails, and the three crests. Set up and form all of the tenons. Note that the tenons on the back rails are not centered on the rail—they are offset toward the front of the cabinet in order to place the rail as close as possible ($1/16''$) to the wall. Groove the back rails to receive the back panels.

Dowel the front crest and top front rail together dry, and dowel the end top rail and crest if you have made them in two pieces. Assemble the posts and the end rails dry, then assemble the remaining rails, also without glue.

Glue up blanks for the two partitions. Recheck partition dimensions from the assembled rails and posts. Trim and put partitions in position.

The partitions are attached to the back rails with screws through the rail into the partition. At the front, they are attached to the center cleats, both top and bottom. Rip cleats, attach center cleats; position (no screws) partitions,

install side section cleats with screws only.

Mark the partitions and back posts for grooves for the back panels. The three back panels are made up of random-width planks of $3/8''$ knotty pine. These are beveled to fit the grooves in the post, partition, and rail. They're joined with deep tongue-and-groove joints.

Blank floors and shelves, and trim to dimension. The adjustable shelves for the center section are mounted with Swedish-style invisible supports. Shelves for the side section are supported by pegs fitted into half-round recesses on the underside of the shelves. The shelves in the side section will need semicircular recesses in the front edges to provide clearance for the corners of the doors when they are opened.

Blank door rails and stiles; form tenons and mortises. Note that these grooves must be stopped to avoid visible notches in the ends of the tenons.

The door panels are made in three pieces each of which are loosely fitted into the door frame (Fig. 1). When installed, there should be random-

CUTTING LIST

KEY	QTY.	PART NAME	MATERIAL	BLANK DIMENSIONS
A	4	Corner Post	knotty pine	1¾ x 1¾ x 43″
B	2	Top Rail	knotty pine	¾ x 2 x 42½″
C	1	Bottom Front Rail	knotty pine	¾ x 3½ x 42½″
D	1	Bottom Back Rail	knotty pine	¾ x 1¾ x 42½″
E	1	Front Crest	knotty pine	¾ x 6½ x 42½″
F	6	End Rail	knotty pine	¾ x 1¾ x 11½″
G	2	End Bottom Rail	knotty pine	¾ x 4½ x 11½″
H	2	End Crest	knotty pine	¾ x 4¾ x 5¾″
J	2	Partition	knotty pine	¾ x 10¾ x 35½″
K	1	Center Floor	knotty pine	¾ x 9¼ x 20″
L	6	Side Floor, Shelf	knotty pine	¾ x 9¼ x 8¾″
M	12 ft.	Cleat	knotty pine	¾ x ⅞″
N	1	Center Shelf	knotty pine	¾ x 10 x 21½″
P	6	End Panel	knotty pine	¾ x 8 x 9″
Q	4	Door Stile	knotty pine	¾ x 1½ x 32″
R	8	Door Rail	knotty pine	¾ x 1½ x 8¼″
S	6	Door Panel (Side)	knotty pine	⅜ x 1⅞ x 8⅞″
T	3	Door Panel (Center)	knotty pine	⅜ x 1¾ x 8⅞″
U	---	Ceiling	knotty pine	¾ x 10⅝ x 40″ (total width, several pieces)
V	---	Back Panel	knotty pine	¾ x 40 x 32½″ (total width, several pieces)

FRONT AND BACK RAILS

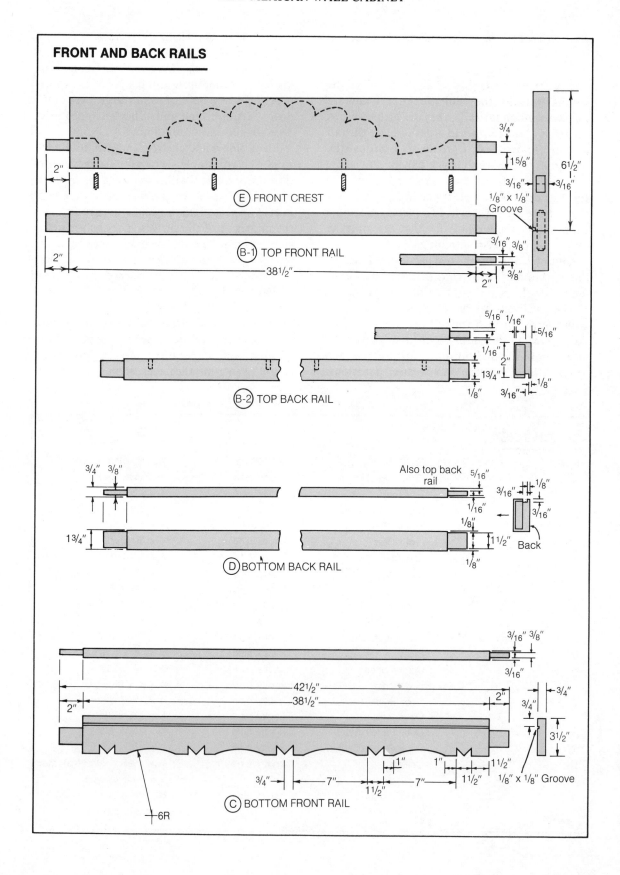

E FRONT CREST

B-1 TOP FRONT RAIL

B-2 TOP BACK RAIL

D BOTTOM BACK RAIL

C BOTTOM FRONT RAIL

CORNER POSTS

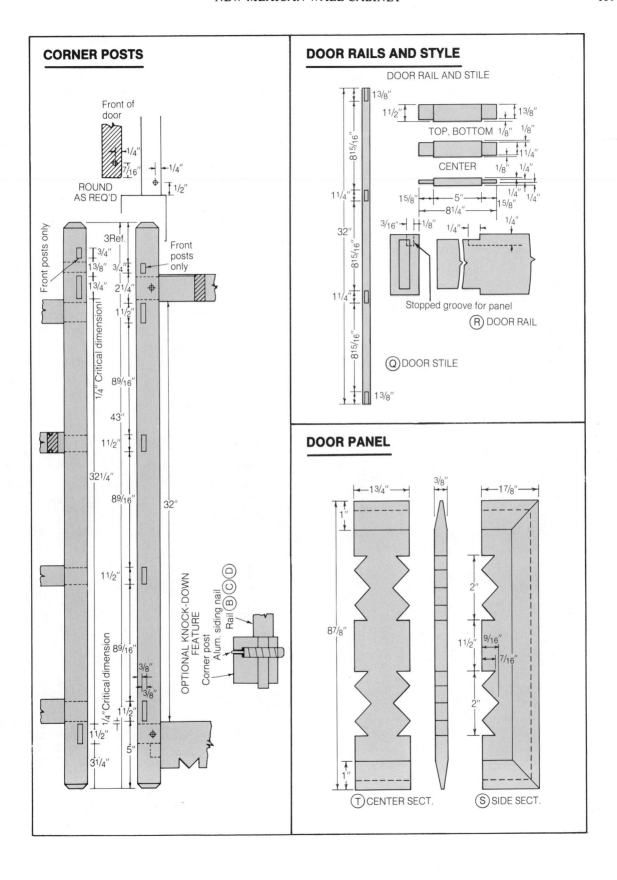

DOOR RAILS AND STYLE

DOOR RAIL AND STILE

TOP, BOTTOM

CENTER

Stopped groove for panel

Ⓡ DOOR RAIL

Ⓠ DOOR STILE

DOOR PANEL

Ⓣ CENTER SECT.   Ⓢ SIDE SECT.

width cracks between the panels. I blanked the door panels in wide pieces for easier handling when raising the panels.This was done with a planer accessory on a radial-arm saw.

The drawing shows the cutout decoration done with 90-degree and 45-degree saw cuts (Fig. 2). I cut those shown with the blade set at 40 degrees from vertical, which I think makes the decoration look a little better. Sand and completely finish the door panels and the inside edges of the door frames before assembling (Fig. 3).

(Note: the doors should not be fitted into the cabinet openings until they are mounted on their pivots.)

The crests can be hand-carved, or they can be routed. Either way, don't cut the crests to final outside dimension until all the carving is complete. I routed them about 1/4" deep.

If you rout, make a reversible pattern from 1/4" plywood. Save the cutouts to use with shims to back up the thin pattern sections while routing.

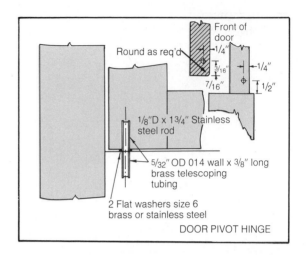

As mentioned, the cabinet can be constructed so it can be knocked down for shipment. The end assemblies are glued up solid. The front and back rail-to-post joints are assembled dry; the post-to-rail locking dowels are glued only at the outer end, and with only enough glue to keep

Fig. 1. Door frame and panel parts. The frames are tenoned. The panels are made in three loose-fitting sections. When installed, there should be random (about 1/16") gaps between the panel sections.

Fig. 2. Notching the door panel. Clamped stop blocks on a long piece of wood facing the miter gauge ensure that all notches are accurately located.

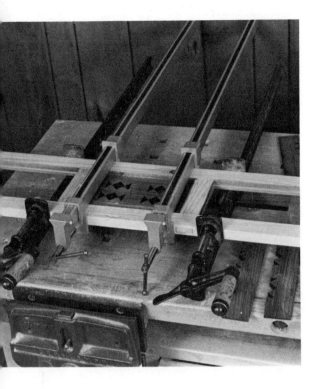

Fig. 3. In first step of door assembly, center rails are tenoned to stiles with prefinished panel sections enclosed. Inside edges of frames were also prefinished.

them in place. Cut-off aluminum-siding nails are placed in the bottom of the dowel holes.

After drilling the dowel holes $1\frac{1}{2}''$ deep, drill a small hole through the post for the shank of the nail. The nail head is captive behind the dowel.

When knock down is desired, the nail can be used to press out the dowels without resorting to violence. The partitions are attached to the rails and cleats with screws only.

Glue up and raise the six panels for the ends. After fitting the panels, sand and finish all inner surfaces and glue up the cabinet end assemblies (Fig. 4).

Drill $\frac{5}{32}''$ holes in the front rails and door frames for the pivot hinges. These shop-made hinges consist of brass tubes pressed into the rails and door frames in which stainless-steel rods are free to turn. Brass washers space the door and frame apart at the bottom.

Reassemble the partitions and rails and fit the doors. Some rounding will be necessary on the front edge of the door on the hinge side. Reattach the end frames for a final check, then disassemble the cabinet for finishing.

Finish the rails, shelves, floor, ceiling, and inboard surfaces of the posts.

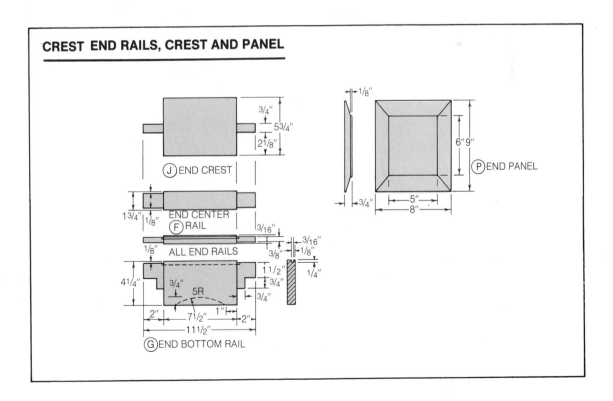

CREST END RAILS, CREST AND PANEL

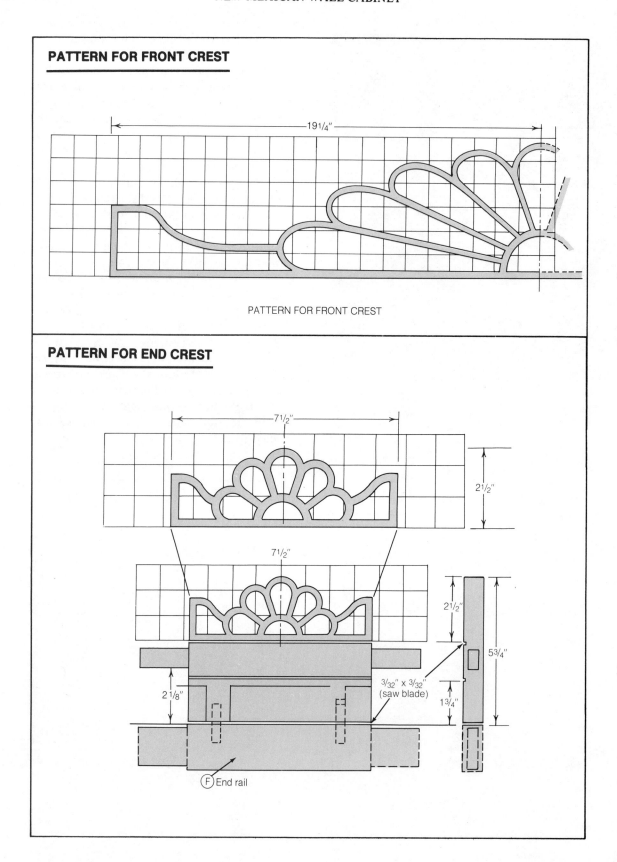

PATTERN FOR FRONT CREST

PATTERN FOR FRONT CREST

PATTERN FOR END CREST

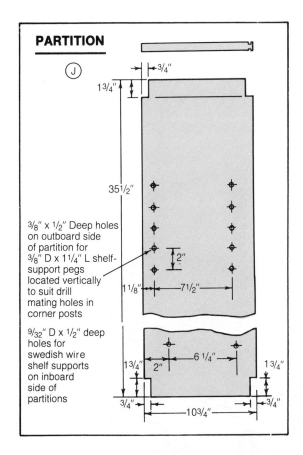

PARTITION

J

3/4"

1 3/4"

35 1/2"

3/8" x 1/2" Deep holes on outboard side of partition for 3/8" D x 1 1/4" L shelf-support pegs located vertically to suit drill mating holes in corner posts

2"

1 1/8"   7 1/2"

9/32" D x 1/2" deep holes for swedish wire shelf supports on inboard side of partitions

1 3/4"   2"   6 1/4"   1 3/4"

3/4"   10 3/4"   3/4"

FINAL ASSEMBLY

Assemble the two bottom rails and the partitions with screws. Insert the back panel boards and attach the top back rail to both partitions. Assemble the door pivots and center the doors vertically in the opening with brass washers under the doors. Now attach the cabinet ends to, the rails (no glue if the cabinet is going to be knocked down). Attach the top rails to the partition (Fig. 5).

Cut off aluminum-siding nails and insert them into the dowel holes in the posts. Apply a small amount of glue to the open end of the dowel holes and drive in the dowels. When dry, trim the tenons flush, complete the sanding of the posts and apply finish.

HANGING

Position the cabinet on the wall and locate and drill holes in the top and bottom back rails for 1/4" diameter lag screws and attach. Drill clearance holes in the back-center bottom cleat to hide the screw heads and replace. Paint the upper-rail screws with dull black paint. Drop all the floors in place and install shelves.

Fig. 4 Gluing is done in stages. At right, center rails are glued and tenoned into one post with second post ensuring alignment (panels are not glued). At left, top rail and crest have been added to assembly. Note that panels and inside surfaces of posts have been stained and varnished before assembly.

Fig. 5. Final assembly. Partitions are attached to lower rails, center back panel boards are inserted in grooves and locked in with top back rail. Doors have been hung on pivots. Here, top front rail is being attached to partitions.

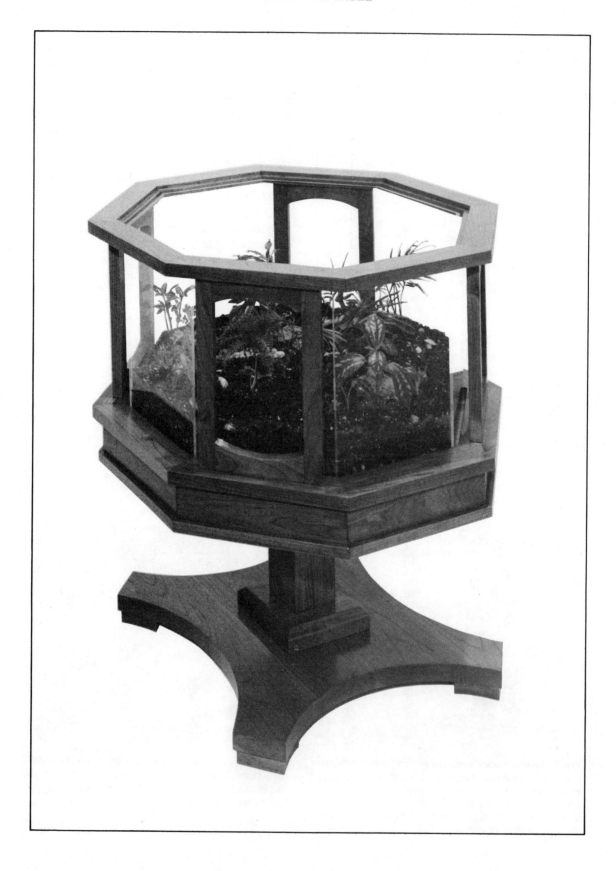

18

TERRARIUM TABLE

Stop fiddling around with tiny terrariums and go big. Turn your friends green with this attractive and impressive octagonal drum table. Under the glass top, there's a huge terrarium—big enough to plant a miniature forest.

The terrarium container is ¼" Plexiglas. The wooden parts could be cherry, mahogany, maple, or almost any other hardwood. I used cherry. The construction is surprisingly simple, but the table requires careful workmanship, as the joints must be strong to support the weight of the terrarium.

A terrarium is a special kind of indoor plant container. Inside is a closed ecological cycle. Besides photosynthesis and plant respiration taking place, a rain cycle is established inside the terrarium once you have watered it.

Water taken up through the roots passes out of the leaves and evaporates into the air, then condenses on the container sides, fogging the Plexiglas. When this moisture builds up sufficiently, it "rains" back to the soil. As long as condensation is present on the sides, there's enough water inside, and you don't have to add any. The glass lid can be propped open for watering, or for evaporation of excess moisture if you put in too much water initially.

Fig. 1. The lid of the terrarium can be propped open for ventilation if the initial watering was too heavy, allowing the excess to evaporate. Normally, the terrarium operates as a closed-cycle ecosystem.

FRAMES AND BASE

Begin construction by sawing sixteen blanks for the two frames. Form a rabbet in the eight pieces for the top frame to seat the glass lid. Next, saw the eight trim pieces. The frame and trim joints should be reinforced with dowels or

TERRARIUM TABLE

EXPLODED VIEW

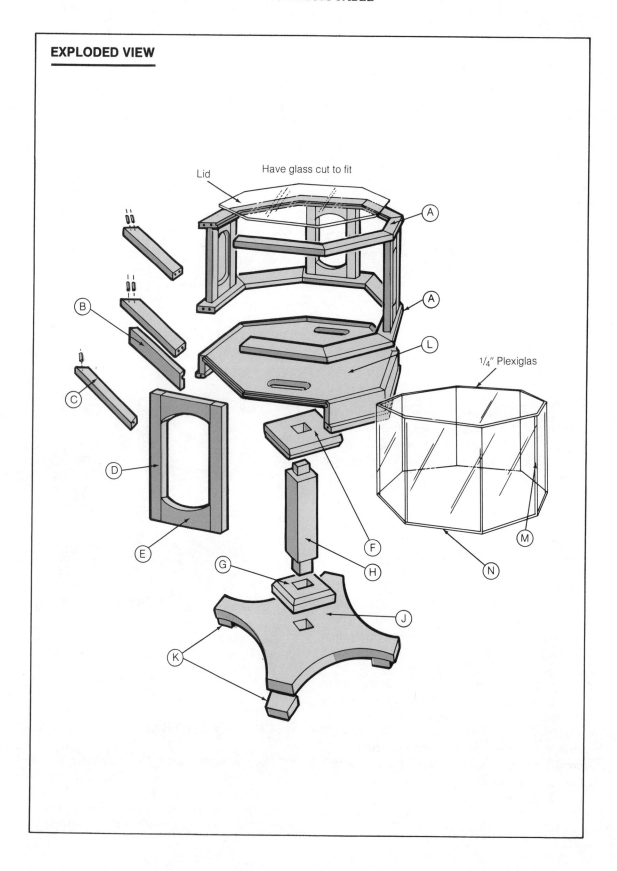

Lid

Have glass cut to fit

1/4″ Plexiglas

A

A

B

C

D

E

F

G

H

J

K

L

M

N

DETAILS

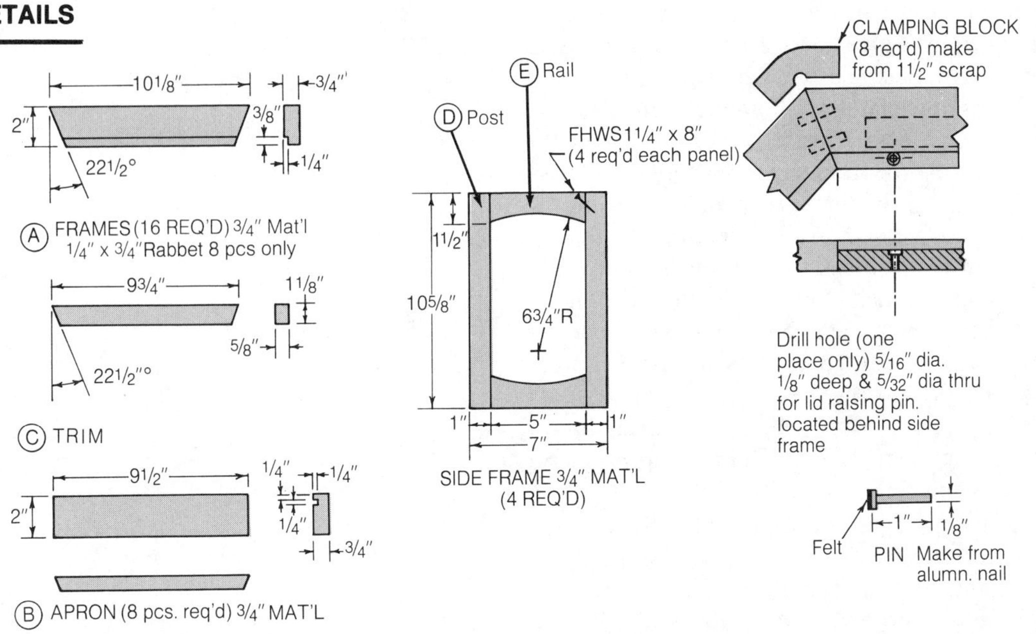
10 1/8"
3/4"
2"
3/8"
1/4"
22 1/2°
A FRAMES (16 REQ'D) 3/4" Mat'l
1/4" x 3/4" Rabbet 8 pcs only
9 3/4"
1 1/8"
5/8"
22 1/2"°
C TRIM
9 1/2"
1/4"
1/4"
2"
1/4"
3/4"
B APRON (8 pcs. req'd) 3/4" MAT'L
E Rail
D Post
FHWS 1 1/4" x 8"
(4 req'd each panel)
1 1/2"
10 5/8"
6 3/4"R
1"
5"
1"
7"
SIDE FRAME 3/4" MAT'L
(4 REQ'D)
CLAMPING BLOCK
(8 req'd) make
from 1 1/2" scrap
Drill hole (one
place only) 5/16" dia.
1/8" deep & 5/32" dia thru
for lid raising pin.
located behind side
frame
Felt
1"
1/8"
PIN Make from
alumn. nail

MATERIALS LIST

QUANTITY	DESCRIPTION
8 board feet	¾" cherry
5½ board feet	1¼" cherry
1 piece 22" x 22"	¾" plywood
1 piece 24"x 48"	¼" clear transparent Plexiglas G

CUTTING LIST

KEY	QTY.	PART NAME	MATERIAL	BLANK DIMENSIONS
A	16	Frame	cherry	¾ x 2 x 10⅛"
B	8	Apron	cherry	¾ x 2 x 9½"
C	8	Trim	cherry	¾ x 1⅛ x 9¾"
D	8	Post	cherry	¾ x 1 x 10⅝"
E	8	Rail	cherry	¾ x 1¾ x 5"
F	1	Top Plate	cherry	1¼ x 8 x 8"
G	1	Base Plate	cherry	1¼ x 6 x 6"
H	1	Shaft	cherry	3 x 3 x 13⅛"
J	1	Base	cherry	1¼ x 19½ x 19½"
k	4	Foot	cherry	¾ x 2¾ x 3⅝"
L	1	Shelf	plywood	¾ x 22 x 22"
M	8	Side	Plexiglas	¼ x 8½ x 11⅝"
N	1	Bottom	Plexiglas	¼ x 19¾ x 19¾"

splines: I used $1/4''$-by-$1''$ dowels, two in each frame joint and one in each trim joint.

When you glue the frames, you can clamp them with a single band clamp (Fig. 2) plus weights or C-clamps to hold the frame flat. Use clamping blocks to ease the band around the angles. Glue the frames in three steps—each half separately, then join the two; each time using the rest of the parts as an alignment jig.

Next, saw the eight apron pieces, and dado them for the shelf. Counterbore and drill holes for the screws attaching the apron to the lower frame. Cut an octagonal blank for the shelf from $3/4''$ plywood (as the shelf won't show, it doesn't have to be hardwood veneer). Saw lift holes for removing the terrarium. Glue the apron pieces around the shelf.

When gluing up the blank for the base, have the grain run as shown in the plan, and reinforce the joints with $3/8''$ by $2''$ dowels. The shaft joints should also be reinforced with blind dowels if you have to glue. Saw the base to outline, saw and bevel plates, form $1\frac{1}{2}''$-square tenons, top and bottom, on the shaft, then saw and file close-fitting $1\frac{1}{2}''$-square mortises in the plates and base.

The side frames are assembled with butt joints, each joint reinforced by a diagonal screw. Saw the feet; the curve of their sides should follow the sweep of the base curve.

Sand all parts, then assemble the table with screws. The side frames are fastened to the top frame with screws through the crosspiece of the side frame, into the frame. As the joining must be

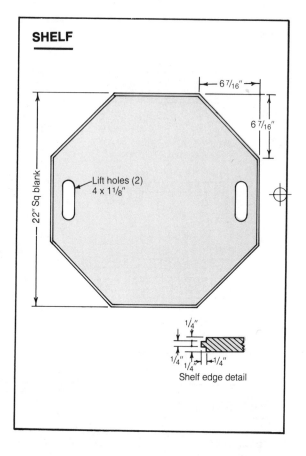

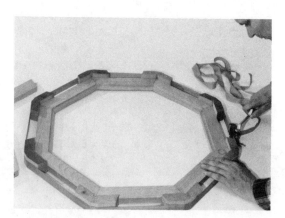

Fig. 2. Clamp the octagonal frames for gluing with a single nylon band clamp. Blocks at the joints ease the band around the corners.

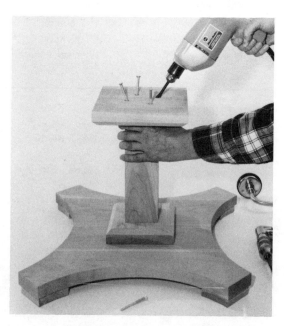

Fig. 3. To assemble the table, bore holes diagonally through the plates and screw them to the shaft. Attach the feet to the base, then the base to the baseplate.

identically located eight times, make a fixture to eliminate repetitious measurement. After joining all side frames to the top, attach the bottom frame with screws through the frame. Lastly, bore the shouldered hole for the lid raising pin.

Now fasten the plates to the shaft with angled screws (Fig. 3); attach the feet to the base, then the base to the baseplate. Center the shelf on the top plate so two of the feet are located under the lift holes and attach with eight screws close around the edge of the top plate.

Align the shelf and apron under the bottom frame with feet located under side panels, then screw together through the deep counterbored holes in the apron. Next, screw the trim to the apron.

BASE AND SHAFT

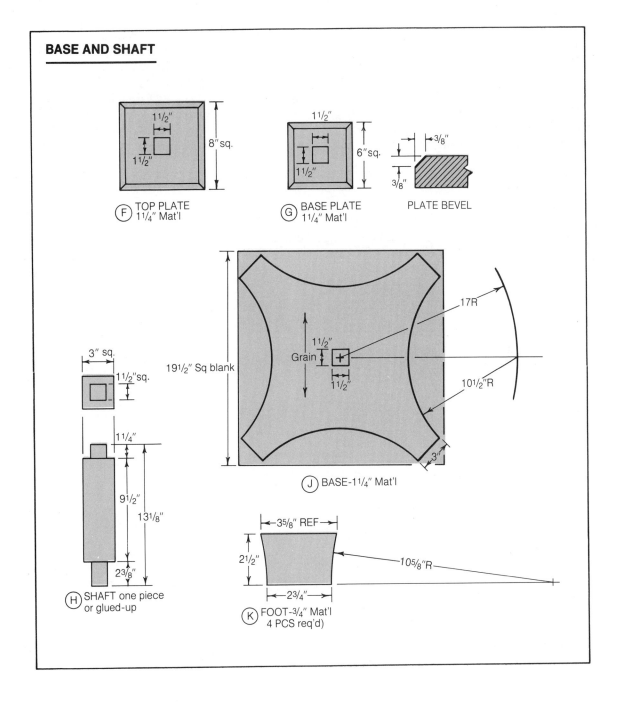

F TOP PLATE
1 1/4" Mat'l

G BASE PLATE
1 1/4" Mat'l

PLATE BEVEL

J BASE-1 1/4" Mat'l

H SHAFT one piece
or glued-up

K FOOT-3/4" Mat'l
4 PCS req'd)

TERRARIUM

The terrarium is made from $1/4''$ Plexiglas. You can buy Plexiglas, adhesives, and tools from plastics supply houses (check the Yellow Pages). You can cut the parts to accurate dimension on a table saw with a special Plexiglas blade. Leave the protective paper on the Plexiglas until assembly. If you use a saber saw, use a metal-cutting blade with 14 tpi, then scrape the edge smooth with a sharpened piece of metal, such as the back of a hacksaw blade.

The parts are joined by capillary cementing, with a bead of thickened cement around the bottom and 4″ up each side as leak insurance.

Before cementing, the sawn edges must be given a satin finish. I used a bench belt sander with shop-built vertical and $67\frac{1}{2}$-degree fences,

and a 150-grit, silicon-carbide, wet-or-dry belt. (Lapidary supply houses generally carry these belts; you will go through two.) Finish the edge with 320-grit paper, wet, by hand. Be careful not to round the edges.

Now remove protective paper and tape the pieces together with masking tape. I clamped the sides with band clamps before taping, mainly to get the sides positioned for the bottom joint. Don't go overboard applying pressure, or you won't be able to get any solvent into the side joints.

Gluing is simple: With the joint to be glued horizontal, apply the solvent, IPS Weld-on #3, methylene cloride (MDC), ethylene dicloride (EDC), or 1-1-2 trichlorethane, with a hyperdermic applicator from the inside of the terrarium (Fig. 4). Although the quantities of the solvents used

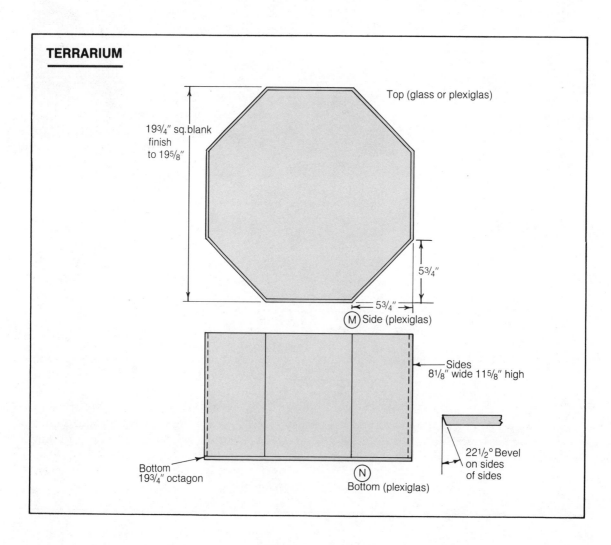

TERRARIUM

Top (glass or plexiglas)

$19\frac{3}{4}''$ sq. blank finish to $19\frac{5}{8}''$

$5\frac{3}{4}''$

$5\frac{3}{4}''$

Ⓜ Side (plexiglas)

Sides $8\frac{1}{8}''$ wide $11\frac{5}{8}''$ high

Bottom $19\frac{3}{4}''$ octagon

Ⓝ Bottom (plexiglas)

$22\frac{1}{2}°$ Bevel on sides of sides

Fig. 4. Assemble Plexiglas sides and bottom of the terrarium container with masking tape, then apply cement.

are minute, have some ventilation in the room.

When all the joints are done, reinforce with beads of thickened cement. Do the side joints two at a time with the side between lying flat—this stuff doesn't set as fast as model airplane cement and will run. Dribbles of either solvent or cement can be cleaned off when dry with a fingernail followed by cotton wheel and buffing compound,

The lid of the terrarium can be either Plexiglas or crystal glass (what you get today when you ask for plate). Glass has better scratch resistance, but you can buff scratches out of Plexiglas. If you use glass, take the frame along and let the glazier fit it, and have the edges of the glass seamed.

I finished the table with two coats of #235 Cherry Minwax, two coats of polyurethane satin varnish, and wax.

PLANTING A TERRARIUM

Potting mix, stones, pieces of wood—everything that goes into a terrarium except the plants—must be sterilized. Buy sterilized soil and use your kitchen oven for everything else (400° F, 20 minutes).

Rinse the container throughly with plain water. The soil layer should be about 4″ deep, but not necessarily level. On the bottom, heap crushed stones for drainage, then a layer of charcoal, then potting mix.

Don't add fertilizer—growth is the last thing you want to encourage. Get your plants from a store specializing in house plants; don't use any dug up in your yard because they will bring all kinds of pests into your closed-world terrarium. Finally add water, but treat your terrarium like a martini—keep it on the dry side.

19

✣✣✣

THREE-TIERED PLANT STAND

The design origins of our plant stand go back to the late 18th century when it would have been called a "muffin stand" and used to serve cakes and desserts. Then , it would have been all made of wood, and the shelves would have had rims to keep the dishes from sliding off while the stand was carried to the table.

Muffin stands were made in many styles over the years, and they turn up occasionally in antique shops. A traditional all-wood muffin stand has been reproduced in the Bartley Collection of Antique Furniture, but I have taken the traditional design a big step forward to a more contemporary appearance with polished, crystal-clear Plexiglas shelves.

The plant stand is made of cherry, but other strong hardwoods such as maple could be used. I would not recommend mahogany.

Building the plant stand is not difficult, but some of the steps will have to be done carefully, and you will need a jig or two to get the holes drilled straight.

CONSTRUCTION

Begin by making full-size patterns for the legs and top pieces on heavy paper or posterboard.

Trace the outlines of the parts on $3/4''$ stock and saw all parts to rough outline. Sand the four legs to exact dimension except for the top two inches of the three long legs.

Locate and cut the notches for the shelves. While some slight looseness can be tolerated in the notches of the long legs, the single notch in the front leg must fit the Plexiglas tightly so the joint, and not the screw, provides rigidity.

Because of the absence of straight lines on the parts, jigs have to be made in order to drill and countersink the screw holes in the notches accurately (Fig. 1).

When making the jigs, undercut them so they can provide support for the workpiece only for an inch or so at each end. (When the legs are cut from the stock, some normal warping may occur, and the legs may not be exactly alike). Note that in each case the notches in the leg are used to key the leg into the jig.

Face-off the tops of the two side legs. Cut the two pieces of $3/4''$ plywood $11\frac{3}{4}''$ and $9\frac{3}{8}''$ long, place them in the bottom and top notches of the side legs to align them for fitting the short joining piece. Drill for dowels and glue up with fast-curing epoxy.

When clamping the joints, replace the piece of plywood in the top notches with a length of 6-32

PERSPECTIVE VIEW

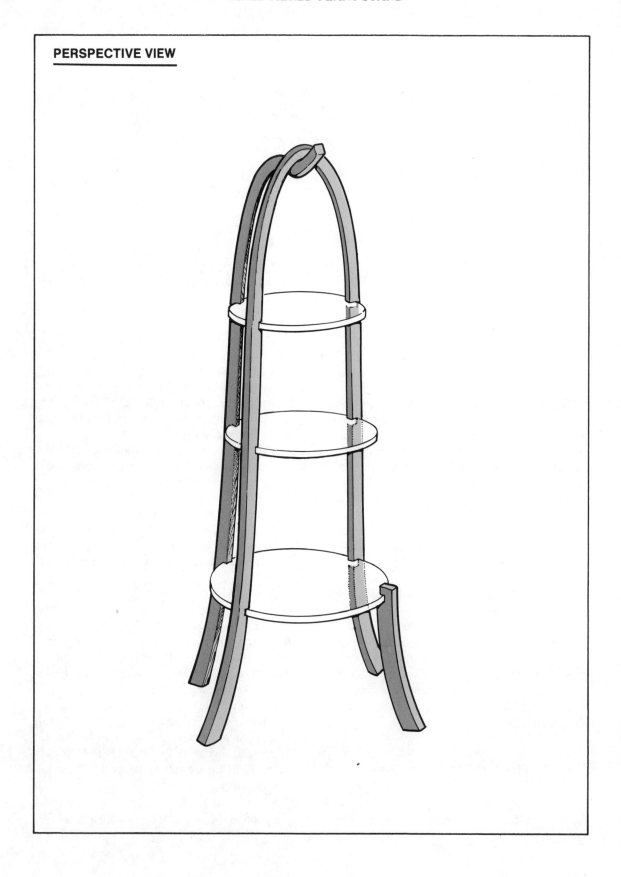

LEG PATTERN

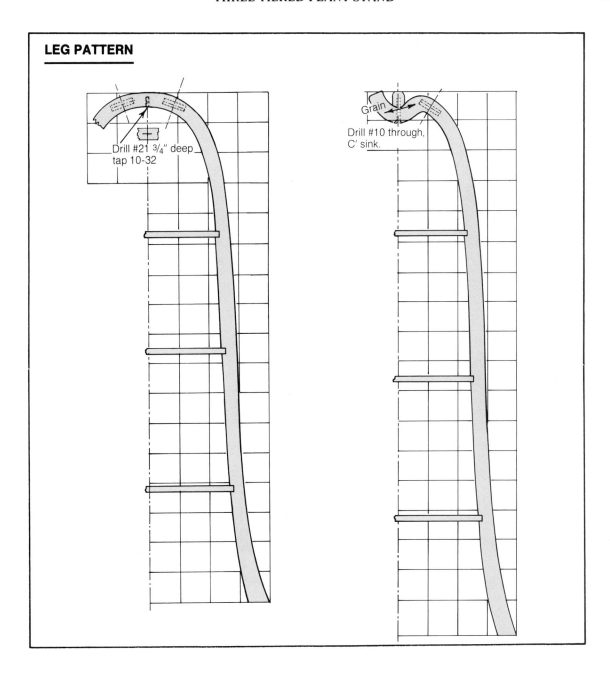

Drill #21 ³/₄″ deep tap 10-32

Grain
Drill #10 through, C' sink.

MATERIALS LIST

QUANTITY	DESCRIPTION
1 piece, 12″ x 36″	³⁄₈″ Plexiglas G
1 piece, 6″ x 40″	³⁄₄″ cherry
10	Brass 8-32 x 1″ flathead machine screws
1	Brass 10-32 x 1½″ flathead brass machine screw

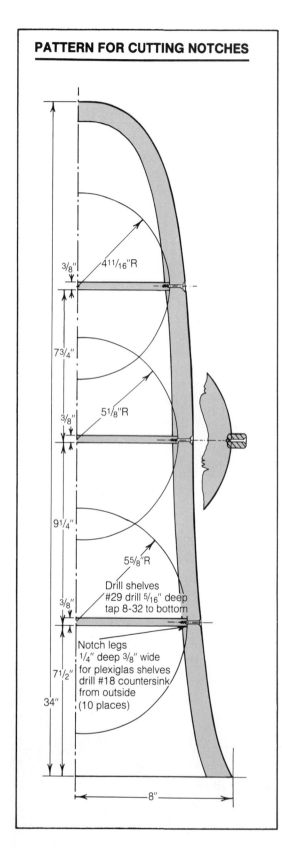

PATTERN FOR CUTTING NOTCHES

$4^{11}/_{16}$"R

$^3/_8$"

$7^3/_4$"

$5^1/_8$"R

$^3/_8$"

$9^1/_4$"

$5^5/_8$"R

Drill shelves
#29 drill $^5/_{16}$" deep
tap 8-32 to bottom

$^3/_8$"

Notch legs
$^1/_4$" deep $^3/_8$" wide
for plexiglas shelves
drill #18 countersink
from outside
(10 places)

$7^1/_2$"

34"

8"

Fig. 1.

threaded rod. Use nuts on the ends of the rods to help draw the joints together. Next, attach the hook to the top of the back leg. When the epoxy has cured, trim and sand the leg assemblies to finish dimensions.

Rout a $^3/_{16}$" radius on all leg edges (except the bottoms). Use a $^3/_{16}$" rounding-over bit equipped with a ball-bearing pilot.

The back and side legs are joined with a single 10-32 machine screw at the top (Fig. 2). Drill and countersink a through #10 hole in the hook of the back leg, and a $^3/_4$"-deep #21 hole from the bottom of the side leg. Thread the #21 hole with an ordinary 10-32 tap.

Finish the wood parts of the plant stand with two coats of Minwax cherry stain, followed by three coats of polyurethane varnish (sanded between coats), and wax.

Make patterns for the three shelves and trace them onto the protective paper covering the Plexiglas. Leave the protective paper on the plastic until all sawing, drilling, and edge polishing have been completed.

The shelves can be sawn with either a saber saw or a scroll saw using a metal-cutting blade with 14 tpi, a slow blade speed, and a slow feed.

To put a transparent finish on the edges,

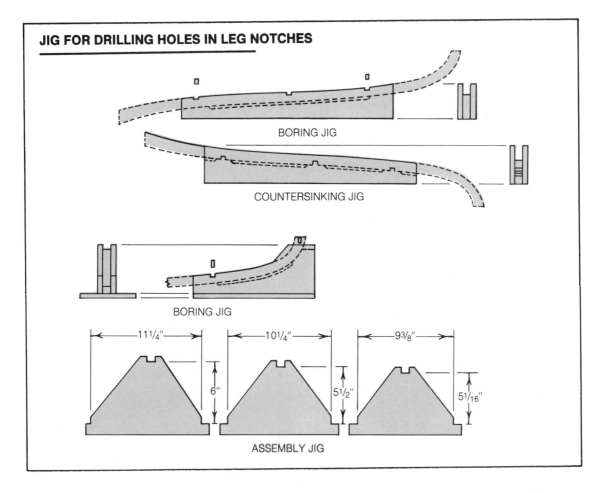

JIG FOR DRILLING HOLES IN LEG NOTCHES

BORING JIG

COUNTERSINKING JIG

BORING JIG

11¹/₄″   10¹/₄″   9³/₈″

6″   5¹/₂″   5¹/₁₆″

ASSEMBLY JIG

machine-sand to dimension with 150-grit paper, hand-sand with wet 320 and 400 wet-or-dry paper, buff with cotton wheel and compound.

Now locate holes in the edges of the shelves as shown in (Fig. 3), drill #29 holes and tap 8-32 threads. Finish threading with a bottoming tap.

Use soapy water as a lubricant and blow out chips frequently.

When installing the shelves with the 8-32 machine screws, it might be necessary to shorten some of the screws to get a tight bottom-of-the hole fit.

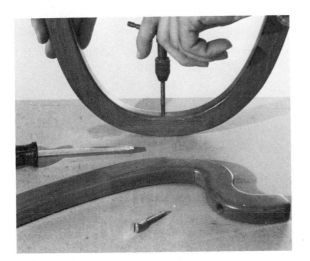

Fig. 2.

Fig. 3.

20

FEDERAL TAMBOUR DESK

The tambour desk typifies the highest refinement of design and workmanship of New England cabinetmakers of the American Federal Period (1780–1830). Foremost among the cabinetmakers making these desks were John Seymour and his son Thomas, of Boston.

Over the years I have built several desks, but never a tambour of this style. The project was always put off, mainly because of the lack of solid information. Studying photographs doesn't provide enough information to build a desk with a design as involved as this one. Recently, I had the opportunity to examine a Seymour tambour desk in a museum, and then two others.

In any piece of furniture, the relationship of all parts is crucial to the appearance of the whole. The rails, writing surface, and flap of the original Seymour desk are only 5/8″ thick. It is this 5/8″ dimension that helps give the desk its lightness and elegance. Although the design of this desk was inspired primarily by these Seymour desks, the dimensions and details match no one particular desk. It is not a reproduction.

The desk is not an easy project. Accuracy is important; carelessness with dimensions in the

Fig. 1. Tambour desk with flap open.

SIDE AND FRONT VIEWS

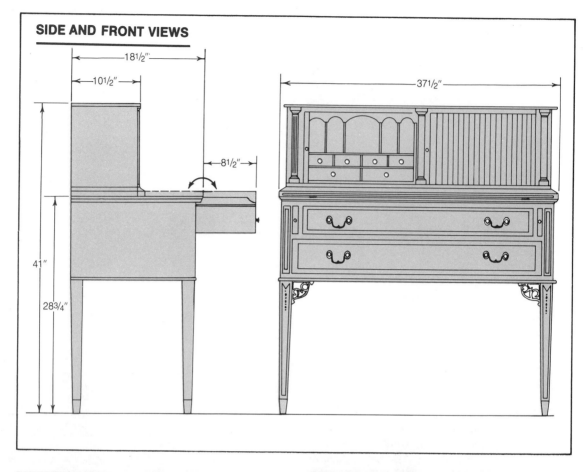

Fig. 2. Detail of column and partitions.

Fig. 3. Detail of writing surface.

MATERIALS LIST

QUANTITY	DESCRIPTION
40 board feet	$\frac{13}{16}$" mahogany
3 board feet	¼" mahogany
10 feet	1¾" x 1¾" mahogany (4 30" pieces)
20 board feet	$\frac{13}{16}$" poplar
6 board feet	¼" poplar
16 square feet	¼" birch plywood (nominal thickness)
6 square feet	⅛" birch plywood
2 square feet	⅛" maple
1½ square feet	⅛" ebony veneer
6 square feet	fiddleback mahogany veneer (In flitch, 2 pieces)
2	¼" inlay strip #B43, Constantine
1	⅛" inlay strip #B2, Constantine
4	Brass rosette pulls, 3" boring #E33-124 Ball and Ball
4	Round brass knobs, ½" #25258, Mason & Sullivan
12	Brass ring pulls paxton hardware
½ yard	Silk cloth (sari weight)

CUTTING LIST

Key	QTY.	PART NAME	MATERIAL	BLANK DIMENSIONS
A	4	Leg	mahogany	1⅝ x 1⅝ x 30"
B	2	Side	mahogany	¾ x 10½ x 15"
C	1	Back	mahogany	¾ x 10½ x 34"
D	3	Front Rail	mahogany	⅝ x 2¼ x 35½"
E	1	Back Rail	poplar	⅝ x 1½ x 35½"
F	6	Side Rail	poplar	⅝ x 3 x 15¼"
G	3	Center Rail	poplar	⅝ x 2 x 15½"
H	2	Partition	mahog pop	⅝ x 3¾ x 17¼"
J	4	Drawer Guide	poplar	¾ x ¾ x 15"
K-1	2	Skirt Front, Back	mahogany	⅜ x 1⅜ x 38"
K-2	2	Skirt Side	mahogany	⅜ x 1⅜ x 19"
L	2	Flap Support	mahogany	⅝ x 3¾ x 17"
M	2	WS Spacer Block	mahogany	⅝ x 1½ x 11½"
N	2	WS Frame	mahogany	⅝ x 1½ x 18½"
P	1	Writing Surface	mahogany	⅝ x 10 x 35"
Q	1	WS Back Rail	mahogany	⅝ x 1½ x 35"
R	1	Flap	mahogany	⅝ x 7 x 35"
S-1	2	Flap Frame Side	mahogany	⅝ x 1½ x 8½"
S-2	1	Flap Frame Front	mahogany	⅝ x 1½ x 37½"
T-1	2	Molding Side	mahogany	⅝ x 1¼ x 11½"

EXPLODED VIEW

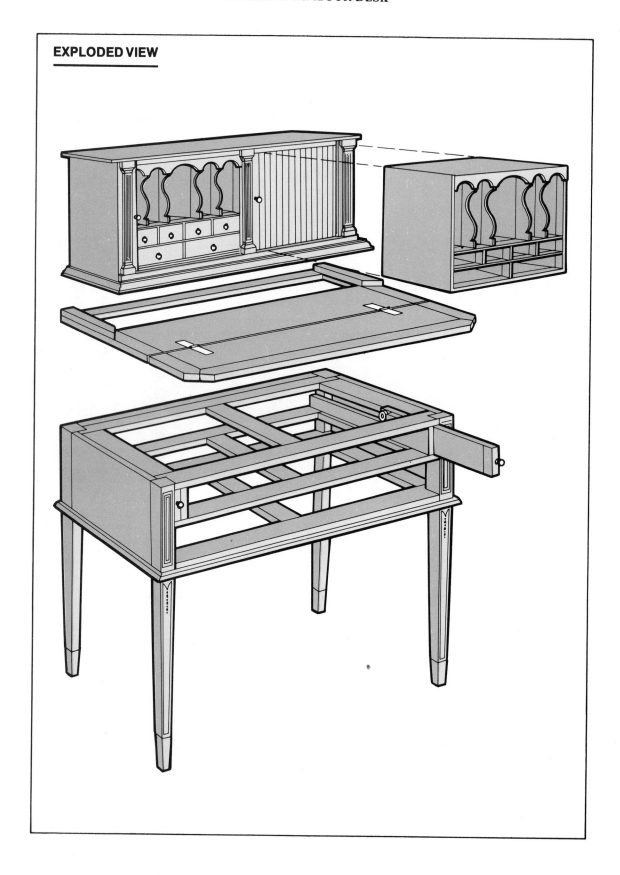

Key	QTY.	PART NAME	MATERIAL	BLANK DIMENSIONS
T-2	1	Molding Front	mahogany	⅝ x 1¼ x 37½"
U	1	Box Floor	mahog/pop	¾ x 10½ x 37½"
V	2	Box End	mahogany	¾ x 9¼ x 13¼"
W	1	Box Center Partition	mahogany	¾ x 8¾ x 10¾"
X	1	Box Top	mahogany	¾ x 10½ x 37½"
Y	2	Box Front Rail	mahogany	¾ x 1¾ x 35"
Z	1	Box Back Rail	mahog/pop	1⅛ x 1⅛ x 34"
AA-1	2	Cleat, Box	poplar	¾ x ⅞ x 7¾"
AA-2	2	Cleat, Compartment	poplar	¾ x ⅞ x 7¼"
BB	1	Box Back	mahogany	½ x 11¾ x 34¾"
CC	10	Column	maple	⅛ x 1 x 12"
DD	2	Lower Drawer Front, Back	poplar	¾ x 4⅝ x 33¾"
EE	2	Lower Drawer Side	poplar	¾ x 4⅝ x 16¼"
FF	1	Lower Drawer Bottom	birch ply	¼ x 15⅛ x 33⅛"
GG	1	Lower Drawer Overlay Front	mahogany	¼ x 4⅞ x 34"
HH	2	Upper Drawer Front, Back	poplar	¾ x 3⅝ x 30⅞"
JJ	2	Upper Drawer Side	poplar	¾ x 3⅝ x 16¼"
KK	1	Upper Drawer Bottom	birch ply	¼ x 15⅛ x 30¼"
LL	1	Upper Drawer Overlay Front	mahogany	¼ x 3⅞ x 31⅛"
MM	8	Comp. Top Bottom, Shelf, Floorbirch ply	¼ x 6⅝ x 15"	
NN	4	Comp. Side	poplar	⅜ x 6⅝ x 10 7/16"
PP	2	Comp. Back	birch ply	⅛ x 10¾ x 15¾"
QQ-1	1	Comp. Partition, Stock	birch ply	¼ x 6½ x 24"
QQ-2	2	Comp. Partition, Stock	birch ply	¼ x 6 x 24"
RR	13 ft.	Comp. Edge Trim	mahogany	1 7/32 x ¾"
SS-1	8	Comp. Scrolled Trim	mahogany	¼ x 1½ x 6"
SS-2	2	Comp. Scrolled Partition	mahogany	¼ x 1⅜ x 15"
TT-1	8	Comp. Lg Dr Front, Back	poplar	¼ x 1 15/16 x 6 15/16"
TT-2	8	Comp. Lg Dr Side	poplar	¼ x 1 15/16 x 6 15/16"
TT-3	4	Comp. Lg Dr Bottom	birch ply	⅛ x 1 15/16 x 6 15/16"
TT-4	4	Comp. Lg Dr Overlay Front	mahogany	¼ x 1 11/16 x 6 5/16"
UU-1	16	Comp. Sm Dr Front, Back	poplar	¼ x 11 11/16 x 3 5/16"
UU-2	16	Comp. Sm Dr Side	poplar	¼ x 11 11/16 x 6⅞"
UU-3	8	Comp. Sm Dr Bottom	birch ply	⅛ x 3 11/16 x 6⅝"
UU-4	8	Comp. Sm Dr Overlay Front	mahogany	¼ x 1 11/16 x 6 5/16"
VV	A/R	Slat (100 required)	mahogany	⅜ x 36 (total w) x 10 9/16"
WW	2	Tambour Lead Strip	mahogany	9/16 x ⅝ x 10 1/16"
XX	4	Bracket	mahogany	¼ x 3½ x 3½"
YY	1	Box Center Post	mahogany	¾ x ⅞ x 10⅝" (+ trim)
ZZ	1	Box Side Trim	mahogany	¾ x 1⅜ x 10¾"

MAJOR ASSEMBLY

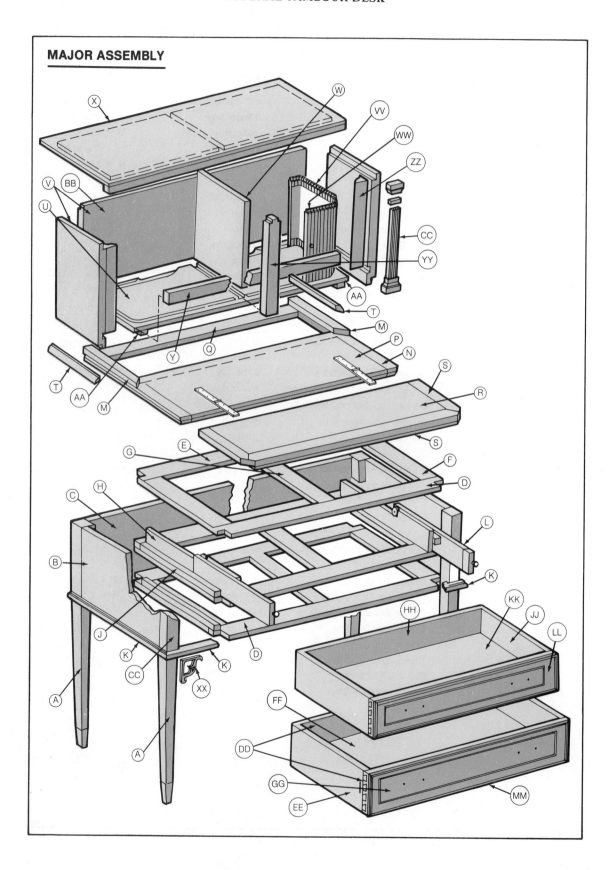

LEG DETAIL

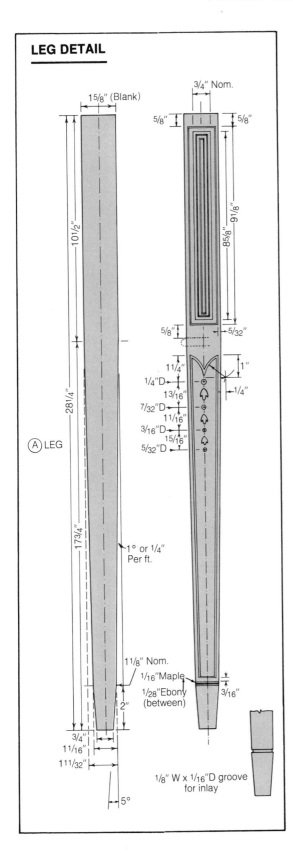

upper part of the desk will result in a tambour that doesn't slide.

The desk can be divided into five projects: the carcase, consisting of the legs, sides, back, and drawer frames; the box and tambours; the writing surface and flap; the two compartments; and the fourteen drawers.

LEGS

The legs are the hardest part; start with them. Dress the blanks $1\frac{5}{8}''$ square end to end. The legs have a double taper. Make the extra taper at the bottom of the legs after the inlay work has been completed. The long leg taper (all sides) is 1 degree (or $\frac{1}{4}''$ in 12'').

Clamp a straightedge to your bench, cut a gauge block $1\frac{9}{32}''$ wide, and mark the ends of the legs for this long taper. As the grain in my leg stock was too wavy for tapering on the jointer, I cautiously cut off most of the waste on the table saw, leaving $\frac{1}{16}''$ to be removed by sanding on a bench belt sander. It was then a simple matter to get the tapers even and matching with the straightedge and gauge block.

All of the inlay on the legs is $\frac{1}{16}''$ thick, rather than the usual veneer thickness of $\frac{1}{28}''$. This makes handling the inlay easier, and allows more leeway in sanding the legs.

The rectangular inlay decoration at the tops of the legs and the columns decorating the front of the tambour box were all made up at the same time, using $\frac{1}{8}''$ maple and $\frac{1}{28}''$ ebony veneer. (If you have only $\frac{1}{40}''$ ebony veneer available, use a double thickness.)

Glue up maple-veneer-maple-veneer sandwiches 1'' wide and 12'' long (Fig. 4). For the columns, clamp these glued sandwiches to the sides of an additional piece of maple. For the leg decorations, miter to length and add mitered sections across the ends.

Face one side of each sandwich and glue to the sides of a pine handle. Rip columns $\frac{3}{16}''$ thick, and leg inlays $\frac{1}{16}''$ thick. A Dremel table saw will rip these very nicely, leaving a smooth surface and little waste (Fig. 5).

Rip a supply of $\frac{1}{16}''$ x $\frac{1}{16}''$ inlay strips from maple for the legs and drawers.

VENEERING INLAY AND COLUMN

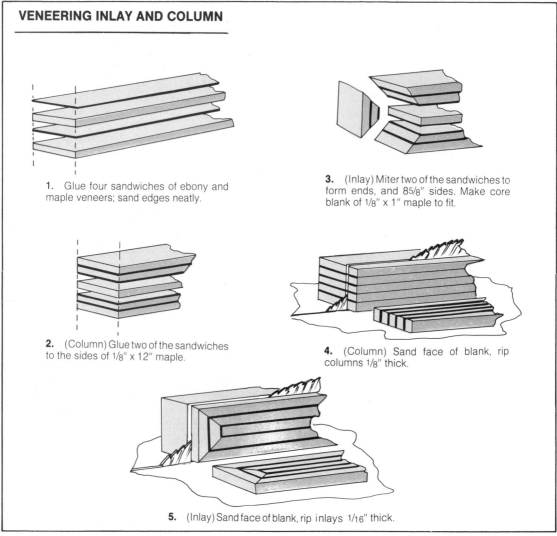

1. Glue four sandwiches of ebony and maple veneers; sand edges neatly.

3. (Inlay) Miter two of the sandwiches to form ends, and 8⅝″ sides. Make core blank of 1/8″ x 1″ maple to fit.

2. (Column) Glue two of the sandwiches to the sides of 1/8″ x 12″ maple.

4. (Column) Sand face of blank, rip columns 1/8″ thick.

5. (Inlay) Sand face of blank, rip inlays 1/16″ thick.

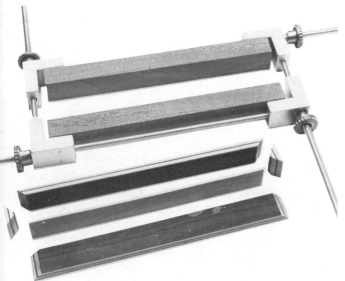

Fig. 4. Gluing up column and rectangular inlay blanks. Both start with four-layer sandwiches, 12″ long by 1″ wide. Sandwiches consist of alternating 1/8″ maple and 1/28″ ebony veneers. For the columns, the sandwiches are glued /8″ maple. For the inlay, the center piece of 1/8″ maple is boxed by mitered sections of the sandwiches.

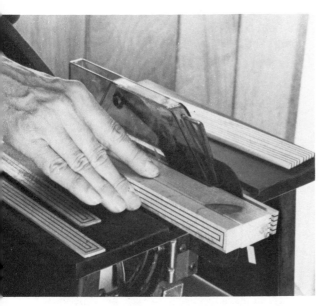

Fig. 5. Sawing inlays and columns. Face the glued-up blanks and glue them to a pine handle. Then rip columns 3/16″ thick, inlay 1/16″.

Fig. 6. Routing jig with dummy leg in place for test routing. Two setups are required per leg: one for the long taper and one for top portion of leg forming carcase post.

Make a fixture for routing the front leg front surfaces (only) for the maple inlay strip, and for the recess for the rectangular inlay at the top of the front legs. The one shown in Fig. 6 was cobbled together from scrap and worked out quite well. Before routing the legs, make up an accurate dummy leg to use for trial cuts. Two setups are required, first for the tapered part of the leg, then for the straight upper section. The fixture can be shimmed for the rectangular inlay cutout.

Two routers were used: an ordinary baseplate router for the straight grooves and the inlay recess; and a Dremel Motor Tool with the router attachment plus a shop-made pivot for the curved strips (Fig. 7). For the straight grooves, the router was guided by the edge of its base plate. After the 1/16″ grooving, the 1/16″ bit was replaced with a 1/4″ bit for the rectangular recess and 7/16″-wide shims were tacked inside the jig.

Fitting the inlay into the recess was approached cautiously as any slight error would be visible and difficult to hide. Several pieces of chipboard were tack-glued to the ends of the jig and removed one by one as the inlay recess was rerouted. This produced the necessary accurate vertical centering. (The inlay must be centered relative to the carcase top and bottom drawer frames.) The 7/16″ side shims produced a recess

Fig. 7. Routing the curved inlay on leg. The groove for this inlay is routed with a Dremel hand grinder using the router accessory and a shop-made pivot. The pivot fits in holes in either side of the routing jig to rout the arcs.

that was slightly too narrow; they were removed and sanded down to correct the recess width.

Glue the strip inlays and the rectangular inlay into the leg. When dry, sand the long tapers on the legs to final dimension. At this time, sand the back legs to the same taper, and rough the lower tapers.

Make a plywood fixture to clamp on the legs to locate the holes for the maple circles. This fixture clamps over the upper end of the taper and is positioned from the top of the leg.

The maple circles should not be cut from dowels as the end-grain will not finish light in color. Saw oversize circles from 3/16" maple and glue them to the ends of short dowels smaller in diameter than the finished circles will be. Chuck the dowels in a lathe or drill press and sand the maple circles to the diameter of the holes in the legs (Fig. 9).

The bellflowers are also graduated in size. Glue patterns to 1/8" maple and saw them out and sand edges neatly. Trace the bellflowers in position on the legs and chisel out the recesses. A set of miniature chisels is a great help here.

Rout grooves around the foot of each leg (all four legs) for the 1/8"-wide inlay trim which goes on all sides of all legs (Fig. 10). Glue in the inlay. Finally, sand the lower taper to final dimension (Fig. 11).

CARCASE

Cut blanks for the sides, back, and drawer frames, Although it is conventional practice to plane each part to thickness before gluing up panels and frames, I blanked and glued everything full thickness and took it all to the local cabinet shop and let them run the stock through their 36"-wide belt sander, starting with an 80-grit belt and finishing up with a 150-grit surfacing. The cost is $12 for most jobs, their minimum charge. If you can find someone with a wide belt sander, blank everything else at this time and have it all done at one time. The time saved and the flat, very flat, results are worth every cent of the cost.

Blank back and sides. Drill mating dowel holes and assemble legs, sides, and back dry, with full-length dowels. Check to see that the legs are square vertically. If not, apply correction to the mating side or back surface.

Fig. 8. Inlay strip is 1/16" by 1/16" rather than 1/28", the size of the purchased strip. This square strip is easier to glue in the groove, and allows more leeway in sanding the legs. Check the inlay strip after you rip and sand it for wide areas that won't fit in the grooves.

Fig. 9. Making circle inlays. Dowel and end-grain cannot be used as it will appear too dark when finished. Instead, glue pieces of 3/16" maple to short dowels. When dry, sand the maple flush with the dowel on a lathe or drill press. Keep leg on lathe table for frequent checking.

Fig. 10. Using leg-rounding jig to groove for ⅛" inlay trim. Clamp the jig to untapered upper section of leg.

Fig. 11. Sanding bottom taper of leg. Foot is positioned exactly at the end of sander table.

LEG AND RAIL ASSEMBLY

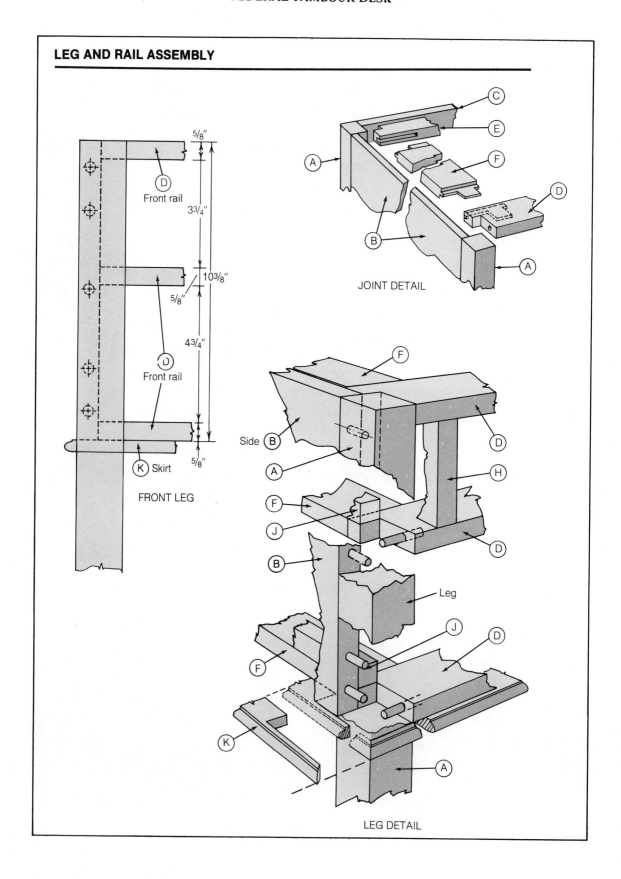

5/8"

D
Front rail

3 3/4"

10 3/8"

5/8"

4 3/4"

D
Front rail

K Skirt

5/8"

FRONT LEG

C
E
A
F
D
B
A

JOINT DETAIL

F
Side B
A
F
J
B
Leg
D
H
D
J
D
K
A

LEG DETAIL

Blank parts for the three identical frames. I mortised and tenoned them; they could also be doweled. Glue up the frames, notch corners (Fig. 12), and fit them into the desk carcase.

Dowel the frames to the front legs, but do not glue (Fig. 13). Blank drawer guides, drill pilot holes in the guides for screws to attach them to the desk sides and frames. Glue and screw the guides to the frames. To do this, clamp the guides to a frame, disassemble the desk and glue and screw the parts together. If you plan locks on the drawers, mortise the frames for the strikes. Make the partitions forming the flap support compartments and screw them between the top and middle frames (with the bottom frame temporarily removed).

Before assembling the carcase, sand all interior surfaces. Then glue and dowel the sides between the front and back legs, one side at a time. Assemble the side to the rest of the desk dry to assure that there is no misalignment, particularly leg rotation.

Glue and dowel the back to one side, using the other side and the frame as a jig (Fig. 14). Next, glue and screw the top and middle frames to the back and the side, one at a time, using the other carcase parts as a jig. Now attach the two partitions between these frames with screws. Attach the bottom frame to the back and side; then glue and dowel the second side (Fig. 15).

DRAWERS

The drawers are made with half-blind dovetails. Drawer fronts are faced with fiddleback mahogany veneer on a core of $1/4''$ plywood or mahogany. If you are going to apply cock beading, use plywood; if not, use mahogany for appearance. Drawer locks should be mortised

Fig. 12. Notching frame corners for legs. Extended faceplate on miter gauge and clamped-on stop block insure that all indentical frames will have identical notches.

Fig. 13. Doweling frames to front legs. First drill dowel holes in legs, then locate them in frames, one frame at a time. Do not use glue at this point.

Fig. 14. Attaching frame to side-back carcase assembly. First, assemble legs and sides, then dowel back to one side assembly.

Fig. 15. Last step in assembling the carcase is attaching the second side. After joints are closed, desk will be inverted on bench for clamping.

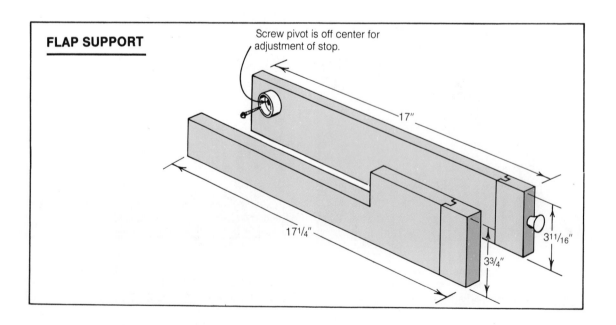

FLAP SUPPORT

Screw pivot is off center for adjustment of stop.

17"

17¼"

3¹¹/₁₆"

3¾"

DRAWER AND FRAME

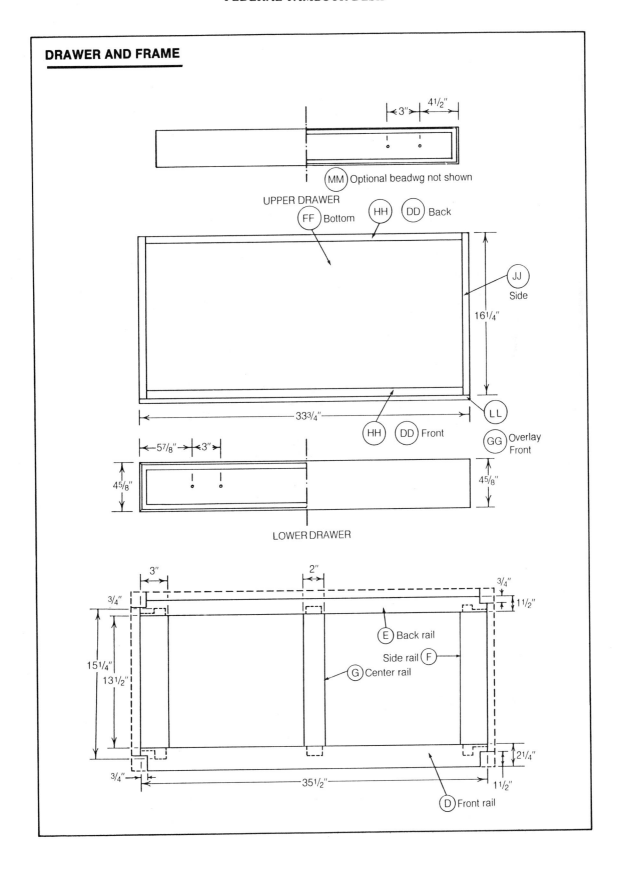

MM Optional beadwg not shown

UPPER DRAWER

FF Bottom HH DD Back

JJ Side

16¼"

33¾"

HH DD Front

GG Overlay Front

LL

5⅞" 3"

4⅝"

4⅝"

LOWER DRAWER

3" 2" ¾"

¾" 1½"

E Back rail

Side rail F

G Center rail

15¼" 13½"

2¼"

¾" 35½" 1½"

D Front rail

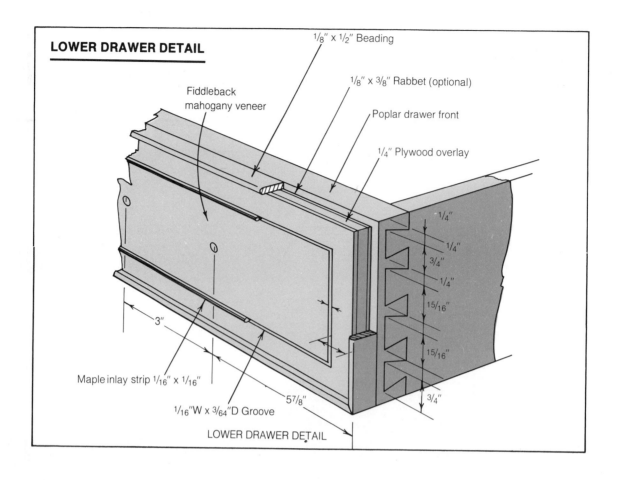

LOWER DRAWER DETAIL

$1/8'' \times 1/2''$ Beading

$1/8'' \times 3/8''$ Rabbet (optional)

Poplar drawer front

$1/4''$ Plywood overlay

Fiddleback mahogany veneer

$1/4''$

$1/4''$

$3/4''$

$1/4''$

$15/16''$

$15/16''$

$3/4''$

$3''$

Maple inlay strip $1/16'' \times 1/16''$

$1/16''$W x $3/64''$D Groove

$57/8''$

LOWER DRAWER DETAIL

before you assemble the drawers. I used old piano-key ivory to make the shield escutcheons.

BOX

Blank the parts for the box—top, floor, two sides, and the center partition. The floor is made of poplar and mahogany for economy. Until the track is routed, the floor and top must be exactly the same size. Blank the center partition $8^3/4''$ wide so the back edge will be flush with the back of the floor and top blanks for initial alignment.

Clamp the floor and top back-to-back with inside faces up and rout the dado (see Fig.17) for the center partition. (This partition will provide the primary alignment for routing the tracks.) Make a key (also shown in Fig. 17) to fit the dado

and lock the floor and top together (but spaced $1/8''$ apart) with edges aligned. Drill dowel holes up through the floor, the key, and into the top.

The same routing templet is used for both sides of the box. Blank the track routing templet; it is dimensioned for a $1/4''$ bushing and a $1/8''$ router bit. Attach the templet to the floor with three flathead screws (Fig. 18). Note their locations. Key and clamp the floor to the top and drill three $3/8''$ holes up through the floor and templet and into the top (Fig. 19).

Remove the top and rout the track in the first side of the floor. Remove the screws, locate the templet on the top with three dowels through the $3/8''$ holes, attach the templet with screws, and rout the track in the top. Repeat the steps for the tracks in the other side.

Position the partition in the dadoes and drill

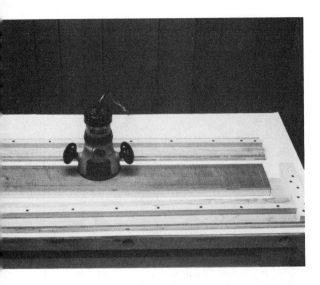

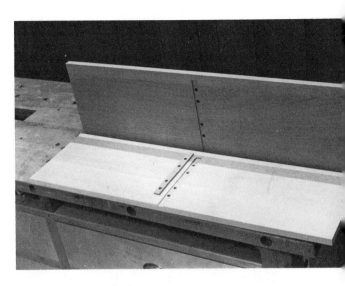

Fig. 16. The same jig can be used to rout the inlay in both drawers dimensioned properly. If optional beading is to be used on drawers, form rabbet after gluing inlay and sanding the drawer front.

Fig. 17. Box floor and top are initially blanked to identical dimensions in order to serve as jigs for aligning center partition and sides. Rout dado for center partition with floor and top back-to-back. Key shown is made to fit dado and align parts for drilling matched dowel holes.

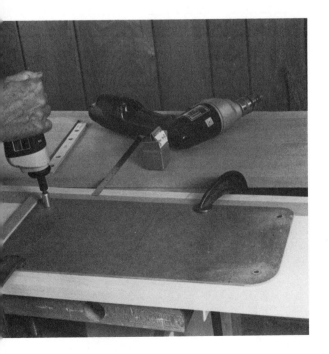

Fig. 18. Installing track-routing templet on floor. Attach templet to floor with countersunk flathead wood screws. After routing track, clamp top to templet and floor, using center-partition key for alignment.

Fig. 19. With floor and top aligned by key, and track-routing templet sandwiched between, drill three randomly spaced holes for dowels through the floor and templet and into top.

BOX: EXPLODED VIEW

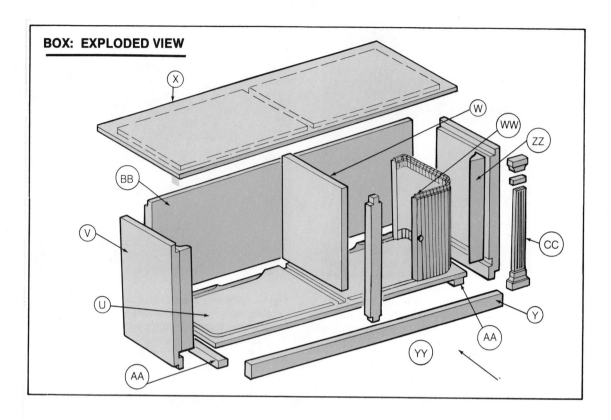

BOX: TOP AND FRONT VIEWS

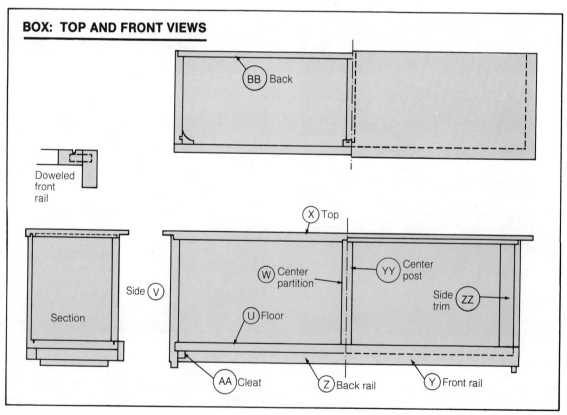

Doweled
front
rail

BB Back

X Top

W Center
partition

YY Center
post

Side V

Section

ZZ Side
trim

U Floor

AA Cleat

Z Back rail

Y Front rail

BOX BLANKS

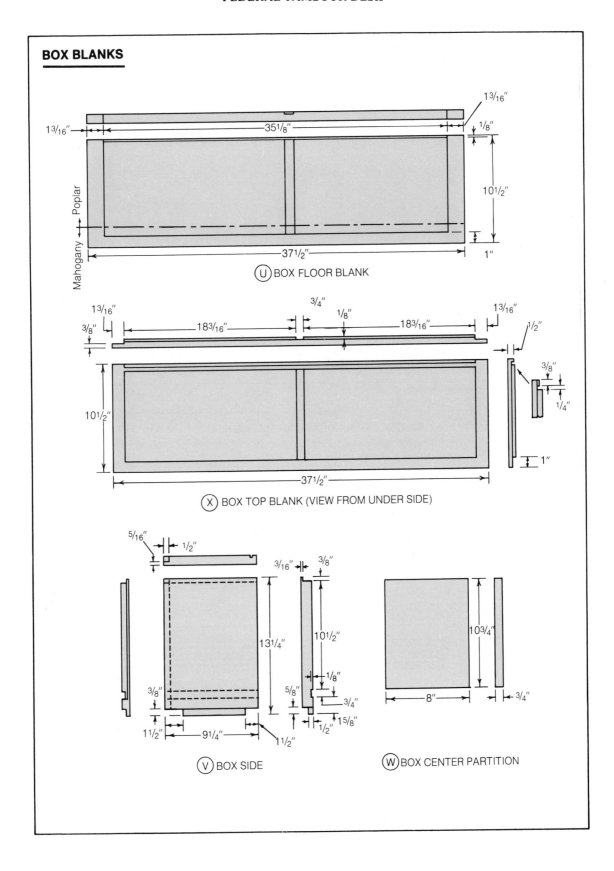

U BOX FLOOR BLANK

X BOX TOP BLANK (VIEW FROM UNDER SIDE)

V BOX SIDE

W BOX CENTER PARTITION

TAMBOUR TRACK

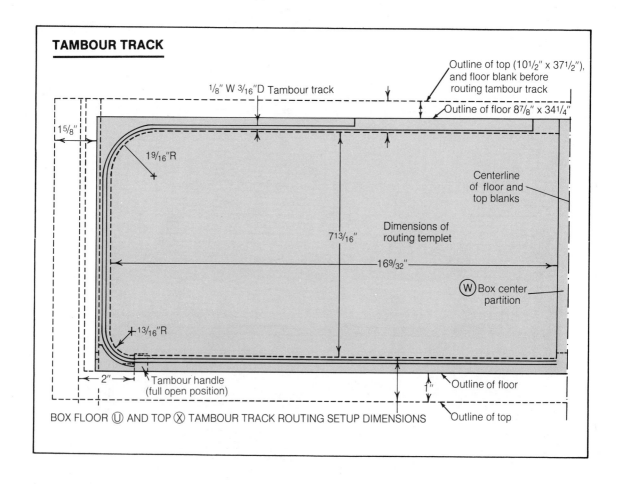

1/8″ W 3/16″D Tambour track

Outline of top (10 1/2″ x 37 1/2″), and floor blank before routing tambour track

Outline of floor 8 7/8″ x 34 1/4″

1 5/8″

1 9/16″R

Centerline of floor and top blanks

Dimensions of routing templet

7 13/16″

16 9/32″

W Box center partition

13/16″R

2″

Tambour handle (full open position)

1″

Outline of floor

BOX FLOOR Ⓤ AND TOP Ⓧ TAMBOUR TRACK ROUTING SETUP DIMENSIONS

Outline of top

COLUMN

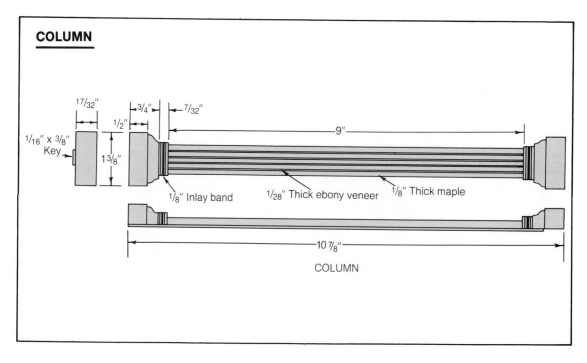

17/32″

3/4″

7/32″

1/2″

9″

1/16″ x 3/8″ Key

1 3/8″

1/8″ Inlay band

1/28″ Thick ebony veneer

1/8″ Thick maple

10 7/8″

COLUMN

mating dowel holes in the partition (use dowel centers to transfer the top holes).

Measure the separation between the floor and top, then blank, rabbet, and dado the two box sides. Cut the floor and center partition to dimension and rabbet the underside of the top. Drill dowel holes and screw pilot holes; assemble the box dry. Blank rails and cleats, and attach with screws only. Blank the box side trim pieces rough and glue them to the sides. Sand the combined front surfaces.

Make the center post. If you do not plan to have a lock on the tambour, it can be solid. Dado the sides and center post for the column tenons.

For details on making the tambour, see the special section at the end of this chapter.

COLUMN DETAIL

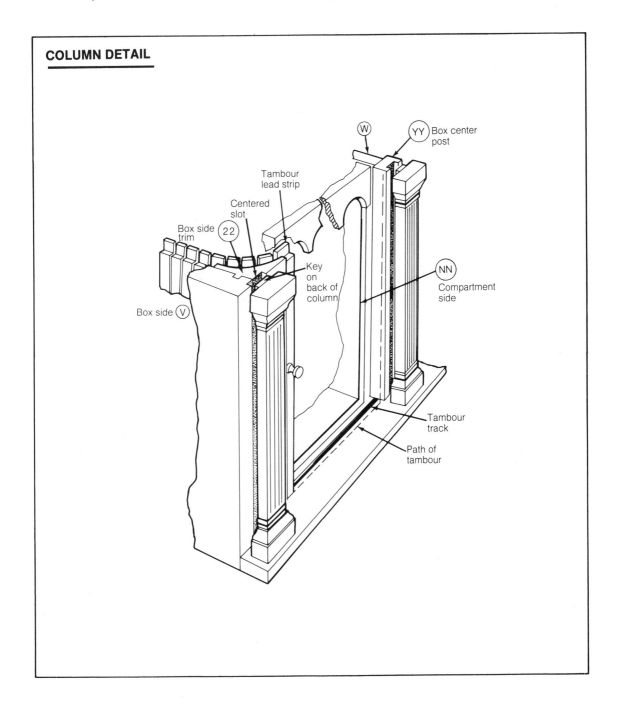

THE COMPARTMENTS

The biggest problem with designing compartments for a tambour desk is keeping the compartment box and drawer knobs clear of the tambour and the tambour lead strip.

One feature of the first Seymour desk I looked at that I liked very much was the interior of the compartments—they were painted medium blue. I changed the drawer and pigeonhole arrangement, but I kept the blue paint.

The compartments—there are two of them—are built of $\frac{3}{8}''$ poplar (sides) and $\frac{7}{32}''$ plywood. The front of the compartments is trimmed with mahogany, tongue-and-grooved to the plywood. This wasn't done as a cost-saving measure, but to make it possible to paint and stain the two parts of the compartment separately. The compartments are attached to the box center partition and by cleats at the outboard sides to the floor.

The drawers have through dovetails, which appear as half-blind after the fiddleback-mahogany-veneered facings are attached.

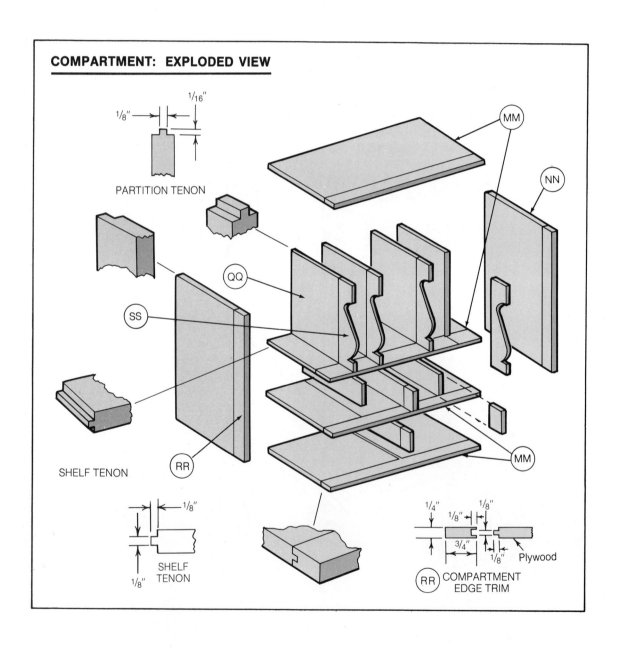

COMPARTMENT: EXPLODED VIEW

$\frac{1}{8}''$ $\frac{1}{16}''$

PARTITION TENON

MM

NN

QQ

SS

SHELF TENON

RR

$\frac{1}{8}''$

SHELF TENON

$\frac{1}{8}''$

MM

$\frac{1}{4}''$ $\frac{1}{8}''$ $\frac{1}{8}''$

$\frac{3}{4}''$ $\frac{1}{8}''$ Plywood

RR COMPARTMENT EDGE TRIM

COMPARTMENT: DIMENSIONS

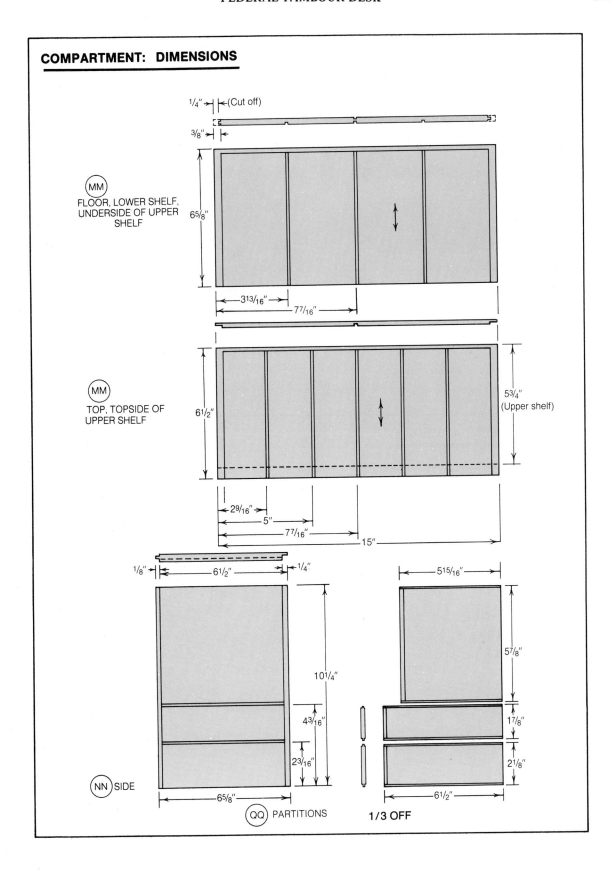

1/4" ← →(Cut off)

3/8" →

(MM)
FLOOR, LOWER SHELF,
UNDERSIDE OF UPPER
SHELF

6⁵/₈"

3¹³/₁₆"

7⁷/₁₆"

(MM)
TOP, TOPSIDE OF
UPPER SHELF

6¹/₂"

5³/₄"
(Upper shelf)

2⁹/₁₆"

5"

7⁷/₁₆"

15"

1/8" → 6¹/₂" 1/4"

5¹⁵/₁₆"

10¹/₄"

5⁷/₈"

4³/₁₆"

1⁷/₈"

2³/₁₆"

2¹/₈"

(NN) SIDE

6⁵/₈"

(QQ) PARTITIONS

6¹/₂"

1/3 OFF

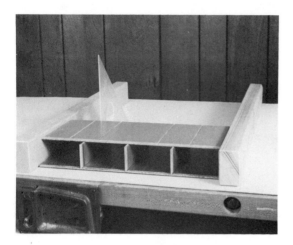

Fig. 20. Assemble upper drawer section. Paint all pigeon-hole surfaces blue before assembly; stain and varnish drawer partitions.

Fig. 21. Assemble bottom and one side, using other side and top as jig. Note bracing to prevent thin top and bottom from buckling under clamping pressure.

COMPARTMENT ASSEMBLY

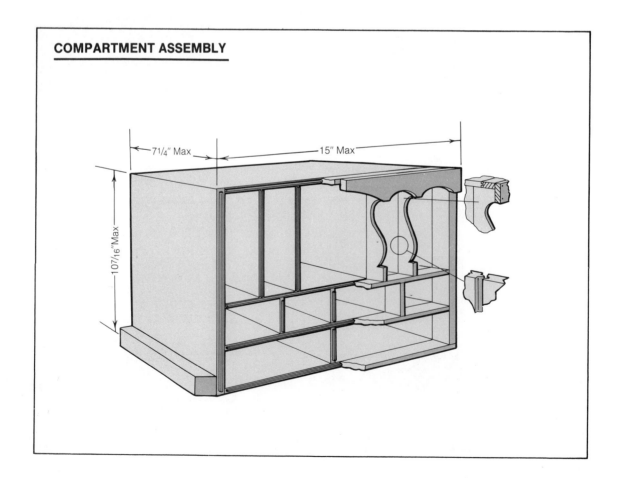

Fig. 22. Assemble side and floor with drawer section plus lower drawer partition.

Fig. 23. Add section side; then with top clamped as a jig, glue in pigeonhole partitions (to shelf only). Then glue top to compartment assembly.

Fig. 24. The front of the compartment is trimmed with mahogany, tongue-and-grooved and nailed to the plywood carcase.

DRAWER: DETAILS

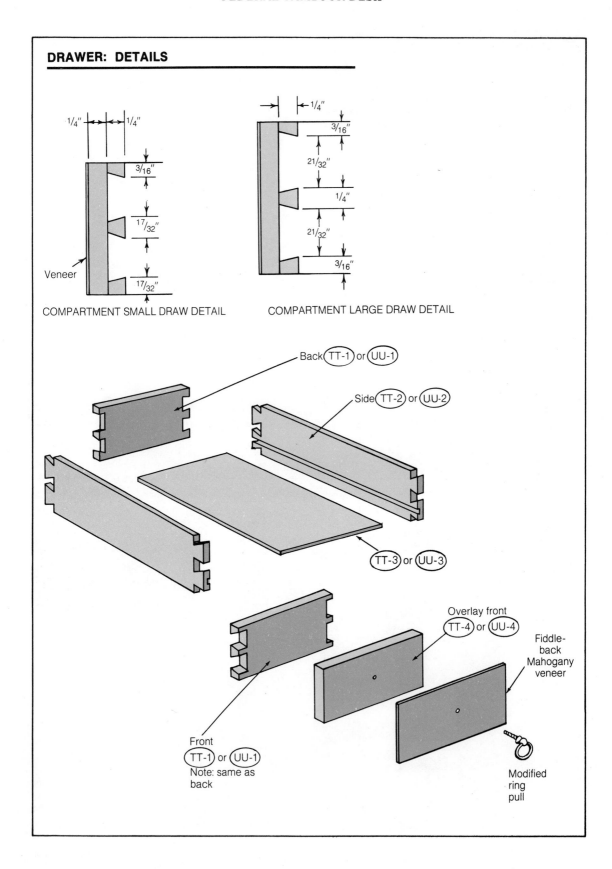

COMPARTMENT SMALL DRAW DETAIL

COMPARTMENT LARGE DRAW DETAIL

Veneer

Back TT-1 or UU-1

Side TT-2 or UU-2

TT-3 or UU-3

Overlay front
TT-4 or UU-4

Fiddle-
back
Mahogany
veneer

Modified
ring
pull

Front
TT-1 or UU-1
Note: same as
back

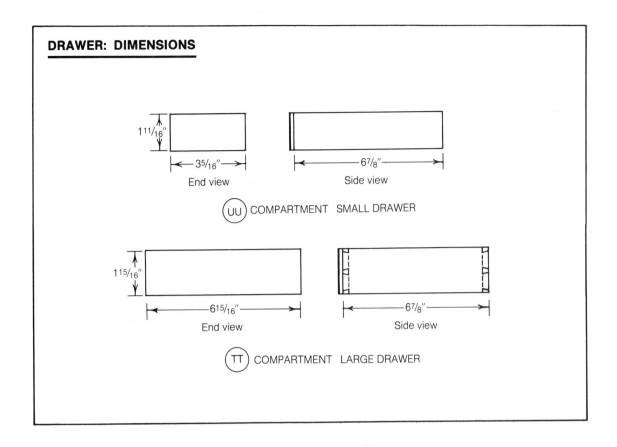

DRAWER: DIMENSIONS

1¹¹/₁₆″

3⁵/₁₆″

End view

6⁷/₈″

Side view

(UU) COMPARTMENT SMALL DRAWER

1¹⁵/₁₆″

6¹⁵/₁₆″

End view

6⁷/₈″

Side view

(TT) COMPARTMENT LARGE DRAWER

Fig. 25. Compartment drawers are dovetailed at all corners. Dimension drawer parts initially for tight fit; then sand finished drawer so it moves easily.

Fig. 26. Ring pulls for drawers require rework. Pull out screw; drill brass post #43, thread 4-40 and insert ³/₈″ piece or 4-40 threaded rod, which can be run into #43 hole in drawer front.

Fig. 27. A single blank supplies all column bases. Rout the ends and cut off the bases. Note grain direction.

Fig. 28. A single blank supplies all column trim pieces. Rabbet the sides for the inlay and glue it in place. Then rout the ends, glue in inlay, and cut off the trim piece.

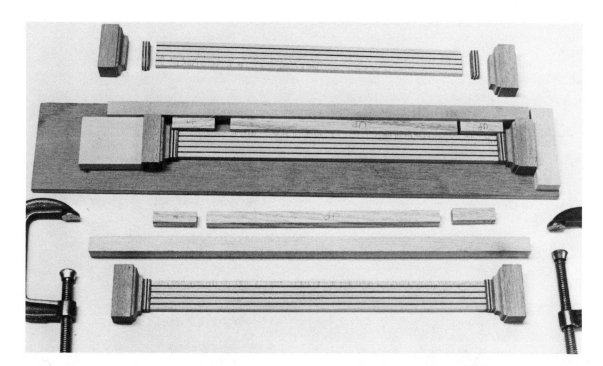

Fig. 29. To assemble the column (above), hold all parts in alignment for gluing in a jig (one piece glued to base, the other one loose). Shims center column and trim.

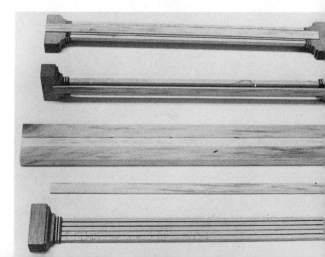

Fig. 30. Glue a 1/16″ x 3/8″ tongue to back of the column for alignment and secure attachment to the front of the desk box. Fixture shown centers the tongue.

WRITING SURFACE AND FLAP

The writing surface is attached to the carcase by screws through the top frame. The box fits into the opening in the writing surface and is attached by its sides with screws into the sides of the writing surface frame.

Assemble the writing surface and flap (Fig. 35); mortise for hinges (Fig. 36). Blank the spacer blocks and rout the molding.

Rabbet the edge of the top and the edge of the flap for the ³/₄"-wide inlay strip. Note that the flap edge rabbet is stopped. Glue in the inlay and sand all surfaces of the writing surface, flap, and box.

Assemble the box. Glue the center partition to

the floor using the rest of the box as a jig; glue and screw the ends of the floor, one at a time. If alignment isn't perfect, the tambour will stick. Then, glue and dowel the top.

BRACKETS

The brackets are not functional—just decorative. As this desk was being made for a specific person, her initials came to mind as I was doodling the bracket design. If you prefer not to make an initial bracket, you could cut any design that pleases you on the scroll saw. It needn't be anything fancy.

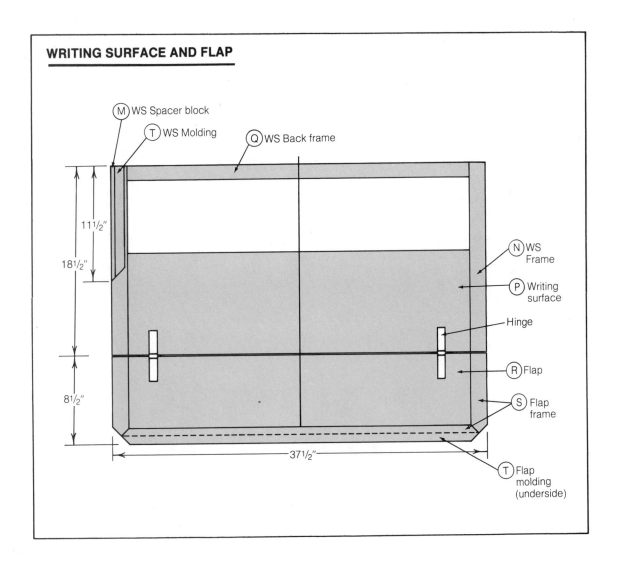

WRITING SURFACE AND FLAP

WRITING SURFACE

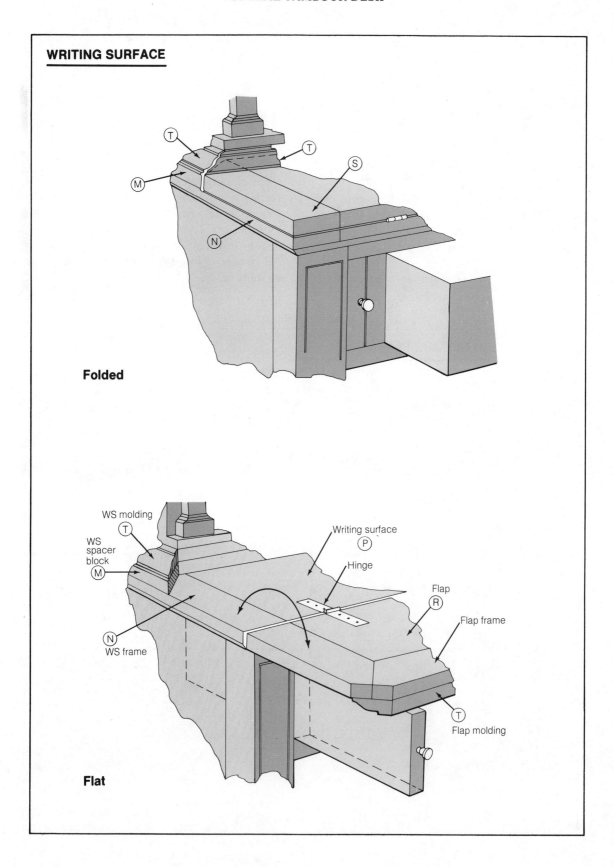

Folded

WS molding
(T)

WS spacer block
(M)

(N)
WS frame

Writing surface
(P)

Hinge

Flap
(R)

Flap frame

(T)
Flap molding

Flat

Fig. 31. Front frame of the flap (left) is doweled for ease of alignment. The side frames are tenoned for joint strength. Mortising for the flap hinges (right). Router is boxed in on all sides for this critical routing. The mortise must be enough to bring the facing surfaces of the folded flap and writing surface almost in contact, to help prevent the wood from warping.

Fig. 33. Brackets are blanked from two pieces of 1/4" mahogany glued together with grain at right angles and sawed on a scroll saw. Attach brackets to legs and skirt with #3 flathead wood screws, angled from the back.

TAMBOURS—HOW TO DESIGN
AND MAKE THEM

Tambours are flexible doors made of wood slats glued to a backing of cloth. If the slats are horizontal, and the tambour moves vertically to open and close, it is usually called a "rolltop" (Fig. 34). If the slats move horizontally, it is called a tambour, or tambour door (Fig. 35).

The advantage of a tambour, besides its attractiveness, is that the door is out of sight when open. The disadvantages are that space must be provided inside the cabinet for the retracted door, and the cabinet must be very

carefully constructed if the tambour is to operate freely.

Tambours are now most popular in the form of oak rolltop desks. They were also popular in Louis XV and XVI, Sheraton, Hepplewhite, and American Federal furniture.

The design of any piece of furniture that will have a tambour door should start with the door and track. The piece of furniture must be designed around the tambour and track, not the other way around. The boxlike structure that

Fig. 34. A rolltop is a vertically opening tambour.

Fig. 35. Example of a horizontally opening tambour.

Fig. 36. A vertical tambour on a cabinet. A tall tambour such as this must be counterbalanced with springs or weights to prevent it from slamming open or closed under its own weight.

contains the tambour tracks must be square and rigid. The tracks must be mirror images of each other in form and location.

Tambour slats are usually rectangular in cross-section, with flat or rounded exposed front surfaces, but they can also be square. The slats are usually shouldered at the ends to form tongues (tenons), which ride in the tracks. Tambour slats have tongues for three reasons:

1. *Appearance*. The overhanging shoulder hides the groove when the door is closed.

2. *Stability*. The wider a slat tongue is relative to its thickness, and the closer the plane of the tongue is to the cloth holding the slats together, the less chattering there is going to be during tambour movement.

3. *Tracking*. Everything else being equal, a narrow tongue will take a tighter curve in the track than a thick tongue.

However, in vertical "rolltop" tambours without any sharp turns, such as in a rollrop desk, the value of the tongues can be questioned. The slats disappearing into the desk ends whole look a lot better than slats displaying $1/6''$ to $1/8''$ or more of tongue. Slats without tongues are also a lot stronger. The Hepplewhite Rolltop Desk (Chapter 9) has slats without tongues.

For a vertical slat, the lower tongue must be long enough to ride on the bottom of the track groove. The shoulder on the slat should clear the floor by $1/32''$ (desk and small box tambours) to $1/16''$ (large cabinet tambours). The upper tongue should have $1/16''$ minimum clearance to the bottom of the inverted groove.

For a horizontal "rolltop" slat, the tongues at both ends must be long enough so that neither shoulder can rub the side of the carcase. End play of the assembled tambour should not be less than $1/16''$ for short slats up to 12"), $1/8''$ for longer slats. The same end play should be provided for horizontal slats without tongues.

Design starts with drawing the plans for the track and tambour slat, and determining whether the tongue can take the curves. For a tambour that opens horizontally it is usually esthetically desirable to make the front curve as tight as possible. (The curve at the back of the cabinet usually does not have to be as tight.)

You can draw and plot curves and walk little rectangles representing the end of the tongue through the plotted curve as carefully as you can,

but the real test is to rout a sample groove, rip some scrap to the dimension of the tongues, tape the dummy tongues together with duct tape, and try pushing them through the curved groove (Fig. 37). If the slats will run around the curve without being waxed, you have your dimensions.

If, when you have your tambour built, the slat tongues bind in the groove at the curves, there are three things you can do, depending on how bad the binding:

1. Sand the tongues slightly thinner.

2. Round the outside corners of the slat tongues, or chisel a small bevel.

3. Rout the track groove wider at the curve.

These cures are appropriate both in the design stage and final assembly.

Watch out for excessive weight in tall vertical tambours. Unless restrained with counterbalancing springs or possibly weights, they can really come slamming down, and can fall shut under their own weight.

Over a period of time, a carcase can warp, and change dimension with variations in humidity. Warping can mess up the alignment of the track

Fig. 37. The best way to determine if your planned tambour slats will be able to negotiate curves in the track is to make a mockup. This is the mockup used for the desk.

and cause binding; expansion can so widen the track that the tambour falls out.

Contraction can lock the tambour in place until next summer. The carcase members that hold the tracks apart (the sides of the tambour desk, for example) must have the grain running the same direction as the tambour slat grain to equalize expansion.

There are several ways to improve the structural soundness of a carcase. A false back positioned in front of the retracted tambour is one good way. If the space behind the tambour is open—a shelf for books, for example—partitions must be provided anyway to keep whatever you store there from interfering with the movement of the tambour, and to protect the tambour from accidental damage. You could get yourself in the bad situation of not being able to open the tambour because its movement is totally blocked. This means the tambour track at the sides must also be boxed in.

In desks, the space behind the tambour usually is occupied by a compartment containing small drawers and pigeonholes. These compartments are best built as separate integral units that can be inserted into the desk from the rear. They must be accurately positioned and securely fastened so they can't shift around and block the tambours.

When dimensioning and allowing clearances, the critical clearance at the front is between the pulls on the drawers and the back of the tambour lead strip.

TRACK GROOVE SIZE

Track grooves vary in width, depth, and curve radius. The dimensions on the desk are width, $1/8''$; depth, $3/16''$; radius at the front, $1''$ (fairly tight for a tambour of this size). The radius at the back is larger. The tongues on the slats are $3/32''$ thick and $3/8''$ wide. This construction is light and delicate, in keeping with the design of the desk. (The museum desk I examined had even lighter dimensions.)

A more exposed tambour in a cabinet front, or a rolltop desk, should have a track width of $3/16''$ to $3/8''$ and be $1 1/2$ times deeper than wide.

Tongues should be at least twice as wide as thick; the slat itself can be rectangular or even square—it's the tongue proportions that affect tracking.

Tambour handles—lead strips—are usually thicker and wider than the rest of the slats. This means the lead strip usually can't be tracked in from the back with the rest of the tambour as it won't fit through the narrow openings and can't negotiate the tight turns. The lead strip is therefore normally attached with screws after the tambour is in place. If it is necessary to repair the tambour, the strip has to be removed.

The lead strip can be attached by sandwiching backing cloth can be sandwiched between the back of the lead strip and a clamping strip of wood attached with wood screws, as in A, B, and C of the drawing on page 237.
The problem with these attachment methods is keeping the cloth pulled tight under the clamping strip while you tighten the screws. Method C would work beter than A or B.

There also may be a problem tilting the lead strip into the tracks (the lead strip must have tongues so it doesn't flap loose).

The desk tambour lead strip is attached as

TAMBOUR DETAIL

Backing cloth

...ue closer
...h
...o face

Clearance

$1/2''$

End of tongue rests on bottom of track

BASIC CARCASE DESIGN

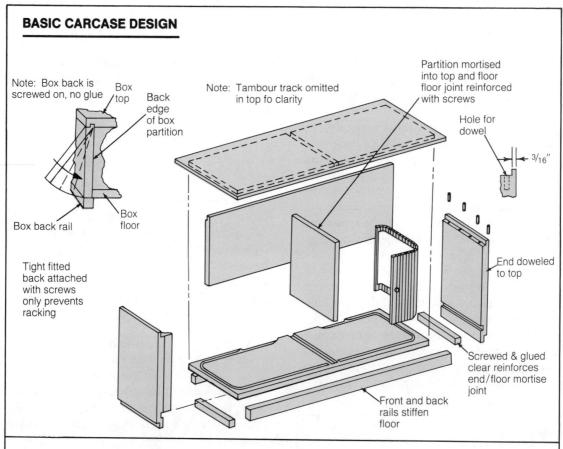

Note: Box back is screwed on, no glue

Box top

Back edge of box partition

Box back rail

Box floor

Tight fitted back attached with screws only prevents racking

Note: Tambour track omitted in top fo clarity

Partition mortised into top and floor floor joint reinforced with screws

Hole for dowel

3/16"

End doweled to top

Screwed & glued clear reinforces end/floor mortise joint

Front and back rails stiffen floor

CARCASE DESIGN WITH FALSE BACK AND SIDES

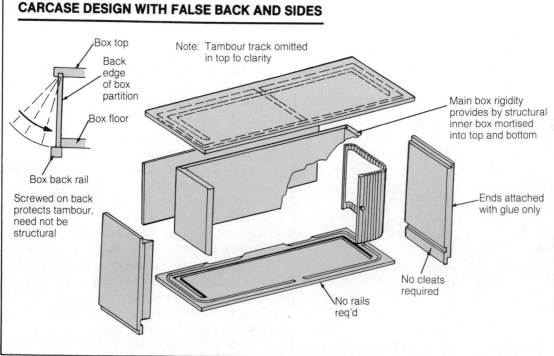

Box top

Back edge of box partition

Box floor

Box back rail

Screwed on back protects tambour, need not be structural

Note: Tambour track omitted in top fo clarity

Main box rigidity provides by structural inner box mortised into top and bottom

Ends attached with glue only

No cleats required

No rails req'd

shown in *D*. The front portions of two slats are ripped off so that slat will fit into the dado in the lead strips. The backing cloth is glued to three sides of these strips for secure attachment. The tambour and lead strip are assembled on the bench and holes for the 6-32 flathead machine screws drilled and tapped.

A templet should be made for routing the track grooves, and some means used to position it accurately on the two separated parts of the carcase. A single templet should be used—one that can be reversed top and bottom, left and right. In the tambour desk, I drilled holes through the floor, templet, and into the top for three locating dowels for each side (a different set for each side): the center partition, mortised into the floor and top, was used as a reference for locating the templets.

At the back of the carcase, an entry slot must be provided for getting the tambour into the carcase. A cloth-backed tambour has a very limited ability to curve backward, so this slot should be as long as possible.

Once the tambour is in the carcase and the lead strip attached, stops should be put in the groove to limit how far the tambour can open so the lead strip doesn't bang against the carcase opening. This tends to cause the lead strip to separate from the rest of the tambour.

RIPPING TAMBOUR SLATS

You can rip tambour slats from blanks, shape and sand them, and then finish them individually. Or you can, as I prefer, shape and finish-sand the slats before they are ripped from the blank. I also believe that the slats should be completely finished (except for the back surface) before they are glued to the cloth.

Prepare blanks for ripping tambours the exact length needed to fit the tracks without any end-to-end clearance allowance. (This procedure simplifies routing the tongues after the slats are assembled into the tambour. The upper ends of the slats can be sanded to provide the needed clearance afterwards.) The thickness of the blank should equal the width of the slats.

Finish-sand the sides of the blank (it's easier now than after ripping). The ripping procedure is simple; finish-sand both edges of the blanks,

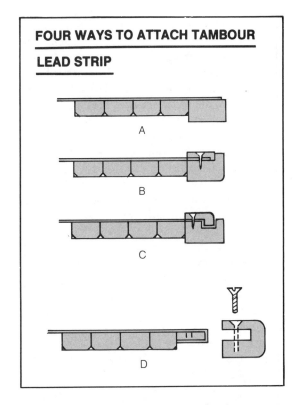

FOUR WAYS TO ATTACH TAMBOUR LEAD STRIP

A

B

C

D

round edges if required in the design, rip off a slat from each edge (working from both edges gives you slats warped in opposite directions, if you are going to encounter warping).

Now finish-sand edges and repeat. When your blanks get too narrow to handle safely, edge-glue them, or glue waste wood between them and continue.

How many slats? First, you need enough to close the opening, less twice the width of the lead strip. I like to add additional slats so the tambour will be wide enough to go completely around the tight curve at the front when the tambour is closed, so I never have a slat leading around the curve—always following. You should rip some extra slats to cover yourself for bad warp, bad appearance, and goofs. How many—some say an extra 30 percent—depends on how the ripping goes.

GLUING THE SLATS

The slats are glued to a flexible backing, usually light canvas. Linen is another good material. For small tambours such as in this desk, use silk (real silk). I bought material marked "sari weight silk." Be sure to leave some extra cloth length at the ends—for attaching the lead strip. Leave cloth at both ends in case you have a problem and have to switch ends. The cloth should also be kept clear of the slat tongues—at least ½" away.

You will need a fixture to hold the tambour slats in position for gluing on the cloth backing and for routing the tongues. The fixture described was designed specifically for the desk tambour. It can be used, with new side strips, for any smaller tambour. The two sides have to be identical for the tongue-routing jig to work.

Start with a ¾" plywood board 1" larger than the slat length, and 6" larger than the required width of the tambour. Attach identical strips to the sides of the board to position the ends of the slats. Attach the strips with brass screws, with the screws positioned well away from the slats and interference with the router bit.

Add a strip at one end of the board, carefully squared. Lay a set of slats in the fixture and screw down the second end strip with the beveled

inner edges positioned so wedges can be used to compress the slats sideways to close the gaps and take out any warp. (If slats are warped, they should be arranged so the warp directions are random and thus balanced out.) The slats are now in position (Fig. 38) for gluing on the cloth backing.

Stretch and staple the backing cloth on the underside of the backing cloth frame. Keep the staples close to the outer edges. Bolt on the locating cleats and check positioning on the base. By using this frame the cloth can be dropped on the glued slats without any accidental misalignment or lateral movement.

When the glue is dry, remove the cleats and the exposed staples at the ends. Slit the cloth free of the side frame and lift off the frame.

The slats are routed from both sides to form the tongues. The routing jig can be set to locate the shoulder once, then shifted to do the tongues on the other end, and then the other sides of the tongues.

What is the best glue to use for the backing

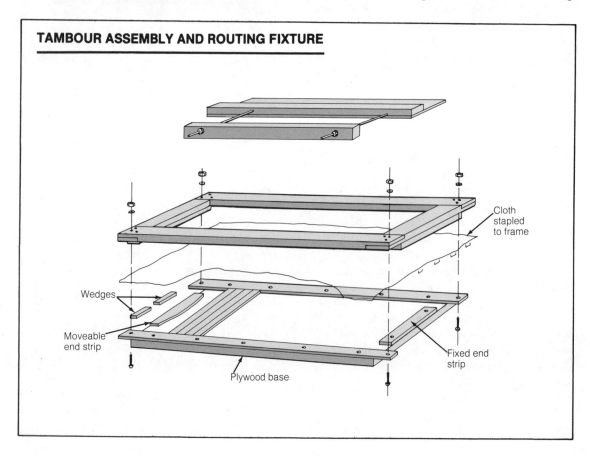

TAMBOUR ASSEMBLY AND ROUTING FIXTURE

Cloth stapled to frame

Wedges

Moveable end strip

Fixed end strip

Plywood base

Fig. 38. Clamping slats in the fixture. Wedges compress slats to close gaps and straighten out any warp that may be present. Measure top and bottom width of clamped slats to be sure tambour will be square. Mark side strips for location of last slat.

cloth? I used white glue on the Hepplewhite desk rolltop, some also recommened hide glue, but I have never tried it. White glue is good for big tambours. You should glue a few slats at a time, and be careful not to get excess glue that would saturate the cloth and make it stiff where it is supposed to act as a hinge between slats, or get glue between the slats.

For the tambour desk, I tried something new, and it works beautifully. 3M has adhesive transfer tapes that roll adhesive onto a work piece with a gun; the interleaved backing paper winds off as you transfer the adhesive. Type 524 is widely used paper-to-paper; 3M recommends type 669 (which is less easily obtained) for cloth-to-wood. I used type 524. The initial adhesion is good enough if the tambour is careful handled;

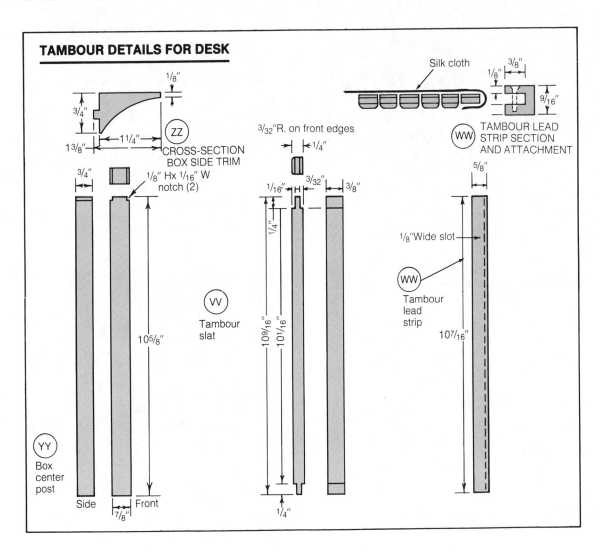

TAMBOUR DETAILS FOR DESK

the adhesion gets stronger with time, very much stronger.

I stretched the silk cloth on the frame, then rolled the adhesive crosswise on the slats, making sure there were no big holidays (Fig. 39). After positioning the frame and silk on the slats (Fig. 40). I pressed the cloth onto the adhesive with a wallpaper edge roller (Fig. 41).

The routing jig was adjusted for tongue length (Fig. 42), clamped to the base, and the tongues shouldered. To prevent tearing on each slat,

extremely light cuts must be taken—1/64″ at a time is not overdoing it (Fig. 43).

After a trial fit in the track, the upper end tongues should be sanded 1/16″ short. (Check the lower tongues first to make sure the clearance between the tongue shoulders and the floor is correct.) Now finish-sand the tongues. Stain and finish with a penetrating finish, such as tung oil, to give them a smooth hard surface without building up the thickness. Do not use filler on the tongues.

Fig. 39. Apply transfer adhesive to slats with special gun in almost-touching strips. Leave no large holidays.

Fig. 40. Drop frame with stretched, stapled backing cloth onto adhesive-coated slats. Cleats on frame and side strip protecting ends prevent lateral movement as adhesive comes into contact.

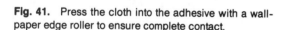

Fig. 41. Press the cloth into the adhesive with a wallpaper edge roller to ensure complete contact.

Fig. 42. To form tongues on slats, convert the fixture to a routing jig. Adjust nuts on threaded rods to position the router bit at shoulder of tongue.

Fig. 43. Routing the tongues. To avoid chipping the slats, the maximum depth of cut should be 1/64″ per pass. After a trial fit, sand upper tongues 1/16″ short.

21

〰〰

FINISHING FURNITURE

FURNITURE FINISHES

All furniture finishes are either clear finishes that display the grain and figure of the wood, or opaque finishes that obscure the grain and figure of the wood under a smooth, solid color or pattern of colors. Although all of the furniture shown in this book has a clear finish, that is not to say that a clear finish is better or more historically correct than an opaque finish.

Clear finishes are just more popular today. In their time a lot of Queen Anne, Hepplewhite, Louis XIV, XV, and XVI furniture was painted or gilded rather than stained, and Early American furniture was customarily painted.

STAINS

It may appear murky in the can, but stain is an essentially transparent liquid that changes the color of a wood without obscuring the grain and figure. A stain can also enhance the contrast in the wood figure. Wood can be stained lighter than its natural color if bleached first. Filler can enhance grain and figure.

You cannot believe printed color charts. They are not reliable guides to how the stain will look on your wood even if they show it on pine and you are using pine. It is not the fault of the manufacturer—it's in the limitations of color printing.

The names given stains aren't too standardized either. Ten brands of fruitwood will all give different colors. "Fruitwood" means whatever color the manufacture wants it to mean, and what he thinks you think fruitwood should look like.

Test stain on scrap wood before using it. Let it dry, then coat with clear spray-can lacquer to see how it will look under a clear topcoat. Once you have applied the wrong stain, or too much stain, you are in trouble. The only way to correct a bad stain job is to strip and sand, or paint it over with an opaque finish.

There are many kinds of stains, and they handle differently. Some are easy to work with, some are not. Naturally, the difficult ones produce the best coloring.

OIL STAINS

Oil stains are the most widely used kind. They come in cans ready to use, and are easily applied by brushing or wiping. As they dry slowly, they can be wiped with a cloth to even up the color.

There are two kinds of oil stains—those colored by finely ground pigments and those colored by dyes. They are very different.

Most stains sold in paint and hardware stores are oil pigment stains. If the can says stir well, it is a pigment stain.

Oil pigment stains are made by adding finely ground tinting colors to a mixture of linseed oil, mineral spirits, and other petroleum distillates. While dyes actually dissolve in the liquid vehicle, powdered pigments remain powder—even after you brush it on the wood. A surface layer of microscopic pigment particles colors the wood.

This coating does not give a clear, transparent finish, but oil pigment stains have a big advantage; the colors are permanent.

Oil dye stains are called penetrating stains. The colors in these stains soak into the wood surface and are transparent. However, the stains are not as permanent as water stains; in other words, the color fades.

Oil dye stains are troublesome on softwoods such as pine as they usually leave porous areas almost black. The surface to be stained is customarily first wiped with dilute linseed oil or shellac to limit penetration. (Use 1 part boiled linseed oil mixed with 4 parts mineral spirits, or 1 part shellac and 4 parts alcohol. If you use shellac, sand lightly before staining.)

WATER STAINS

Water stains consist of a water-soluble colorant and water. Water stains penetrate more deeply than any other stain. Water-soluble powdered aniline dyes are mixed with hot water to provide quarts of concentrated stain which is diluted (and tested) before use. They are cheap, too. An ounce of powder—enough to make a quart of concentrate—costs less than $2.

Analine-dye water stains are transparent and more brilliantly colored than any other stain. They are also essentially permanent. But they are hard to work with. They raise the grain (even after you have sanded to stop the grain from raising).

Water stains are harder to work with. The best way to apply water stain is with a spray gun, but you can also brush or sponge it on. Don't use water stain on veneer; it will swell the wood, cause cracks, and weaken the glue.

ALCOHOL STAINS

Alcohol, or spirit, or NGR (non-grain-raising) stains seldom raise the grain; when they do, it is slight, and easily sanded.

They dry very quickly, giving them little chance to penetrate into the wood. But you can stain, seal, fill, and varnish (one coat) in one day.

The colors of alcohol stains are transparent and brillant, but in time fade badly in sunlight or strong artifical light. Some colors are better than others. Use alcohol stains primarily for dark-colored finishes.

If you seal alcohol stain with dilute shellac, do as little brushing as possible. The shellac dissolves the stain and it bleeds into the shellac. The stains are usually sold as liquid concentrates.

VARNISH STAINS

Varnish stains are simply varnish to which enough colorant has been added to produce a definite color. I have yet to find one that works.

PAINT

You can use alkyd or oil-base interior flat wall paint as a stain on open-grained wood to get any color desired. Thin the paint with mineral sprits until it's watery, brush out throughly, then wipe off the excess before the paint can dry.

FILLERS

The surface of woods such as oak, ash, mahogany, and walnut are covered with large, visible pores. You can't sand them away.

You fill these pores with filler, which can be applied to raw wood but is usually applied after staining. If applied over shellac or dilute varnish sealer, the filler can be sanded from the surface and left only in the pores. The sealer keeps the filler from penetrating and staining the surface.

Wood fillers are also used to provide a smooth, unblemished surface for paint. (Under paint, ZAR Wood Patch, thinned 5–10% with water, makes an excellent filler. Use plastic tools—metals react with the filler vehicle.)

Fillers are packaged as concentrated pastes that must be thinned before using. These pastes are essentially finely powdered sand, boiled linseed oil, mineral spirits, and japan drier. Paste filler is naturally gray, but is also sold with a pigment to match a finish color.

Paste filler should be thinned to the consistency of cream for oak, and a little thinner for mahogany and walnut. Use mineral spirits. Don't use wood-distilled turpentine in a filler because it won't dry well, and not drying is a regular filler problem. Filler can be tinted with universal colors.

Unless you want to accentuate the visibility of the pores in the wood after filling, the filler color should be the same as the stain. Experiment on scrap before using darker or lighter fillers.

If the surface to be filled has been sealed, sand it. Apply filler with a stiff-bristled brush. Brush the filler on with the grain, then brush across the grain. The filler is not going into the pores without hard brushing. Stir the filler frequently.

Wait until the surface has dried dull (10 to 15 minutes). Now start rubbing off the surface filler across the grain only. Use a rough cloth, such as burlap. You only want to take the filler off the surface—if you rub with the grain, it will come out of the pores too. Use terry cloth if you haven't any burlap. Next, rub across the grain with a soft cloth, then with the grain for a final cleanup.

Filler thinned to the right consistency will roll up and crumble off the wood when you rub with burlap. If the filler is hard to remove, you probably waited too long to start wiping, or you filled a larger area than you could handle. The filler has to be removed from the surface quickly, before it dries hard. Rub down with a cloth wet with mineral spirits. When dry, try filling again. Filler that lifts out of the pores when you rub usually has too little japan drier in it. Add japan dryer to your thinned filler—try one ounce per pint.

Did the filler fill the pores? Check with an oblique light across the surface and a magnifying glass. To get the pores completely filled, you will probably need a second filling.

Let the filler dry twenty-four hours. Don't cheat. If not thoroughly dry, the filler packed in the pores can bleed through topcoats and sometimes cause them to lift off—usually when you are sanding between coats.

GLAZING

Glazing is either a second stain of a different color to break up the monotony of large, plain areas, or a thin paint applied over stain or enamel to change the color.

Glazing is used to match up different colored woods (this is called shading). Glaze over stain produces a subtle color change. Over enamel, the change is more drastic, as happens in an antiqued finish.

The procedure is simple. Wipe, brush, or spray the glaze on, wipe off the varying amounts to get the effect you are looking for. To highlight areas, use steel wool. Stain coats should always be sealed before glazing.

Glaze can give an instant appearance of age. A dark glaze in the corners of a panel can add interest to an otherwise plain area, and it can be used to accentuate carvings and moldings.

Spattering is a form of glazing in which specks of glaze are spritzeled onto the surface, usually by flicking droplets off the ends of the bristles of a stiff brush. Like all glazing, spattering should not be overdone.

TOPCOATS

It is the final coating on your piece of furniture—the clear, transparent, essentially colorless protective topcoat—that makes or breaks a piece of furniture and justifies all the hours spent designing, building, sanding, scraping, staining, filling, sealing, and possibly glazing it. Picking the best topcoat is not easy.

There is a wide choice of material and there is no one, absolutely best, all-around coating. Some provide better physical protection to the surface, others are better at enhancing the color and figure of the wood. Better "protection" can be defined in terms of water-, alcohol-, and scratch-resistance, but what is meant by better appearance defies definition. A natural, open-grained finish? A mirror-smooth, polished "piano" finish? A "hand-rubbed" satin or antique finish? A finish with the "patina" of age, whatever that is.

Clear topcoats are of three types: surface finishes in which a film of the finish material is built up on the wood surface; penetrating finishes which soak into the pores of the wood leaving a relatively thin surface coating; and padding finishes in which a very thin surface coating is applied. Some finish systems are easy to work with, some difficult, some just plain tedious.

And when it comes to furniture topcoat materials, we all have our prejudices. Some are no good, others we swear by. I started out using varnish, or rather my father used varnish. My contribution to the finish cycle was rubbing down between coats. Despite this odious division of labor, I stuck with varnish later on when doing my own finishing—dust, bubbles, brush marks, sags and all. I was convinced varnish was the only good furniture topcoat.

Somewhere along the line I took a wood finishing course offered by Constantine's and got coaxed into using lacquer—brushing lacquer. With the right brush and technique, and very low temperature baking, the problems with varnish were avoided except that I always got a sore throat after lacquering. That was finally licked by sucking a sourball when lacquering.

I never did like shellac as a topcoat finish, probably because of not being able to get fresh shellac during World War II, but later I began successfully using a padding finish on some furniture, and a padding finish is essentially shellac. Today, we have a host of polyurethane and other synthetic resin varnishes, and tung oil in all kinds of formulations.

Varnish is the finish today, especially polyurethane varnishes. No sanding between coats, hand-rubbed stain and antique finishes right out of the can. Can you get as good a finish on your furniture projects with these modern miracle concoctions as you can using one of the traditional materials and finishing procedures?

I did some testing. Old and new topcoat materials and procedures were compared on woods such as pine, mahogany, cherry, and teak. Finishes were tested in four groups; penetrating, padding, and two surface-film groups, gloss and satin/antique. For the new finishes, manufactures' directions were followed at first, then I experimented.

The primary criterion in the testing was appearance; water and alcohol-resistance was checked, and ease of application was noted.

To answer the original question, "Are today's new materials actually better than the old materials, and do the new short-cut methods really work as well or better than the traditional methods?" The answer came out yes and no, depending on the finish.

TESTS: PENETRATING OIL FINISHES

Old: Linseed Oil
New: Watco Danish Oil, Tungseal
Wood: Teak, Mahogany, Pine

Penetrating oil finishes as a group are the easiest to apply, with no worries about brush-marks, dust, bubbles, or sags. Although the recommended procedures vary from product to product, essentially you slobber it on, wait, then wipe off the excess. The only real precautions are not waiting too long before wiping to avoid a gummy surface, and careful disposal of oily rags as they can spontaneously ignits.

Linseed Oil

Some craftsmen swear by linseed oil, others condemn it as a finish that is all work and no results. There are two kinds of linseed oil sold—raw and boilded (polymerized). Raw linseed oil cannot be used as it will never dry. Boiled linseed oil will dry eventually. To use, boiled linseed entine (not petroleum-based paint thinner) to one part oil.

You brush on the mixture liberally; allow to penetrate, is cut with two parts turpwipe dry. Repeat daily for seven days, then weekly for amonth. Some say you should then continue once a month for a year, then once a year for the rest of your life, but I think that may be exaggerating the problem with linseed oil a bit. However, in the test, four months after the last application I culd still smell the finish, indicating that it was not dry.

Watco Danish oil

Penetrating finishes contain a mixture of oils, synthetic and natural resins, and petroleum solvents. The oil in Watco is linseed oil, Watco has a revised application procedure: Lay on a wet first coat, the immediately wet-sand with 600A wet-or-dry paper before wiping off the excess. The second coat is applied normally and wiped; then, after twenty-four hours, waxed. The 600A burnish is supposed to produce a smoother surface.

Tungseal

Tungseal contains tung oil and synthetic resins. The first coat is applied and wiped, or it can be allowed to dry and then be buffed with steel wool. The second coat is applied and wiped, then waxed (optiona). One or two additional coats are recommended for soft wood.

Test Results

There wasn't much difference in the sheen pruduced by all three. Application was easy, and done quickly except with linseed oil. The linseed oil finishing schedule was arbitrarily declared completed after one month.

Half of each sample surface was waxed and puddles of water and puddles of dilute alcohol (Gordon's Gin) were left overnight straddling waxed and unwaxed surfaces. Faint rings, easily wiped off, were left on the waxed surfaces, but not on unwaxed.

Conclusion

Linseed oil was in no way superior to the packaged penetrating oil finishes, and not worth the effort needed for application.

TESTS: PADDING FINISHES

Old: French Polish
New: Padlac, Rapid Pad, Padover
Wood: Myrtle Burl, Walnut, Mahogany

French Polish

French polish is a rubbed-on shellac topcoat. It is applied to the wood in very thin coats by rubbing it on with a pad moistened with alcohol, and lubricated with linseed oil (if required). Orange shellac is preferred over white shellac because it dries better. Even after many coats, the coating is so thin the orange color is not visible.

The technique is time-consuming and very difficult to master, but the result is supposed to be a finish unsurpassed for bringing out the color and figure of wood. Unfortunately, it is not water and alcohol-resistant, nor is it as durable under normal wear as varnish or lacquer.

To apply French polish, make a rubbing pad of lint-free cloth with a wad of surgical cotton inside. Dribble a little shellac inside the pad, and disperse it by tapping the pad on the palm of the hand or clean paper. Now put a few drops of alcohol on the pad surface and proceed with padding. If the wood surface is too tacky, add a few drops of linseed oil to the pad. The oil should be used sparingly as all of it has to be eventually rubbed off completely.

Padlac, rapid pad, padover

These are prepared substitutes that do not require the use of alcohol or oil in the application. Everything said about French polish applies equally to these modern equivalents, except that they are easier to apply successfully.

Surface preparation for padding a topcoat is very important, as the surface film is so thin, even after may coats, that it will not correct surface defects. Padding finishes should not be used on any open-grained wood. The wood, usually veneer or marquetry, must be thoroughly sanded. A sealer coat of diluted shellac should be applied by brush before padding.

The traditional filling procedure is to sprinkle the surface with pumice and pad it into the sealed surface with alcohol and a burlap pad. In England they used plaster of paris (to which powdered color could be added) with water. I prefer applying coats of shellac and sanding between coats until the wood is filled. If the wood is too porous for that kind of filling, don't attempt a padded finish.

The procedure is the same as that for French polish. Load the pad with about ¼ ounce of padding lacquer and tap it on clean paper to disperse the liquid. You don't want a wet spot, just a damp pad. Now rub the pad on the surface with a circular motion, keeping it moving. Never start on the surface—always slide on and off, or you will leave a sitz mark. Put a thin coat on the whole surface, then wait twenty-four hours. Repeat until you have four coats on. Now apply two or more coats with the grain or in a straight-line rub, to eliminate swirl marks left by the first coats. Wax is optional.

Besides being a one-step finish system for bare wood, a French padded-finish polish can be applied over stain (be careful of raised grain). It can be applied as a refinishing topcoat over varnish, lacquer, or shellac, or it can be used to finish off spot repairs. French polish is a most versatile finish.

How do the new padding materials compare with the traditional French polish? I tried Padlac, Rapid Pad, and French polish on myrtle-burl veneer samples, along with a gloss varnish finish applied the traditional way to a fourth sample.

The results? Constantine's Padlac produced a finish that as far as I can determine is identical to the finish obtained with traditional French polishing. Rapid Pad builds fast—it is a one-session commercial padding material. If you are in a hurry, use it. The Rapid Pad and varnish finishes appeared to be almost as good, but were soft enough to be scratched with a fingernail. If you want a padded finish use a product such as Pad Lac or Rapid Pad or Quolasole. None of the padded finishes resisted water or alcohol.

SURFACE FILM TOPCOATS

These varnish, lacquer, or shellac topcoats are applied to the wood surface in films with discernable thickness that form a dry skin on the surface of the wood. To some extent they will soak into open wood pores, but essentially they remain on the surface. The coating can be crystal clear, or it can be clouded by measured amounts of silica to simulate a satin or antique (dull) finish without the handwork usually associated with these finishes.

Varnishes

Varnishes are formulated from oils, resins, and chemicals, all dissolved in petroleum solvents. When applied to a surface, the varnish dries either by simple solvent evaporation, or by chemical reaction with the oxygen in the air. There is no one universal all-purpose varnish—varnishes are formulated for particular uses.

Spar varnish has to resist the weather, including sunlight, extreme temperature, water, and dimensional changes of the wood it is coated on. Varnish for a bar top must resist water, alcohol, detergents, and have a good and long-lasting gloss. Floor varnish has to be more flexible than a bar-top varnish and have good abrasion resistance, with a high gloss being much less important. These varnishes are not satisfactory for interior furniture.

Polyrethane varnishes are today the most widely used kind of furniture varnish. They are formulated from drying oils, alcohols, and iso-cyanates, combined chemically. They dry rapidly to a very hard, abrasion resistant finish, but they darken with age. There are gloss polyurethane varnishes, and satin and antique polyurethanes made by adding different quantities of fine silica to the varnish.

Alkyd varnishes have been around longer. They are made from drying oils, organic acids, and alcohols, chemically combined. Alkyd varnishes are slower drying than the polyurethanes. However, they are recommended for light-colored woods because of their paler color, and the fact that they do not darken with age as most other varnishes do. These varnishes are also made in several sheens. Although most tung oil and phenolic resin varnishes are formulated for exterior use, some are made for furniture finishing. All tung oil varnishes darken with age.

Lacquer

Varnish originally meant any unpigmented liquid applied to a wood surface in a thin coating for decoration and protection; the word lacquer has also changed in meaning. The word is derived from lac, the gum resin that is produced from lac insets. Japanese and Chinese lacquers were not made from lac resin, nor are they related to what we now call lacquer.

Today's lacquers are formulated from nitrocellulose and other bases, resins, plasticizers, and solvents. Lacquer is cheap and fast drying. A lacquer topcoat is less prone to chipping than most varnishes. Most wood funiture commercially manufactured today has a sprayed lacquer finish. You can also buy nitrocellulose lacquers formulated for application by brush, but finding brushing lacquer in quart cans is getting difficult.

Lacquer still has one advantage over varnish—it is colorless, and stays that way. The varnishes described as "water white" are actually still a pale yellow.

Shellac

Shellac was once widely used as a topcoat, but low resistance to water and solubility in alcohol limits shellac to use today primarily as a sealer. The basic material in shellac is the resinous material called lac deposited by insects on twigs in India. The lac is purified and turned into orange-colored flakes. Orange shellac is chemically bleached to produce white shellac. Shellac as you buy it is simply these flakes dissolved in alcohol. In the tests, surface films were divided into two groups for evaluation—as satin or antique finishes, and as high-gloss finishes.

TESTS: SATIN AND ANTIQUE FINISHES

Old:	Shellac Gloss ZAR, hand-rubbed to a stain finish
New:	Antique ZAR, Wood Glo (Constantine's) Deft Clear Wood, Finish, Satin Minwax, Satin Varathane
Wood:	Mahogany, Pine, Cherry

How good are the traditional old finishes and procedures—shellac, lacquer, and varnish with many coats throughly sanded between, finishing with pumice and rottenstone—compared to the modern, mostly polyurethane varnish finishes, with your choice of sheen formulated in the can?

In the tests, the satin varnishes produced as good a stain finish as could be obtained with the traditional rottenstone and pumice rubdown. Something that I already knew was quite apparent—a satin finish will hide a multitude of small surface defects. Although the finishes did tend to fill pores, they were found to be no substitute for pastewood filler.

The results of the water and alcohol resistance tests were a surprise because almost everyone knows that shellac does not resist either very well. All materials passed the water and gin test, including shellac, which was surprising.

Conslusion:

For a satin or antique finish, the finish obtained with the new products is as good as one obtained with the old rubbing with pumice and rottenstone, but the test revealed a significant shortcoming in application procedure. Light sanding between coats is absolutely necessary to clean the surface of tiny imbedded particles of dust, etc. There's no such thing as a no-sand brush finish that can be applied under home workshop conditions.

TESTS: GLOSS FINISHES

Old Procedures:

    *Gloss ZAR Varnish
    *Hour Varnish
    Gloss Brush Lacquer
    Shellac
    *Barrett Coachman Varnish

New Materials and Procedures:

    Gloss ZAR Varnish
    Gloss Varathane
    Deft Wood Armor Gloss

Wood:	Walnut, Cherry, Mahogany

*New Materials

What about gloss, "piano," "mirror" finishes? Can you get a good gloss finish out of the can? The answer is no. The only way you can brush on a good gloss finish is to apply a lot of thin coats with thorough drying and thorough sanding between coats. The same finishes, applied with the typical minimum sanding between coats specified on can directions, never got anywhere near glass smooth.

Test Results

Sanding makes the difference. While the new samples all displayed the same pored surfaces as in the previous test, the old heavily sanded-between-coats samples were glassy smooth with the pores, even in mahogany, well on the way to be filled. After rubbing with pumice and oil and rottenstone and oil, compounding and buffing with a lamb's-wool pad, a true high gloss (but glare-free) mirror finish was achieved.

Conclusions

1. As a group, the new gloss finish materials when applied in accordance with container instructions did not produce acceptable gloss furniture finishes.

2. No sanding, or only light sanding between coats, will not produce a blemish-free gloss surface regardless of the brush-on material used. Sanding between coats must be thorough. Be careful, however, not to cut through edges when you sand.

3. Gloss varnishes, shellac, and lacquer can be applied and rubbed to beautiful mirror finishes using the old-time procedures.

4. Brushing lacquer has no advantage over varnish today, except that it is more colorless, and darkens less with time.

5. Shellac is still the best choice for a mirror finish on antiques and other furniture not subject to wear, or exposed to moisture and alcohol spills. If any finish has instant patina, shellac rubbed to a mirror finish does.

HOW TO IMPROVE YOUR FURNITURE FINISHING

1. There is no way you are going to get a good brushed varnished, shellac, or lacquer topcoat without sanding between coats, with particular attention to sanding before the final coat. Containers that say that no sanding between coats is required mean that you don't have to sand the coat on the wood to give it a tooth so the next coat will adhere. If you want a smooth finish, sand between coats.

2. Except for the sanding before the last coat, the sanding can be with 280- or used 220-grit garnet or aluminum-xide paper, or with 320 or 400A wet-or-dry silicon-carbide paper. Use a felt pad or felt-faced wood sanding block to keep the sanding even. A small-orbit pad sander, such as the Porter-Cable #33 Speed Bloc, is invaluable for this sanding because of the freedom from scratching and the good one-hand control. Sand until the surface is dull except for pores and depressions, then rub the surface with 0000 steel wool to dull these spots too.

3. For the final sanding, use 320 or 400A wet-or dry silicon-carbide paper lubricated with paint thinner. Use a felt block to keep the paper flat on the work.

When sanding is completed, go over the wood with 0000 steel wool as before. Clean thoroughly and let dry. Don't be impatient with this drying as all of the solvent must be gone before the final coat.

4. Do not rush your finishing. You can't wait too long between coats. (You are going to sand anyway.) A whiff of thinner left in a pore after cleaning will put craters in what you thought was going to be your final coat, but instead is now your next to last coat—at best.

5. With a padded finish, don't try to put too much on at one session. Quit while you are ahead. With too much of a build-up in one session, the surface starts grabbing the pad too much for you to retain control.

6. I have stopped using bristle brushes for everything except applying exterior house paint. I have found that disposable polyfoam brushes are not only more economical, but they do a far better job applying varnish than any bristle brush no matter how expensive. They lay on a thin coat, without brush marks or dropped bristles. I buy the brushes in quantity directly from the manufacturer (see appendix).

Although the poly brushes are not marked for shellac or lacquer, they can be used for both of these finishes. The only problem is that a side-seam adhesive on the foam lets go after short use. The brush can't be left in solvent for the next coat, and you can't even clean it; you might have to trash a brush in the middle of a lacquer or shellac coat. But after use in varnish, these brushes can be rinsed and downgraded for stain or paint. Another point: With poly brushes you always know you have a clean brush for varnishing.

OPAQUE FINISHES

Furniture can be painted a solid color, and left that way, or the solid color can be the base for a more exotic finish. Either way, use alkyd enamel. This type of enamel comes in flat, semi-gloss and gloss, and in a wide spectrum of colors. Latex paint is not as good, even though you will be told so in stores that don't carry alkyd paint.

Latex paint should not be used in any furniture work. It cannot be sanded and rubbed down to as smooth and even a finish as alkyd and other oil paints.

By definition, enamel is a varnish with enough pigment added to produce an opaque coating. An undercoater is different from an enamel. Its low resin content provides better adhesion to the wood surface.

The surface to be painted must be clean and free of defects. Sand wood smooth and repair all scratches and indentations. If the wood is open-grained and you do not want the grain showing through the enamel, fill the wood.

Minor defects in the surface are sometimes easier to repair after the first coat has been applied—because you can see them better.

For the first coat, use a prepared undercoat or an enamel thinned slightly. Thinned enamel is often more practical when you are working with a deep color—prepared undercoats are white and cannot be tinted much.

When the undercoat is thoroughly dry, sand it. If it doesn't powder off, it is not dry. Sanding provides a tooth for the next coat and levels out any ripples and brushmarks. Dust the surface, wipe with a tack rag, and apply the first coat of enamel. Brush on a thin coat. Brush out all sags. When dry, sand and apply a second coat.

The final coat can either be rubbed down with pumice and water to a soft polished surface, or sanded and a finish coat of varnish brushed on and rubbed down. Varnish over white and other light colors should be tested first because most varnishes will give a definite yellowish cast to the finish.

APPENDIX

SOURCES OF SUPPLY

Artisanos Imports, Inc.
222 Galisteo Street
Drawer G
Santa Fe NM 87501
Southwestern hardware and ceramic tile

Ball and Ball
463 West Lincoln Highway
Exton PA 19241
Reproduction American hardware

Albert Constantine and Son, Inc.
2050 Eastchester Road
Bronx NY 10461
Finishing materials, veneer, hardwood, hardwood plywood, cabinet hardware

Craft Products Co.
2200 Dean Street
St. Charles IL 60174
Clock movements, parts, musical movements

Craftmans Wood Service Co.
2727 South Mary Street
Chicago IL 60608
Finishing materials, veneer, hardwood, hardwood plywood, cabinet hardware

Door Store
Washington DC, New York NY
Queen Anne legs

Educational Lumber Co., Inc.
P.O. Box Drawer 5373
Asheville NC 28813-5373
Softwood and hardwood lumber in quantity

Factory Lumber Outlet
(Iaccorino and Son)
200 Shrewsbury Street
Boylston MA 01505
Hardwood, domestic and imported

Garret Wade
161 Avenue of the Americas
New York NY 10013
Brass hardware, tools

Horton Brasses
Nooks Hill Road
Cromwell CT 06416
Brass cabinet hardware

Klockit
P.O. Box 629
Lake Geneva WI 53147
Clock movements, parts, musical movements

S. LaRose, Inc.
234 Commerce Place
P.O. Box 21208
Greensboro NC 27420
Clock movements, parts, musical tools

Mason and Sullivan
586 Higgins Crowell Road
West Yarmounth MA 02673
    Clock movements, parts, musical movements

Mohawk Finishing Products, Inc.
Amsterdam NY 12010
    Professional finishing supplies

Paxton Hardware Co.
Upper Falls MD 21156
    Cabinet hardware, all periods including Victorian

Small Parts, Inc.
6901 N.E. Third Avenue
P.O. Box 381736
Miami FL 33238-1736
    Metal tubing, bar stock, etc., small quantities

Smith Supply, Inc.
120 West Lancaster Avenue
Ardmore PA 19003
    Cabinet hardware

TALAS
Division of Technical Library Service Inc.
213 West 35th Street
New York NY 10001
    Leather

Woodcraft
41 Atlantic Avenue
Box 4000
Woburn MA 01888
    Tools

The Woodworker's Store
21801 Industrial Boulevard
Rogers MN 55374
    Hardware, wood, veneer, finishing supplies

Woodworkers Supply of New Mexico
5604 Alameda Place NE
Albuquergue NM 87113
    Tools, hardware

BIBLIOGRAPHY

Feirer, John L., *Furniture and Cabinet Making,* Peoria, IL: Bennett Publishing Company, 1983

Frid, Tage, *Tage Frid Teaches Woodworking; Joinery: Tools and Techniques*, Newtown, CT: Taunton Press, Inc. 1979.

Furniture From The Hispanic Southwest, Santa Fe, NM,: Ancient City Press, 1984.

Gottshall, Franklin H., *Heirloom Furniture*, New York: Bonanza Books, 1957.

Gottshall, Franklin H., *Masterpiece Furniture Making*, Harrisburg, PA: Stackpole Books, 1979.

Gottshall, Franklin H., *Period Furniture Design and Construction*, New York: Bonanza Books, 1937.

Gottshall, Franklin H., *Provincial Furniture Design and Construction*, New York: Crown Publishers, Inc., 1983.

Greenlaw, Barry A., *New England Furniture at Williamsburg*, Williamsburg, VA: The Colonial Williamsburg Foundation, 1974.

Hinckley, F. Lewis, *A Directory of Antique Furniture*, New York: Bonanza Books, 1953.

Joyce, Ernest, *The Encyclopedia of Furniture Making*, New York: Sterling Publishing Co., Inc., 1979.

Montgomery, Charles F., *American Furniture: The Federal Period*, A Winterthur Book, New York: The Viking Press, 1966.

Osburn, Burl N., and Osburn, Bernice B., *Measured Drawings of Early American Furniture*, New York: Dover Publications, Inc., 1975.

Shea, John G., *The American Shakers and Their Furniture (with measured drawings of museum classics)*, New York: Van Nostrand, 1971.

Symonds, R.W., and Whineray, B.B., *Victorian Furniture*, London: Country Life Limited, 1962.

Williams, A.D., *Spanish Colonial Furniture*, Salt Lake City: A Peregrine Smith Book, Gibbs M. Smith, Inc., 1982.